C000068194

"I am honored to provide an endorsement for *Intelligence Analysis in the Digital Age*. Sponsored by my close colleague and treasured friend, Kjell Grandhagen, this work is a masterful treatise on the subject of intelligence, and I consider it a must-read for either the interested citizen or expert practitioner – whether Norwegian or American."

James R. Clapper, *Former US Director of National Intelligence*

Intelligence Analysis in the Digital Age

This book examines intelligence analysis in the digital age and demonstrates how intelligence has entered a new era.

While intelligence is an ancient activity, the digital age is a relatively new phenomenon. This volume uses the concept of the "digital age" to highlight the increased change, complexity, and pace of information that is now circulated, as new technology has reduced the time it takes to spread news to almost nothing. These factors mean that decision-makers face an increasingly challenging threat environment, which in turn increases the demand for timely, relevant, and reliable intelligence to support policymaking. In this context, this book demonstrates that intelligence places greater demands on analysis work, as the traditional intelligence cycle is no longer adequate as a process description. In the digital age, it is not enough to accumulate as much information as possible to gain a better understanding of the world. To meet customers' needs, the intelligence process must be centred around the analysis work – which in turn has increased the demand for analysts. Assessments, not least predictions, are now just as important as revealing someone else's secrets.

This volume will be of much interest to students of intelligence studies, security studies, and international relations.

Stig Stenslie is Professor at the Center for Intelligence Studies at the Norwegian Defence Intelligence School (NORDIS), Norway.

Lars Haugom is Senior Adviser at the Norwegian Defence Establishment.

Brigt Harr Vaage is Director of Operations in the Norwegian Intelligence Service (NIS). He was Director of the NIS' Analysis and Assessment Division (2014–2020).

Studies in Intelligence
General Editors: Richard J. Aldrich and Christopher Andrew

For more information about this series, please visit: www.routledge.com/
Studies-in-Intelligence/book-series/SE0788

Intelligence Analysis in the Digital Age

Edited by Stig Stenslie, Lars Haugom, and Brigt Harr Vaage

Routledge
Taylor & Francis Group

LONDON AND NEW YORK

First published 2022
by Routledge
2 Park Square, Milton Park, Abingdon, Oxon OX14 4RN

and by Routledge
605 Third Avenue, New York, NY 10158

Routledge is an imprint of the Taylor & Francis Group, an informa business

© 2022 selection and editorial matter, Stig Stenslie, Lars Haugom, and Brigt Harr Vaage; individual chapters, the contributors

The right of Stig Stenslie, Lars Haugom, and Brigt Harr Vaage to be identified as the authors of the editorial material, and of the authors for their individual chapters, has been asserted in accordance with sections 77 and 78 of the Copyright, Designs and Patents Act 1988.

All rights reserved. No part of this book may be reprinted or reproduced or utilised in any form or by any electronic, mechanical, or other means, now known or hereafter invented, including photocopying and recording, or in any information storage or retrieval system, without permission in writing from the publishers.

Trademark notice: Product or corporate names may be trademarks or registered trademarks, and are used only for identification and explanation without intent to infringe.

British Library Cataloguing-in-Publication Data
A catalogue record for this book is available from the British Library

Library of Congress Cataloging-in-Publication Data
A catalog record for this book has been requested

ISBN: 978-0-367-76697-9 (hbk)
ISBN: 978-0-367-76699-3 (pbk)
ISBN: 978-1-003-16815-7 (ebk)

Typeset in Times New Roman
by Apex CoVantage, LLC

Contents

viii *Contents*

Illustrations

Figure

Boxes

Table

Notes on contributors

Wilhelm Agrell is Professor of Intelligence Analysis at Lund University. He has written several books on security policy and intelligence. Together with Gregory F. Treverton, in 2015 he published the book *National Intelligence and Science* (Oxford University Press). His latest book sheds light on the Swedish intelligence service during the Cold War. Agrell has also written a number of novels and youth books, including stories that often take place in the intelligence world.

Espen Barth Eide is a Norwegian politician and political scientist. He is a member of the Norwegian parliament, deputy chairman of the board of the Center for Humanitarian Dialogue in Geneva, and board member of the Stockholm International Peace Research Institute (SIPRI) and the Norwegian Institute of International Affairs (NUPI). From 2014 to 2017, he was Director of the World Economic Forum and Special Adviser on Cyprus to UN Secretary-General Ban Ki-moon. He was Minister of Defence (2011–2012) and Minister of Foreign Affairs (2012–2013) in Jens Stoltenberg's second cabinet. He holds a Cand. Polit. in political science from the University of Oslo.

Patrick Cullen is a senior researcher in the Security and Defence research group at NUPI. His work concerns security and defence issues, including terrorism and political violence, piracy and counter-piracy, US foreign and defence policy, private military/security companies, warning intelligence and strategic foresight, and the future of warfare and hybrid warfare. Prior to coming to NUPI, he worked at Eurasia Group as a political risk consultant in Washington, DC. He currently heads the multinational MCDC Counter-Hybrid Warfare project on behalf of the Norwegian Ministry of Defence.

Vegard Engesæth is an international politics expert who has extensive experience in political risk advisory and threat intelligence in the corporate sector. He holds an MSc degree in international politics from the School of Oriental and African Studies and degrees in political science and China studies.

Kjell Grandhagen was head of the Norwegian Intelligence Service (NIS) from 2010 to 2016. In 1974, Grandhagen graduated from the Infantry Officer Candidate School, and in 1978 he graduated from the Norwegian Military Academy.

Grandhagen then took the Norwegian Army Staff College and studied at the École supérieure de guerre interarmées in Paris. In addition to a number of commander positions in the Armed Forces, Grandhagen served overseas in the Multinational Force and Observers (MFO) in Egypt and in the Nordic-Polish Brigade in the SFOR in Bosnia and Herzegovina, where he was first chief of staff and then commander.

Kristian C. Gustafson is Deputy Director of the Brunel Center for Intelligence and Security Studies, Brunel University, and Director of the Center's MA programme in intelligence and security studies. He holds a doctorate from Downing College, University of Cambridge. Gustafson previously served for ten years as a Canadian army officer and lectured in war studies at the Royal Military Academy, Sandhurst. In 2013, together with Philip H.J. Davies, he published the book *Intelligence Elsewhere: Spies and Espionage Outside the Anglosphere* (Georgetown University Press).

Lars Haugom is Senior Adviser at the Norwegian Defence Establishment. He is a political scientist, holding a master's degree from the University of Oslo. Haugom has previously been a lecturer in Middle East studies at the University of Oslo and a research fellow at the Norwegian Institute for Defence Studies. Currently, he is working towards completion of his PhD project on civil-military relations in Turkey. He has extensive experience from political research on the Middle East and North Africa, intelligence analysis, and management of intelligence processes in the Norwegian Armed Forces. He has published on a range of topics related to politics and security in Turkey and the Middle East.

Cato Yaakov Hemmingby is an experienced senior security practitioner in government service and affiliated with the Center for Research on Extremism (C-REX). From 2012 to 2020, he was a research fellow at the Norwegian Police University College, focusing on terrorism, societal security, and intelligence. His academic background is in Middle Eastern studies and Modern Hebrew, and he holds a PhD degree in risk management and societal security from the University of Stavanger. He visited the Hebrew University of Jerusalem in 2008 and was a guest researcher at John Jay College of Criminal Science in New York in 2014. Hemmingby has written and co-authored several publications, including *The Dynamics of a Terrorist Targeting Process: Anders B. Breivik and the 22 July Attacks in Norway* (Palgrave Macmillan, 2016, with Tore Bjørgo).

Sir David Omand began his career at GCHQ. After working for the Ministry of Defence for a number of years, Omand was appointed Director of GCHQ from 1996 to 1997. His next post was as Permanent Secretary at the Home Office. He was intelligence and security coordinator at the British Prime Minister's Office in the period 2002–2005, with special responsibility for counterterrorism strategy. He was for seven years a member of the Joint Intelligence Committee, which coordinates intelligence information for the British government. He is now visiting professor at the War Studies Department, King's College

London, and honorary professor at Corpus Christi College, University of Cambridge. Omand has highlighted various aspects of intelligence in his extensive authorship, which include the books *Securing the State* (Hurst & Company, 2010) and *Principled Spying: The Ethics of Secret Intelligence* (Georgetown University Press, 2018, with Mark Phythian).

Tore Pedersen is Professor of Intelligence and National Security at NORDIS: Norwegian Defence Intelligence School, where he serves as Chair and Director of the Centre for Intelligence Studies. He is also Appointed Professor of Psychological Science at Bjørknes University College, Norway. He is currently Visiting Senior Scientist at the Department of Informatics and Computer Science at the University of Oslo, Norway, and Visiting Professor at the Department of War Studies at King's College London. He holds a Norwegian National accreditation as Military Intelligence Specialist, he is Elected Fellow of the Royal Society of Arts (RSA) UK, and he has served in various International Academic Evaluation Committees, including the IMSISS advisory board. He is currently engaged in experimental research on cognitive aspects in the intelligence domain and human–technology interaction.

Kira Vrist Rønn holds a doctorate in philosophy from the University of Copenhagen. She is currently a lecturer at the Metropol Police College and was previously a fellow at the University of Copenhagen and an analyst and developer for the Danish National Police. Her professional areas of interest include intelligence work, professional ethics, police strategies, and types of knowledge in police work.

Stig Stenslie is Professor at the Center for Intelligence Studies (CIS) at NORDIS. He is a political scientist, holding a Dr Philos. from the University of Oslo. Stenslie has been a visiting researcher at, among others, the National University in Singapore and Columbia University in New York. He has previously published a number of books on the Middle East and China, including *49 Myths about China* (Rowman & Littlefield, 2014, with Marte K. Galtung), *Regime Stability in Saudi Arabia: The Challenge of Succession* (Routledge, 2011), and *Stability and Change in the Modern Middle East* (I.B. Taurus, 2011, with Kjetil Selvik).

Knut Magne Sundal is an instructor at NORDIS. He has a master's degree in political science from the University of Oslo and in military studies from the Norwegian Defence University College, and is currently working on his PhD. He has been serving as an intelligence professional since 2000.

Bjørnar Sverdrup-Thygeson is Senior Advisor at the Norwegian Defence Establishment. Formerly Research Fellow at the Norwegian Institute of Foreign Affairs, he specialises in Chinese foreign policy and international relations theory. He holds a doctorate from the London School of Economics, MSc in Modern Chinese Studies from the University of Oxford, in addition to degrees from the universities in Norway and China. Sverdrup-Thygeson has published on a range of topics related to Chinese foreign policies of the past and present.

Brigt Harr Vaage is Director of Operations in the NIS. He was director of the NIS' Analysis and Assessment Division (2014–2020). Vaage graduated from the Norwegian Military Academy and holds a *cand. mag.* degree from the University of Oslo and an MSc in international relations from the London School of Economics. He has previously worked for the Norwegian Ministry of Foreign Affairs and NATO, as an attaché in Serbia and Montenegro; he has been a senior military officer in the Ministry of Defence and a military adviser at the Norwegian Institute for Foreign Affairs (NUPI).

Njord Wegge is a political scientist with an expertise in international relations. Wegge obtained his PhD from the University of Tromsø in 2013. He has published extensively on issues relating to international relations and security in the Arctic, hybrid warfare, and intelligence oversight. Wegge has worked as a senior research fellow at the Fridtjof Nansen Institute, at the Norwegian Institute of International Relations, as well as for the Norwegian Parliamentary Intelligence Oversight Committee. He has been a visiting scholar to UC Berkeley, USA.

Foreword

Kjell Grandhagen

What does an intelligence service actually do? I have had to answer this question many times, both as intelligence chief and afterwards. And most often I have responded in a populist way: It gives our government the answers it cannot find in the newspapers.

Now, of course, it is true that an intelligence service should be able to provide better and deeper answers than can be read in easily accessible open sources. But it is still far from the whole truth. Indeed, it would appear somewhat surprising if the intelligence service's conclusions were fundamentally different from what one could read in open sources. In this respect, today's world is too transparent, and the media's source access is very good. But if the picture painted of the world and the main conclusions are not significantly different in an intelligence product, one will usually find a degree of detail, a source of richness, and, thus, a degree of credibility that exceeds what one finds in a newspaper article.

Another characteristic of the intelligence services' products is the analytical process that leads to their conclusions. Intelligence places great demands on its collection and basically requires verified information from various independent sources. Preferably, the sources should also be of a different nature, such as human contacts and electronic collection. But the analytical process does not stop there; collected material is assessed against a comprehensive database of historical information and against the analysts' deep knowledge of their field of work. And to top it all, the assessments are thoroughly reviewed by colleagues and responsible leaders in the hierarchy before they are finally released to customers in the government apparatus.

An intelligence service is entirely dependent on the customers' trust. This is achieved by delivering intelligence within the mandate given by the authorities. Although intelligence has many striking similarities with research, the differences are also large. Many intelligence analysts might wish for the opportunity for greater freedom of action in choosing themes and focus, but this can be difficult. The resources are limited and must be focused on answering the questions the government and state apparatus ask through their priority document.

Trust by our political authorities and in the civil service also presupposes, of course, that the intelligence service does indeed present fairly correct predictions. It is not enough to provide a good description of the current situation – one must also be able to predict further development with a high degree of accuracy. Of course, this part of the mission is far more demanding than telling what has happened, and with a significantly greater height of fall. Exactly this aspect represents one of the most difficult dilemmas for intelligence leaders: Should one choose to be on the safe side, describing several alternative directions of development and be open – and perhaps even slightly diffuse – in the conclusions, or should one dare to be clear even if the intelligence is not clear and the risk of error is present. In the world of analysis, this is not a theoretical problem – this is a dilemma one has to live with every single day.

Another key challenge for intelligence services is the high degree of secrecy. Much information and data processed are highly classified. This is not only due to the sensitivity of the information itself but equally to the need to protect the systems that collect the information and the partners across the globe who choose to share information with us. Therefore, information that may also be read in the newspaper can be highly classified in an intelligence service, if it has been collected through a system whose capacity is dependent on protection.

The level of secrecy easily becomes a challenge in contact with the outside world. Even in the political circles, it is difficult to demand respect for the protection of information. It becomes even more challenging when the media calls for answers. The intelligence service's trust and reputation in the population is also at stake.

The simple solution, of course, is to give as little information as possible. Traditionally, intelligence services' answers to the media's questions have been "no comment". If you refuse to answer, you are not saying anything wrong. But in today's society, this does not work. Allegations are being made that the intelligence services are committing illegal activities and are beyond political control. Such claims will go unchallenged if the services choose not to speak out. Even if no specific charges are made, an intelligence service will continuously be suspected of irregularities. This is simply because it is surrounded by myths and mystique because the public does not have a clear picture of what it does and how.

If one chooses to ignore this risk, the result will soon be a falling reputation and reduced trust in the political circles, the media, and the population. Therefore, a modern intelligence service must:

- Seek to be open about what it can be open about. After all, *everything* is not super-classified.
- Publish the main conclusions of its assessments through unclassified reports, without compromising sources, capabilities, and methods.
- Set the premises for an open public exchange on important elements of foreign and security policy through qualified situational descriptions.
- Welcome independent, democratic control of its activities.

Intelligence has become a demanding craft. During the Cold War, the work was characterised by long-term processes, where the main focus was about securing access to information that formed a "normal picture". From this, one could then find deviations that could indicate that threats arose or disappeared. Today, the picture is different. The number of actors an intelligence service must monitor is multiplied, and includes states, organisations, and individuals. Available information has also largely shifted from the physical and analogue space to the digital. The amount of collected information has increased exponentially, and the requirement for response time has been greatly sharpened.

In Norway, the intelligence service has gone from being an almost purely military service to becoming an important provider of assessments for a broad range of the state apparatus. In particular, the ministry of foreign affairs has become an important customer for the service. The service's assessments play an increasingly important role in the government's work, from long-term planning to dealing with emerging crisis situations.

These changes place great demands on the adaptability of the service. First and foremost, it has had to expand its area of expertise from the purely military to the geopolitical domain. Secondly, it has had to reorient the collection structure both to a wider part of the world and into the digital sphere.

However, for a small country like Norway, there will always be major limitations in what you actually can collect on your own. Therefore, the establishment and maintenance of a comprehensive international cooperation network are crucial. There is no room for free-riders. Only those who can add something of interest to the partners will receive something back. In other words, intelligence is a commodity where one must carefully weigh the value of what one gives and what one receives. In addition, there are, of course, some absolute limits related to respect for human rights and legal restrictions.

Analysis is, as shown in this book, at the very core of intelligence production, and it is a fascinating craft. Its products in the form of assessments, reports, and briefings, which often reach the highest political level, require a high degree of humility and integrity: humility towards the consequences of the decisions that the analysis eventually leads to, integrity in relation to the requirements of objectivity, thoroughness, and unaffectedness. With such a seriousness hanging over them, analysts can easily become overcautious and passive. This must be countered by a culture that stimulates intellectual creativity and an acceptance that it is sometimes allowed to make mistakes – as long as you learn from them.

Experience shows that both analysts and customers benefit from establishing a close dialogue throughout the intelligence process. In this way, the focus of the product is sharpened and both parties learn along the way. But the contact must also not be too close – it can affect the analyst's independence by making the customer's expectations too controlling, and it can also lead the customer to draw conclusions and make decisions before the process is completed and all factors are considered.

Going back a little bit in time, the analyst's biggest challenge was the lack of information – "had I only had this single piece of evidence" was an often heard sigh. Even today, analysts have to live with the fact that they lack important puzzle pieces, but they also have to face another challenge: they "drown" in data. The access to information has exploded both with an ever-increasing flow of information and, perhaps especially, with the ability to store information that can be quickly retrieved when needed. These huge amounts of information threaten to "jam down" the analysts, who gradually use more and more of their valuable time to find relevant information from large, unstructured data stores.

Today, it is important that analysts have good search tools that quickly help them find all the information that may be important to their work. Such tools are based on each piece of information being labelled, or "tagged", so that its relevance can be identified electronically. Analysts are also supported by analytical tools that are able to see patterns, such as networks and connections, in vast amounts of data.

Intelligence is becoming increasingly important in the ever-changing and unpredictable world we now live in. Our government needs insight and understanding beyond those obtained through the media. Such insight must rest on access to information that is not widely known and that has been processed and evaluated according to thorough analytical principles. But intelligence can easily be challenged because it operates clandestinely – on the side lines of a society that is becoming increasingly transparent. Therefore, it is and will be a major challenge to enter into dialogue with the surroundings in such a way that the society is given the insight into the intelligence activities that are possible, while at the same time maintaining the respect for necessary secrecy.

This book is a valuable contribution to the development of the intelligence profession. Skilled intelligence professionals are not only created through practice and experience – they also need a theoretical framework to deal with. This is provided by this book!

Acknowledgements

Former director of the Norwegian Intelligence Service Kjell Grandhagen passed away in 2019. He was therefore never to see this book in print. More than anyone else, Kjell brought the service out into the public domain. He did this by taking the initiative for the service to publish an annual, unclassified report. The value of this report, which bears the name "Focus", is not only to contribute to the public debate on threats to our security and increase the public's understanding of the service's work, but it is also necessary for the service's professional development. In a time characterised by a changeable and complex threat environment, the service relies on being able to test its assessments in the open. Without Kjell's desire for openness, positive attitude, and support, this book would not have come to light. Thank you!

Thanks also to Helge Arnli, Karsten Friis, Trygve Gulbrandsen, Jarl Eirik Hemmer, and Gunnar Kleivenes, as well as a handful of colleagues who insist that their identity not be revealed for valuable discussions and inputs.

1 Introduction

An old activity in a new age

Stig Stenslie, Lars Haugom, and Brigt Harr Vaage

Princes and warlords from all cultures have at all times relied on intelligence to achieve their goals. Intelligence is even referred to as "the world's second oldest profession".[1] In the Old Testament, we can read that Moses sent 12 spies to explore Canaan, the land that God had promised the Israelites. Hieroglyphs from ancient Egypt, the land the Israelites escaped from, testify that the pharaohs had their own organised intelligence service, known as "the king's ears". The Greeks and Romans also had their well-developed network of spies. In ancient texts written by Indian and Chinese military strategists, like Chanakya and Sun-Tzu, the importance of intelligence in order to get an advantage over one's opponent is emphasised. Japanese rulers are said to have used the legendary *ninjas* to gather intelligence. And in South America, the Aztec rulers used so-called *pochtecas*, traders with diplomatic immunity, as spies.[2]

Unveiling what others want to keep hidden and then exploiting this knowledge to one's own advantage have over the centuries been central to intelligence. And because intelligence is conducted at all times in all forms of organised societies, this activity must be understood in light of the societal context in which it operates. As the external circumstances change, the way intelligence is conducted also changes.

The starting point for this book, *Intelligence Analysis in the Digital Age*, is that intelligence in general and intelligence analysis in particular have entered a new era. While intelligence is an ancient activity, the digital age is a relatively new phenomenon. The speed, huge volume, and complexity of information are its foremost characteristics. New technology has reduced the time it takes to spread news to about *zero*, and we are now getting to know about every small event even in the most distant little place almost before it has happened. The book's title emphasises the importance of technology for the pursuit and understanding of intelligence. But the book is not about technology, new collection methods, or the need for more advanced IT systems – although each of these subjects is discussed. Rather, the book employs the concept *digital age* as the expression of an increased pace of change, complexity, and speed of information. These factors, in turn, affect decision-makers' demands for intelligence in support of policymaking. The message of this book is that good and efficient intelligence places greater demands on the analysis work than ever before. Assessments, not least predictions, are as important as revealing someone else's secrets.

How to work with intelligence analysis in the digital age? What kind of questions will customers have answers to? What methods and tools can an analyst rely on, and what are their possibilities and limitations? How to warn of today's subtle threats? How to capture the attention of busy decision-makers? What specific challenges are associated with politicisation and ethics in the digital age? These are among the questions that will be discussed, and hopefully answered, in this book.

We hope this book will be a useful contribution to preparing today's and tomorrow's analysts for the challenges that lie ahead.

Intelligence analysis

The type of "intelligence" we write about in this book is a state-driven activity. The knowledge this activity generates is intended to give decision-makers the best possible basis for making decisions. Taking the Norwegian Intelligence Service (NIS) as an example, its vision is "to contribute to the decision-making basis of the Norwegian authorities with timely, reliable, and relevant knowledge of the world around us".[3] Knowledge is power, not at least in intergovernmental relations. Michael Herman points out that intelligence is a type of power that states possess, that is, "intelligence power".[4] Intelligence is typically directed at matters affecting the security of the state,[5] and a key task for intelligence analysts is to alert key political, civilian, and military decision-makers to potential threats – for example, other countries' military power, terrorism, or cyberattacks. While international law, to a lesser degree, regulates intelligence, the framework for this activity in Western democratic countries such as Norway is regulated by national law. The NIS's task is specified in the Act on the Intelligence Service of 1998, § 3:

> The Norwegian Intelligence Service shall procure, process and analyse information regarding Norwegian interests viewed in relation to foreign states, organizations or private individuals, and in this context prepare threat analyses and intelligence assessments to the extent that this may help to safeguard important national interests.[6]

To achieve and maintain relative intelligence power, the activity is carried out under cover. In particular, the sources and methods of information collection are kept secret. Intelligence is therefore associated with secrecy. Michael Warner even goes so far as to claim that "no secrets, no intelligence".[7] The fact that the intelligence activity is hidden distinguishes it from research and journalism, two activities that it otherwise has much in common with.

Although intelligence is closely linked to various forms of hidden information collection, it does not mean that the activity can be reduced to a question of collection methods alone. According to Sherman Kent, the late history professor at Yale University, who is often referred to as the "father of intelligence studies", the concept of intelligence is used interchangeably with the associated organisation, the activity, and the knowledge generated.[8] The term can thus refer to information and knowledge: "What kind of intelligence do we have on Iran's missile programme?" Or it may refer to the organisation: "The intelligence considers it likely that Iran will develop a nuclear programme." Or it may refer to the activity: "How extensive is the intelligence that foreign powers carry out in Norway?"

Info box 1.1 Intelligence-collection disciplines

It is common to distinguish between human-based collection (HUMINT) and technical collection. HUMINT refers to information obtained through interaction with human sources. Technical collection is a collective term that refers to information acquired through the use of various technical sources – such as a radar or images taken from a satellite. This type of collection includes signal intelligence (SIGINT), image intelligence (IMINT), acoustic intelligence (ACINT), radar intelligence (RADINT), geographic intelligence (GEOINT), and open-source intelligence (OSINT).[9] Today, an increasing share of an intelligence service's information comes from open sources (the Internet, media reports, private intelligence organisations, research publications, etc.). Another increasingly important source of information is social media collection (SOCMINT).[10]

Based on Kent's insights formulated as early as 1949, it is still common to illustrate intelligence as a continuous step-by-step production process. This also applies to the Norwegian Defence Intelligence Doctrine of 2013, according to which the production process is divided into four distinct sub-stages.[11]

The first step is "direction". The intelligence service receives intelligence requirements from decision-makers, referred to as customers in this book, as part of an ongoing intelligence dialogue with them. The various intelligence needs are prioritised, and production and collection plans are developed. The second step is "collection", which involves gathering and processing data. Collection includes inputs from various intelligence-gathering disciplines. The third step is "processing", where data are systematised, analysed, and summarised into products. The products use words of estimative probability that help the customers assess the validity of the conclusions drawn. The fourth step is "dissemination", where the product is communicated to the customer in a suitable form and where it is ensured as far as possible that the content is understood correctly. The product often generates new intelligence needs, and the cycle restarts (Figure 1.1).

Three assumptions can be identified in the traditional intelligence cycle: firstly that it is useful to distinguish between the various functional components of the process, such as collection and analysis; secondly that the components are sequential; and thirdly that they can be shaped into a cycle through the feedbacks of customers, which in turn dictates future needs. This cyclical model is still used in intelligence doctrines and basic military education.

The digital age

In 1989, Tim Berners-Lee invented the World Wide Web. The foundations of the digital age, also known as the information age, had been laid years earlier with

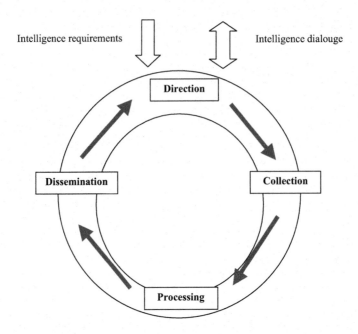

Figure 1.1 The Intelligence Cycle

the invention of internet technology and the rise of home computers. But it was the introduction of the World Wide Web that allowed information to flow freer and more quickly than ever in human history.[12] This important innovation led to the fall of age-old obstacles to human interaction, such as geography, language, and restricted information.[13] In 2005, the global internet population reached 1 billion.[14] By 2012, over 2 billion people used the Internet. By 2016, half of the world's population was connected, and as of 2021 that number had risen to almost two-thirds.[15]

Information is flowing faster and faster – a trend that seriously accelerated in the 2000s with the introduction of social media channels such as Facebook, Twitter, and Instagram – and humanity is accumulating an incredible amount of information. Eric Schmidt, Google founder, points to the long historical lines in an attempt to illustrate this development:

> There was 5 exabytes of information created between the dawn of civilization through 2003, but that much information is now created every 2 days, and the pace is increasing.[16]

As a result of this, "information overload" has become a hallmark of the digital age. The term is used to describe how difficult it is to understand a problem and effectively make decisions when one has too much information. Such situations occur when the amount of information exceeds the ability to process it and both individuals and organisations have limited processing capacity.[17] The topic was discussed already in the nineteenth century by the German sociologist Georg Simmel,[18] while the term itself was popularised by Alvin Toffler in his bestselling book *Future Shock* in 1970.[19] None of them could have foreseen the actuality this topic would get in the digital age, when the rapidly growing volume of easily accessible information arguably makes it increasingly difficult to make decisions.[20]

Nowadays, everybody can access all kinds of information with just a few clicks through Google and Wikipedia – a development that has led some to proclaim the "death of the expert".[21] Of course, there will still be experts – those with more knowledge than other people in individual fields – doctors, lawyers, engineers, and other specialists. But the point is that there are good reasons to believe that easy access to information will gradually weaken people's recognition of expertise. Today, anyone can search for information and become an "expert". "But doctor, I googled it!" is a phrase often heard in consultations – a challenge to any medical expert.[22]

The spread of so-called fake news makes it even more complicated to navigate the ocean of information. False information, spread with the goal of confusing and influencing, is far from a new phenomenon. But the opportunities to spread misinformation have become far greater in the digital age. Social media, in particular, has proven to be a great platform to distribute such information, and the effect is powerful. A research team led by Soroush Vosoughi at the Massachusetts Institute of Technology (MIT) has shown that "fake news" travels far faster than the truth. In a study on Twitter, a major channel for information sharing, researchers found that it was 70 per cent more likely that an untrue tweet would be retweeted than a true tweet. The reason, according to the research team, is that fake news is fabricated to appeal to the reader. They are shocking, they are surprising, and they play on people's emotions.[23]

As a result of huge amounts of information being spread so quickly, thanks to the power of new technology, primarily the smartphone, people's ability to stay focused has dramatically reduced. A study conducted by Microsoft in 2015 concluded that an average human being is able to maintain concentration for only 8 seconds, down from 12 seconds in 2000.[24] At the same time, there is an increasing uniformity in people's focus. Driven by the media's "24-hour cycle", information is spreading today in the form of "hurricanes", which suddenly arise and lie just as quickly. The sensational news of yesterday, which suddenly drew everybody's attention, has lost its charm, and is forgotten today.[25]

Intelligence analysis in the digital age

"Unpredictability has become the new normal." This is the opening phrase of a white paper written by the Norwegian Ministry of Foreign Affairs in 2017.[26] The statement reflects that the Norwegian authorities perceive today's security policy context as less clear and persistent than before. Whether or not the world is actually falling apart is not essential. From an intelligence perspective, the authorities' perceptions are important as they form their intelligence requirements. In other words, the digital age does not change the fundamentals of intelligence. The essence consists in revealing what others want to keep hidden and then utilising the knowledge to one's own advantage. However, the changed context makes it *far more demanding* than before to be an intelligence professional.

The traditional intelligence cycle is no longer adequate as a process description.[27] In the digital age, work is done in parallel with different steps, and steps are often skipped if needed. In order to be able to warn of rapidly emerging threats, the collection and processing cannot be sequenced.[28]

Critics of the intelligence cycle point out that it does not adequately reflect reality. The model is complicated by the fact that many people add arrows and boxes here and there in an attempt to make it more realistic. The question is whether this helps to increase the understanding of the intelligence process. In this book we have chosen a different angle. The starting point is not the cycle but the ones who do the job. For them, a day in the office hardly appears as being a step in a cycle but rather as a set of work processes designed and rooted in the current threat environment, technology, and the broader social context in which they operate. And, as we shall see, today the role of analysts is something far more than an isolated step in a wheel. In the digital age, analysts play a much more central role, from the operationalisation of intelligence needs, through assistance to targeting, processing of information collected, to communicating intelligence to decision-makers. The intelligence process is increasingly centred on the analysis work. It has become analysis-centric. This development places new demands on the analyst.

***

As Sir David Omand shows in Chapter 2, "The Historical Backdrop", it is precisely technological breakthroughs that have opened up new methods for information collection that have repeatedly changed the analyst's role. Now we are facing digitalisation. Broadly speaking, the evolution of intelligence analysis can be divided into five overlapping eras, each reflecting the type of information available at that time. Each era opened up new uses for intelligence. Like the laying down of sedimentary layers of rock, each new era has added new weight and complexity to the analytic task without removing the earlier layers. Today (and tomorrow), the task of the intelligence analytic professionals should be capable of mining the material from each of these five layers. Increasingly specialised branches of analysis are therefore essential to be able to cover the full range of tasks.

In Chapter 3, "Intelligence as Decision-Making Support", Espen Barth Eide argues that intelligence is more relevant than ever to help those navigating Norway in a demanding time. On the basis of his own experience as a key decision-maker in the Norwegian government, Espen Barth Eide argues that the increasing number of decisions that must be made, combined with the decreasing time available before a decision must be made, in total makes it very challenging to be a decision maker in the digital age. For a policymaker to be assured of her or his own decisions, the intelligence service plays an important role as a trusted and non-stop dialogue partner. Rather than secrets delivered in a sealed envelope, a decision-maker in the digital age should be supported with good analysis: sober analysis of both what the world actually is and how it might come to be. In this way, intelligence can help a decision-maker to think of the unthinkable and thus help to reduce the danger of unpleasant surprises.

To enable analysts to answer ever more challenging questions and analyse a growing amount of information, intelligence services are using new analytical methods and tools. In Chapter 4, "The Necessity of Experts", Stig Stenslie takes a critical look at various methods that have been used by intelligence analysts since the early 2000s. An issue that is among the most debated in the intelligence litera-ture is whether intelligence can best be described as an "art" – that is, an activity based on intuition, experience, and knowledge – or as a "science" – that is, work that uses specific analysis methods. Proponents of the latter position attach great importance to the use of so-called structured analysis techniques (SAT). The aim of these techniques is to reduce biases, and hence reduce the risk of intelligence fail-ures, as well as to make the premises on which an analysis is based clearer to the customer. Stenslie argues that SAT might be useful but that these methods cannot replace the subject-matter expert, who is an authority in a particular area or topic.

In Chapter 5, "Open-Source and Social Media Intelligence", Bjørnar Sverdrup-Thygeson and Vegard Engesæth argue that the digital era entails two interrelated tectonic changes to the world of intelligence analysis, one of quantity and one of quality. Firstly, the information revolution entails a massive increase in available open-source material, and second, this information deluge is in large parts driven by interpersonal and social processes bleeding into the open domain on an unprec-edented scale. This transformation in the field of OSINT is thus amplified by the advent of the new field of social media intelligence, SOCMINT. This paradigm shift of information opens up a range of opportunities for intelligence analysis. However, it also necessitates a methodological shift from the traditional intel-ligence issues of dealing with information scarcity to one of performing, more saliently, intelligence analysis under conditions of information excess. For this purpose, there is a continuous development of software tools to help harness the information flows in ways that can best complement and augment the skills of the analyst – whose methodological and cultural skills will still be at the heart of the intelligence analysis process.

In Chapter 6, "Analysing with Artificial Intelligence", Lars Haugom, Cato Yaa-kov Hemmingby and Tore Pedersen discuss technology's role in the analysis pro-cess, especially in the analysis of so-called big data – that is, the huge and rapidly growing volume of digital information generated by new information technology such as smartphones, the Internet, storage clouds, and social networks. So-called artificial intelligence is about to make its entry into a number of fields, such as journalism, finance, medicine, and law, and intelligence analysis is no exception. By discussing the relationship between new technology and intelligence analysts, the authors show that various computer programs are increasingly supporting ana-lysts in their work, especially in the work of analysing large volumes of data and complex causal links. At the same time, they emphasise the limitations of technol-ogy and the analyst's continued important role in the intelligence process. When it comes to making complex intelligence problems meaningful, and communicating these to decision-makers, the machine's algorithms will hardly be able to outperform the human brain and judgement.

Warning is a key task for any intelligence service, but a task that has become more demanding than ever before. The reason is that the threats one faces today are often subtle. Patrick Cullen and Njord Wegge highlight this challenge in Chapter 7, "Warning of Hybrid Threats". These types of threats are challenging to reveal before they turn into a serious problem. One important method used by Western intelligence services since the Cold War is indicator-based warning analysis. Even though this method was developed in the context of a relatively static threat, to warn decision-makers about a possible Soviet attack, the authors argue that indicator-based analysis still is useful in the face of today's more subtle threat image. Cullen and Wegge show how the method can be further developed to help analysts discover hybrid threats.

In Chapter 8, "Futures and Forecasting", Kristian C. Gustafson discusses the utility of so-called horizon scanning methods to warn decision-makers about more subtle threats, which lie far into the future. These methods concern raising customers' awareness of possible alternative futures without necessarily considering their likelihood. They are suitable for capturing subtle, long-term trends and focus particularly on changes as a result of technological breakthroughs.

In the digital age, it has also become more challenging to draw the attention of decision-makers. Every decision-maker has access to vast amounts of information through newspapers and journals, research reports, e-mail correspondences, social media, and so forth, and an intelligence report is thus only one of a great many sources. In addition, an experienced decision-maker will often consider that she or he is equally well-suited, or even better suited, to interpret information as a young "expert" from an intelligence service. In Chapter 9, "Capturing the Customer's Attention", Lars Haugom discusses various aspects of communicating intelligence analysis in the digital age. Importantly, if an analyst's assessments do not receive attention, they have no relevance as support for decision-makers. Today, the competition to be listened to is fierce, not least when it comes to catching the attention of busy decision-makers. Therefore, in order to succeed, an analyst must be able to handle the following challenge: Without compromising on professional substance, an analyst must be able to present her or his assessment of even the most complicated intelligence problem with only a few sentences available.

Furthermore, there are particular challenges associated with politicisation and ethics in the digital age. In Chapter 10, "Avoiding Politicisation", Wilhelm Agrell focuses on the first topic. Throughout history, there are several examples of politicians misusing intelligence services to legitimise and promote a particular policy. Today, this challenge has become even more complex, given the trend of populist politicians dismissing expertise, including intelligence analysts' opinions, and using digital media to spread and establish their "alternative facts".

In Chapter 11, "A Professional Code of Ethics", Kira Vrist Rønn addresses ethical problems related to intelligence analysis in the digital age. More specifically, she discusses the need for professional integrity when confronting fake news and disinformation, and the risk of biases and politicisation when facing decision-makers and their expectations. Rønn especially argues for developing a professional code of ethics for intelligence analysts to assist in handling problems associated with the increasing use of open-source and social media intelligence.

Finally, in Chapter 12, "Towards an Analytic-centric Intelligence Process", Brigt Harr Vaage and Knut Magne Sundal summarise the discussions in the book and describe a new way of working with intelligence adapted to the digital age. While intelligence was previously centred on uncovering "secrets", the work focuses today more on "mysteries". Secrets are something that can be stolen by a spy or discovered by a technical sensor. Mysteries, on the other hand, are something that there is no point in stealing, because what you wonder about lies ahead of time and the actors involved do not know the answer either. During the Cold War, intelligence services were asked by their customers to steal secrets that the opponent was trying to hide, and collection was therefore the core business of any service. Today, on the other hand, customers are rather asking questions related to complex problems and trends, which puts analysis into focus. Vaage and Sundal point out that it is crucial that intelligence services invest in new collection resources to maintain relevance and reliability. But in the digital age, it is not enough to accumulate as much information as possible to gain a better understanding of the world. To meet customers' needs, the intelligence process must be centred around the analysis work – which makes it more demanding than ever to be an analyst.

Notes

1 Phillip Knightley: *The Second Oldest Profession: Spies and Spying in the Twentieth Century*. New York: W.W. Norton & Company, 1986.
2 For early uses of intelligence, see, as examples, Philip H.J. Davies & Kristian C. Gustafson (ed.): *Intelligence Elsewhere: Spies and Espionage Outside the Anglosphere*. Washington, DC: Georgetown University Press, 2013; Francis Dvornik: *Origins of Intelligence Services: The Ancient Near East, Persia, Greece, Rome, Byzantium, the Arab Muslim Empires, the Mongol Empire, China, Muscovy*. New Brunswick, NJ: Rutgers University Press, 1974; Ralph D. Sawyer: *The Tao of Spycraft: Intelligence Theory and Practice in Traditional China*. Boulder: Westview Press, 1998; Sun Tzu (translated by Ralph D. Sawer): *The Art of War*. New York: Barnes & Noble, 1994; Gayatri Chakraborty: *Espionage in Ancient India: From the Earliest Times to 12th Century A.D.* Calcutta, India: Minerva Associates, 1990; Kautilya: *The Arthashastra*. New York: Penguin, 1992; Frank S. Russell: *Information Gathering in Ancient Greece*. Ann Arbor, MI: University of Michigan Press, 1999; Stephen Austin & N.B. Rankov: *Exploration: Military and Political Intelligence in the Roman World from the Second Punic War to the Battle of Adrianople*. London: Routledge, 1995; Rose Mary Sheldon: *Intelligence Activities in Ancient Rome: Trust the Gods But Verify*. New York: Frank Cass, 2005; Rose Mary Sheldon: *Operation Messiah: Roman Intelligence and the Birth of Christianity*. Portland: Valentine Mitchell, 2008; and Ross Hassig: *Aztec Warfare: Imperial Expansion and Political Control*. Norman: University of Oklahoma Press, 1995.
3 See, as an example, "The Intelligence Service: Ethical guidelines (in Norwegian)", February 2016, p. 6, https://forsvaret.no/fakta_/ForsvaretDocuments/2016-05-10-(U)-Etiske-retningslinjer.pdf.

4 Michael Herman: *Intelligence Power in War and Peace*. Cambridge: Cambridge University Press, 1996, p. 2.

5 David Omand: *Securing the State*. London: Hurst & Company, 2010.

6 Act of 20 March 1998 relating to the Norwegian Intelligence Service, https://app.uio. no/ub/ujur/oversatte-lover/data/lov-19980320-011-eng.pdf.

7 Michael Warner: "Wanted: A Definition of Intelligence", in Christopher Andrew et al. (eds.): *Secret Intelligence: A Reader*. London: Routledge, 2009, pp. 3–11.

8 Sherman Kent: *Strategic Intelligence for American World Policy*. Princeton, NJ: Princeton University Press, 1949.

9 For more about intelligence collection, see, as examples, Michael Bazzell: *Open Source Intelligence Techniques: Resources for Searching and Analyzing Online Information*, 5th edition. CreateSpace Publishing, 2016; Mark M. Lowenthal & Robert M. Clark (eds.): *The Five Disciplines of Intelligence Collection*. Washington, DC: CQ Press, 2015; and Robert M. Clark: *The Technical Collection of Intelligence*. Washington, DC: CQ Press, 2010.

10 David Omand, Jamie Bartlett, & Carl Miller: *#Intelligence*. London: Demos, 2012, www.demos.co.uk/files/_Intelligence_-_web.pdf?1335197327.

11 "The Intelligence Doctrine (in Norwegian)", *The Norwegian Defence Establishment*, May 2013, p. 17.

12 On the birth of World Wide Web, see James Gillies & Robert Cailliau: *How the Web Was Born: The Story of the World Wide Web*. Oxford: Oxford University Press, 2000.

13 Eric Schmidt & Jared Cohen: *The New Digital Age: Reshaping the Future of People, Nations and Business*. New York: Alfred A. Knopf, 2013, p. 4.

14 "One Billion People Online!", *eMarketer*, May 18, 2006, https://web.archive.org/ web/20081022105426/www.emarketer.com/Article.aspx?id=1003975.

15 Internet World Stats, www.internetworldstats.com/stats.htm.

16 Eric Schmidt quoted in *New York Magazine*, August 5, 2010, http://nymag.com/daily/ intelligencer/2010/08/googles_ceo_eric_schmidt_finds.html.

17 Cheri Speier, Joseph S. Valacich, & Iris Vessey: "The Influence of Task Interruption on Individual Decision Making: An Information Overload Perspective", *Decisions Sciences*, Vol. 30, No. 2, 1999, pp. 337–360.

18 Georg Simmel: "The Metropolis and Mental Life", in Kurt H. Wolff (ed.): *The Sociology of Georg Simmel*. New York: Free Press, 1950, pp. 409–424.

19 Alvin Toffler: *Future Shock*. New York: Random House, 1970.

20 Peter Gordon Roetzel: "Information Overload in the Information Age: A Review of the Literature from Business Administration, Business Psychology, and Related Disciplines with a Bibliometric Approach and Framework Development", *Business Research*, Vol. 12, 2019, pp. 479–522.

21 See, Bill Fischer: "The End of Expertise", *Harvard Business Review*, October 19, 2015, https://hbr.org/2015/10/the-end-of-expertise; and Tom Nichols: "Death of the Expert", *The Federalist*, January 17, 2014, http://thefederalist.com/2014/01/17/ the-death-of-expertise/.

22 Shankar N. Mundluru et al.: "'But Doctor, I Googled It!': The 'Three Rs' of Managing Patients in the Age of Information Overload", *Clinics in Dermatology*, Vol. 37, No. 1, 2019, pp. 74–77.

23 Robinson Meyer: "The Grim Conclusions of the Largest-Ever Study of Fake News", *The Atlantic*, April 8, 2018, www.theatlantic.com/technology/archive/2018/03/ largest-study-ever-fake-news-mit-twitter/555104/.

24 "Attention Spans", Consumer Insights, *Microsoft Canada*, September 2015, http:// dl.motamem.org/microsoft-attention-spans-research-report.pdf.

25 Se, for example, Howard Rosenberg & Charles S. Feldman: *No Time to Think: The Menace of Media Speed and the 24-hour News Cycle*. New York and London:

Continuum, 2008; and Bill Kovach & Tom Rosenstiel: *Warp Speed: America in the Age of Mixed Media*. New York: Century Foundation Press, 1999.

26 The Norwegian Ministry of Foreign Affairs: "Setting the Course for Norwegian Foreign and Security Policy", Meld. St. 36 (2016–2017), Report to the Parliament (White Paper), www.regjeringen.no/contentassets/0688496c2b764f029955cc6e2f27799c/en-gb/pdfs/stm201620170036000engpdfs.pdf.

27 Gregory F. Treverton & C. Bryan Gabbard: "Assessing the Tradecraft of Intelligence Analysis", Santa Monica: RAND Technical Report, 2008.

28 We are far from the first to claim that the sequential intelligence cycle does not reflect today's intelligence processes. See among others, Wilhelm Agrell & Gregory F. Treverton: *National Intelligence and Science: Beyond the Great Divide in Analysis and Policy*. Oxford and New York: Oxford University Press, 2015, pp. 39–43; Arthur S. Hulnick: "The Future of the Intelligence Process: The End of the Intelligence Cycle?", in Isabelle Duyvesteyn, Ben de Jong, & Joop van Reijn (eds.): *The Future of the Intelligence: Challenges in the 21st Century*. London and New York: Routledge, 2014, pp. 47–57; Mark Phythian (ed.): *Understanding the Intelligence Circle*. London and New York: Routledge, 2013; Peter Gill & Mark Phytian: *Intelligence in an Insecure World*, 2nd edition. Cambridge: Polity Press, 2012, pp. 11–17; and Omand, *op. cit.*, pp. 113–137.

Further reading

Agrell, Wilhelm, & Gregory F. Treverton: *National Intelligence and Science: Beyond the Great Divide in Analysis and Policy*. Oxford and New York: Oxford University Press, 2015, pp. 39–43.

Gill, Peter, & Mark Phytian: *Intelligence in an Insecure World*, 2nd edition. Cambridge: Polity Press, 2012, pp. 11–17.

Hulnick, Arthur S.: "The Future of the Intelligence Process: The End of the Intelligence Cycle?", in Isabelle Duyvesteyn, Ben de Jong, & Joop van Reijn (eds): *The Future of the Intelligence: Challenges in the 21st Century*. London and New York: Routledge, 2014, pp. 47–57.

Omand, David: *Securing the State*. London: Hurst & Company, 2010, pp. 113–137.

Phythian, Mark (ed.): *Understanding the Intelligence Circle*. London and New York: Routledge, 2013.

Warner, Michael: "Wanted: A Definition of Intelligence", in Christopher Andrew et al. (eds.): *Secret Intelligence: A Reader*. London: Routledge, 2009, pp. 3–11.

TV series

Le Bureau des Légendes, 4 seasons, Canal+, 2015–2018.
Rubicon, 1 season, IMDb, 2010.

2 The historical backdrop

Sir David Omand

Buddhists have a teaching that there are three poisons that cripple the mind: anger, attachment, and ignorance, of which ignorance is the most damaging.[1] As the editors show in Chapter 1, the very purpose of intelligence is to reduce ignorance so that our capacity to make sensible decisions can be improved. It is what intelligence analysts strive to achieve on behalf of governments, whether the decision-makers are the diplomats, military commanders, or Secretaries of State, who would be the traditional customers for secret intelligence. To this list we now also must add a multitude of security and police agencies, as well as border, customs, and immigration officers. Much of the information that analysts need to examine in order to answer the questions that are posed may be openly available by looking around, particularly on the Internet – that is, if they know in which direction to look and can distinguish the signal from the noise. There is also information that is hard to get since the holder of the information does not want us to know it. It may be the intentions of a leader of a hostile state poised to invade, the location of a terrorist cell plotting an atrocity, the malware from a group preparing a cyberattack, or the timing of when a criminal gang will commit their next crime. They will go to almost any length to prevent anyone else from acquiring their secrets.

In order to reduce ignorance, finding ways of making the person with the secret give it up is the central purpose of secret intelligence activity. The task of the intelligence analyst is, and always has been, to assess the truth value and significance of collected intelligence, determine how important and relevant they are to the decision maker, whether they should be shared, and what reservations must be made regarding the reliability of the information. Here, the analyst plays a key role in the intelligence process by performing the challenging task of combining collected intelligence of different kinds with available open information on a given subject. The goal is to provide the best explanation of observed events and, if possible, a forward-looking estimate of how events might develop.

The chapter starts by setting out the purpose of secret intelligence and the role of the analyst and explains how the role of the analyst has changed with technology. Digitisation of data has created new demands for actionable intelligence on people, and the possibility to supply such demands from the internet and other digital sources. The chapter concludes by examining how the role of the analyst may change in the future.

Types of decision-making support

At its most basic, there are four kinds of support that intelligence analysis can extend to a decision-maker. These types of decision-making support have remained unchanged throughout the five eras that are described later in the chapter, whether the analyst is working with information from traditional human agents, signals and imagery intelligence, or modern digital intelligence sources.[2]

Situation awareness

The first and most obvious way is to improve the situational awareness of the decision-maker. This includes essential knowledge of the characteristics of the situation being faced, answering questions about "what, who, where, and when". A diplomat needs to know if a hostile government is trying to circumvent a sanctions regime or if the terms of an arms control agreement have been violated. A military commander will need to know the size and composition of the enemy units facing him, and where and when they were last located. Similar demands will come from police and security agencies about terrorist groups or narcotics gangs or from naval units about pirates. Some of that "what, who, where and when" information may come from information accessible from the open internet or from digital databases, including non-secret sources. However, much of the information needed for situational awareness, when it really matters for national security and public safety, is likely to come from intelligence agencies. They will have to find ways of accessing sources and devise methods to overcome the will of adversaries to conceal their secrets.

True situational awareness rests on factual knowledge of the world, but the intelligence analyst can normally only hope to have parts of the information established as facts; the rest will have to be inferred and subject to caveats around reliability. Single-source reports can be graded in different ways according to the status of the source (documentary, technical, regular and reliable human source, etc.). However, an overall assessment also needs to include a caveat to indicate how deep the intelligence base on which the conclusions have been drawn is and present this by carefully choosing validation words. The UK Agencies, for example, would describe a judgement as "highly likely" if it corresponds to a probability range of 75–85 per cent, "likely" if 55–70 per cent, and "improbable" if 15–20 per cent. Such a scale helps provide consistency between analysts and gives the recipient of the judgement a sense of the "betting odds" on it being true. "Intelligence indicates that x is likely to have occurred" would be a typical statement, where "likely" carries the probabilistic meaning of 55–70 per cent likelihood of it being the case.

Explanations

Given a sound situational awareness of what is being faced, the good analyst then needs to construct explanations for why things are as they are, answering the questions that begin with "why, how, and what for". Put in terms of scientific analysis, the goal should be to provide the most convincing explanation of what is going on consistent with the observed data. Strictly speaking, one can only hope to provide the best explanatory hypothesis since any explanation may have to be changed if new evidence arrives that points in a different direction. In deciding between alternative hypotheses (such as the adversary is posturing with a major exercise or alternatively the adversary is trying to conceal preparations for a surprise attack), it is generally the hypothesis with the least evidence pointing against it that is to be preferred, not the hypothesis with the most reporting in its favour. Contrarily, the analyst can fall prey to the inductive fallacy whereby the existence of multiple reports saying the same thing strengthens belief in a hypothesis, when in reality they represent a non-representative sample. We are convinced that all swans are white and have masses of reporting to that effect, but our agent network does not extend to Australia, so the existence of black swans escapes our notice.

The analysts have, above all, to infer from the information available what meaning to ascribe to it in reporting the intelligence to their customers. Even apparent facts need interpretation. As a simple analogy, consider a chicken farm where the chickens conduct an espionage operation against the farmer and hack into his computer. They find that he has placed orders for large quantities of chicken food. Is the key judgement of the chicken analysts that this is good news, that there is more food on the way? Or bad news, that the time has come when the farmer must be planning to fatten up the chickens for the kill? The same raw intelligence report is capable of leading to very different assessments. Which is chosen may well depend upon the framing of the problem in the unconscious mind of the analyst. If this is an organic farm deep in the countryside, with chickens free to roam in the open air, the analyst may find it hard to conceive of the farmer having such a cruel fate in mind. If it is a factory farm with thousands of chickens cooped up in a giant metal shed, the chicken analyst may be all too ready to attribute the worst motive to the farmer.[2]

Any explanatory hypothesis is only as good as the information on which it is based. When fresh intelligence appears showing that the facts appear to have changed, the previously preferred hypothesis will have to be re-evaluated and may have to be rejected in favour of a more convincing alternative. There is no shame for the analyst in revising assessments in such circumstances, however frustrating for the decision-maker who may already have made decisions based on the earlier hypothesis.

Prediction or estimate

Given sound situational awareness, and the best possible explanation of what is going on and of the motives of the parties involved, the analyst may be able to hazard a prediction or estimate of how events will unfold. The latter term is usually preferred since it implies a range of possible outcomes around the one that is judged "most likely". This is the third level in this model of analysis. A good analyst will not just report what she or he believes is the most likely outcome but will also give a sense of whether the distribution of likelihood of that outcome (in statistics this would be equivalent to the standard deviation) is sharply pointed or whether the range of possible outcomes is wide and difficult to pinpoint. An analyst who knows the concerns of the decision-maker (as every good analyst should) may well also highlight much less likely but very troubling possible outcomes. A current example would be the risk that a terrorist group might succeed in smuggling shoulder-launched surface-to-air missiles into Western Europe with which to attack civil airliners. These are the so-called long-tailed distributions beloved of financial analysts – possible but not judged among the most likely outcomes – but were they to occur, then the implications for the decision-maker would be extreme. As the 2008 financial crisis showed, however, even very unlikely outcomes will sometimes happen.

In putting forward an assessment, therefore, the good analyst will distinguish for the customer those key judgements that rest directly on intelligence reporting (with caveats as necessary about their assessed reliability) and those that rest on the analyst's best explanation of what is going on and how the situation might develop (with as necessary a range of estimates, highlighting those of greatest consequence for the decision-maker).

Warning

There is a fourth category of analytic output that needs to be added to the trio of situational awareness, explanation, and estimation, and that is the provision of strategic warning of significant possible future developments. With strategic warning decision-makers can consider whether to take precautions, set new intelligence requirements and priorities, or commission further study to prepare just in case those threats should crystallise. This level of analytic work is intended to provide notice of possible futures, for which direct intelligence reporting is unlikely to be available in time. An example might be an assessment of the risk of terrorist groups attacking critical infrastructure with cyber malware, given the availability of the necessary tools and training from criminal sources on the Dark Net. There may well be no direct intelligence that any group is planning such operations, but that does not mean that such a potential threat might not suddenly materialise. A wise government may well commission work on defensive preparations and instruct intelligence agencies to be alert to any early signs of interest in the technology on the part of hostile groups. In a similar way, intelligence about potentially hostile governments investing heavily in research on quantum computing provides strategic notice of a major threat to the security of key communications – should a workable quantum computer ever be built that works at scale. None has been to date, and it may be decades into the future, but a wise government might start research on quantum attack–resistant cryptosystems just in case. Analysts can prepare papers giving strategic notice of the possible security consequences but are not likely to be able to estimate likelihood in the way that would be possible for short-term threats where current intelligence exists.

Five eras

We can surmise that the fundamental purpose of intelligence analysis as described in the preceding sections has not changed over the centuries, although in previous eras the task would have been conducted instinctively and would certainly not have been conceptualised as a distinct set of disciplines. From historical records, however, we can see how the analytic task began to require specialised training as types of intelligence sources multiplied with advances in technology, most recently the digital revolution. In a first approximation, the development of intelligence analysis can be fitted into five overlapping eras that reflect the kind of information available at that stage, each era opening up new uses to which intelligence could be put. Like the laying down of sedimentary layers of rock, each new era has added new weight and complexity to the analytic task without removing the earlier layers. Today (and tomorrow), an intelligence analyst professional should be capable of mining the material found in each of these five layers. In order to cover the full range of tasks, increasingly specialised branches of analysis are becoming essential.

First era: human agents and encrypted messages

Before the invention of the electric telegraph by Samuel Morse in 1837, the original and most basic form of secret material available for analysis was often limited to reporting from informants and paid agents (forms of human intelligence or HUMINT) and the contents of intercepted and deciphered diplomatic despatches and opened letters (the earliest forms of communications intelligence or COMINT, a branch today of signals intelligence or SIGINT). The crypt-analyst who conducted the decryption belongs to an ancient professional tradition but separate from that of the intelligence analyst, one often associated with extraordinary mathematical aptitude. Well-known crypt-analysts include such figures as the seventeenth-century English cryptographer Royal, Oxford Professor John Wallis, the most talented English mathematician before Newton, together with Antoine Rossignol at the French court under Cardinal Richelieu and Alan Turing at Bletchley Park during the Second World War.[3]

In the pre-telegraph era, the senior palace official who was controlling human agent reporting, and interception and decryption of despatches, could at the same time be the judge (chief analyst) of their significance as well as the end user of the intelligence. Such a user of intelligence knows better than anyone what intelligence is most valuable to have (what today is called setting the requirement) and how it might be used to maximise national advantage, including countering both foreign plotting and domestic sedition. The two outstanding historical examples of this model of intelligence come from England in the reign of Queen Elizabeth I and a little later from France under King Louis XIII. In the former case, the close adviser to the Queen, Sir Francis Walsingham created a network of agents across Europe backed by exceptional cryptographers such as Thomas Phelippes. These agents were able to provide intelligence on the plotting of the

Pope and the monarchs of Spain and France to overthrow the Protestant Elizabeth in favour of the Catholic Mary Queen of Scots, including foiling two invasion attempts and several assassination plots. In the case of France, the close adviser and spymaster to the King was Cardinal Richelieu, outwitting the Austro-Spanish Hapsburg dynasty with a network of spies inside and outside France and ensuring French dominance in the Thirty Years' War. Richelieu too was supported by able cryptographers, notably Antoine Rossignol. Both Walsingham and Richelieu operated intelligence-gathering networks, received the product, had the knowledge and experience to analyse it themselves, and had the authority on behalf of the sovereign to act on it (often brutally where domestic sedition was suspected).

Second era: topological and strategic military intelligence

A second era for intelligence opened with the forming of mass armies in Europe, for example those of legendary commanders such as Napoleon, Wellington, and Blücher. Its value in providing essential information about the enemy, land to be marched over (and its ability to sustain the army), and terrain to be fought over was recognised for the strategic command of large armies and, correspondingly, for fleets such as that of Admiral Nelson. The famous German theoretician of war General Carl von Clausewitz later studied their practice and advised the Prussian Army on the institutionalisation of general staff support to improve the quality of information available to the Field Marshal or General to reduce the inevitable uncertainties of war, although warning that "many intelligence reports in war are contradictory; even more are false, and most are uncertain".[4] Strategic-level military intelligence flourished during the American Civil War, including decryption of Confederate despatches, observation by balloon linked to the ground by an electric telegraph wire, and the interception of long-distance telegraph lines. Later, the French Army set up their military intelligence staff, the Deuxième Bureau, in 1873, following the observation by their military attaches of the Civil War and their own crushing defeat by the Prussian Army in 1871. Other armies followed suit, with the British Army creating its military intelligence branches, including the provision of mapping and topological information to commanders.

Third era: radio and tactical military intelligence

The opening of the third era came with the technological revolution of wireless communication. In July 1897 while on a visit to Italy, Marconi made the first radio contact from ship to shore over a distance of 12 miles. Progress in using and in exploiting wireless radio was rapid and greatly expanded the way that intelligence could be used consistently in war. The first wireless interception station was established in 1914 on the North Sea coast at Scarborough in England, with the purpose of monitoring transmissions from the newly installed radios in the German Grand Fleet and conducting direction finding. Field wireless sets reached the British Army in 1916 and by the following year reconnaissance aircraft were fitted with wireless as well. Now intelligence support was not just useful for strategic decisions but could readily be exploited for operational and tactical use by lower-level commanders using timely information derived from intercepted communications.

The new technology made it possible to gather pieces of intelligence on the enemy, and these scraps of information could be assembled and analysed. As a result, they could warn of an enemy warship or submarine, located by radio direction finding, or pre-empt an artillery barrage by intercepting and piecing together logistic instructions for its preparation. In 1916, it was the Royal Navy's cryptographers (in Room 40 in the Admiralty in London under Rear Admiral "Blinker" Hall) who deciphered the transatlantic telegram they had intercepted from German Foreign Minister Zimmerman offering Mexico an alliance against the United States in return for which Mexico would recover Texas, Arizona, and New Mexico. The British shared the decrypt with President Wilson, who made the message public, helping to precipitate US entry into the war against Germany, an early example of "weaponising" information. By the time peace finally came to Europe in 1918, the centre of gravity of intelligence analysis work had shifted during the course of the war from the diplomatic and strategic (although those still continued to be important functions) to operational military use. Wireless messages, like telegraph messages, were sent in Morse code during the First World War. A major technical advancement came with the invention in the 1920s of radio telephony and voice communication. This provided a new source for intelligence analysts to work on, something that developed much further during the Spanish Civil War and the Second World War.

In a dynamic interaction, not unlike that of the digital revolution of the twenty-first century, the potential availability of all forms of wireless communications stimulated new demands on intelligence agencies during the Second World War, from intelligence officers on the military and naval and air staffs. Efficient systems were needed to ensure the results of interception of signals could be decrypted, leading to the development of the first computer systems. Analysts were under considerable operational pressure to generate reporting quickly, such as indications of a U-boat pack near a convoy or that enemy fighters had been scrambled, so that they could speedily be put to operational use by the military commander who could warn a bomber force already airborne. That pressure of demand for useable intelligence in turn stimulated innovation over new sources of interception and ways of decrypting messages with remarkable results.

In the Cold War that followed, the dominant intelligence requirement for NATO nations was to keep track of the order of battle of Soviet forces and their defence programmes, including on Soviet atom bomb development and on the economy, given its importance for armaments production. Sources for signals intelligence and imagery became highly sophisticated. The huge US national space reconnaissance programme used orbiting and geo-stationary imagery and then signals intelligence-gathering satellites, in turn placing new demands for specialised intelligence analysts.

Fourth era: intelligence and the Internet

The fourth era is that of digital intelligence. Its dominance in current intelligence activity started in the 1990s with the advent of the Internet. The phenomenal development and rapid take-up of internet services resulted from its open protocols enabling any compliant network to connect to and thus be connected with any other internet network. Within a decade the rapid development of the Internet, and the World Wide Web, provided entirely new methods of personal, commercial, and government communication, information sharing such as text messaging and interactive web pages, and file sharing. The development of public key cryptography made online monetary transactions feasible and allowed rapid innovation in applications attractive to business and consumers alike. Voice and video communications began to be carried over the Internet, using, for example, Skype and FaceTime, supplanting much of the terrestrial telephone traffic that used subscriber dialling, not least because such internet calls were not separately charged for.

In parallel, there was the advent of mobile telephones to replace analogue mobile systems. This accelerated the use of new communications channels, and virtual private networks carried on the Internet replaced the old-fashioned diplomatic and governmental wireless networks of the previous era. Mobile telephones themselves became digital internet devices with the functionality of desktop computers.

The digital revolution wrought profound changes in the technological environment in which intelligence agencies operate and generated new sources and methods for analysts to work with this fourth era was described in the 2012 National Security Agency (NSA) strategy by General Michael Hayden (Director of the NSA and later of the Central Intelligence Agency (CIA):

> For decades, Signals Intelligence has sustained deep and persistent access to all manner of adversaries to inform and guide the actions and decisions of Presidents, military commanders, policy makers and clandestine service officers. As the world has changed, and global interdependence and the advent of the information age have transformed the nature of our target space, we have adapted in innovative and creative ways that have led some to describe the current day as "the golden age of SIGINT".[5]

That judgement has much truth in it – although it was a golden age for intelligence agencies, it did not last long. For those who wish to hide their communications the Internet was seen to offer a safe space outside the rule of law, with a wide choice of social media platforms, chat rooms (including those inside online games), drop boxes, and secure apps. The targets of the intelligence agencies began to realise how to protect their communications, and the internet companies following the Snowden allegations introduced more secure devices and end-to-end strong encryption that required no skill on the part of the user.

Companies accelerated the commercial development of highly secure services and devices. Apple made advanced security of their mobile devices from interception a selling point. Social media applications such as Telegram gained market share by having strong end-to-end encryption and became popular with terrorist groups for that reason. At the same time, obtaining readable content from interception was becoming increasingly hard against encryption too strong to be routinely dealt with in any useable time. In part, this has been driving the trend towards "hacking" devices rather than attacking the communications in transit.

Governments came under public pressure to find lawful ways of enabling intelligence analysts to exploit digital data on their suspects and to work with internet companies to enable lawful access to communications content and the communications data of the users of their services. Communications data has, in particular, shown itself to be invaluable for intelligence and law enforcement purposes.[6]

Fifth era: digital forensics and big data

A fifth era for the intelligence analytic profession then opened up in terms of digital forensic analysis, as hacktivists, criminals, terrorists, and hostile states began to realise that the digital medium could be exploited by them. States and non-state actors, including criminal groups based in Russia and China, also developed means of hacking into computer networks and spreading viruses and other malware to conduct cybercrime, cyber espionage, cyber sabotage, and cyber subversion.[7] The role of the cyber analyst developed in order to examine the forensic evidence for an intrusion, to deduce if possible from the computer code involved the nature of the attack, to conduct the equivalent of a counter-espionage damage assessment of what has been stolen, corrupted, or affected by the attack, and then to assess which state or group might be responsible. The analytical difficulty of attributing attacks to a perpetrator is compounded by the inherent anonymity of the Internet and the possibility of deliberate "false-flag" deception where the attacker wishes to deceive the analyst as to authorship of the exploit. A good example is the 2016 hacking of French *TV 5 Monde* at the launch of its broadcasting service. At first, the hacking appeared to have been perpetrated by the self-proclaimed "Cybercaliphat", but further analysis revealed that a Russian group was most likely behind it. Such deception is not unique to the digital medium but is much easier to conduct there.[8]

The private cyber security sector now also employs a large number of these specialist digital intelligence analysts to assess client breaches and advise on cleaning up networks after intrusions. Some of the private sector companies have shown themselves, for commercial reasons, more ready than governments to take the risk of publishing their own forensic attribution conclusions – for example, North Korea was behind the 2016 attempt to steal $941 million from the Central Bank of Bangladesh.[9] The availability of anonymising software, which hides the IP address of the user's device from an intercepting agency, has created further demands from police and security agencies for cyber analysts able to pursue investigations into serious criminal groups using the Dark Web, such as child abuse networks. Analysts now have to understand the nature of advanced persistent cyber threats (advanced since they often involve exploiting vulnerabilities in software that firewalls will not detect – so-called zero-day exploits – and persistent since the attacks will continue until there is a successful penetration). They can thus help detect, classify, and, where possible, attribute cyberattacks, including the theft of intellectual property. Such intelligence analysis can then be used to design and help operate improved security systems for cyber defence. The UK National Cyber Security Centre, for example, is openly described as an important part of GCHQ, the UK signals intelligence agency.[10]

The current era of digital analysis has been marked by insistent demands by police and national security authorities for intelligence on individuals who pose threats to Western nations, especially after the trauma of the al-Qaeda terrorist attacks on New York and Washington on 9/11, 2001, and later on Madrid in 2004 and London in 2005. Although traditional diplomatic and military intelligence requirements have continued, the priority has had to be given to finding and countering those networks and individuals posing a direct and immediate threat to the public. The number of counterterrorism analysts expanded rapidly and specialist centres such as the US National Counter-Terrorism Centre and the UK Joint Terrorism Analysis Centre were set up in the early years of the twenty-first century. Dictators, terrorists, arms proliferators, cyber hackers, people traffickers, narcotics gangs, child abusers, and others in the sights of intelligence, security, and law enforcement agencies had something else in common. As individuals living in the modern digital world, they all were liable to leave traces – digital exhaust – behind them. Such scraps of information pieced together by analysts could begin to reveal the identities (often multiple identities) of such individuals, together with those of their associates, and their location, movements, financing, pattern of life, and intentions.

By a global coincidence, this upsurge in demand for information on suspects came at the same time as the commercial revolution of the Internet, generating an increase in the collection of information on individual users by internet companies and thus the potential ability of police, intelligence, and security agencies to access such information for intelligence and evidential purposes. The Internet has thus made possible new supply opportunities for accessing information, helping to meet those insistent demands for intelligence about suspects. This has in turn driven the development of more ingenious uses of digital data from which intelligence can be derived. The dynamic interaction between digital demand and supply is set to continue.

Other digital intelligence sources have proliferated; these require specialised analysis. These include telemetry (remote measuring and wireless transmission of measurement data), digitised mapping, and multispectral imagery from satellites or streamed from reconnaissance drones, from CCTV and automatic vehicle number plate readers, and from miniaturised video cameras that can be used in surveillance. Access to communications being transmitted by fibre optic cable, satellite, or microwave links provides metadata in bulk as well as the communications content. Intelligence agencies can also derive useful intelligence from digitised personal information collected for marketing purposes by the commercial world from internet and mobile devices. The existence of so much digitised personal data also poses a counterintelligence risk, illustrated by the massive 2015 cyber theft of sensitive personal information from the Office of Personnel Management on US government employees, including the secret agencies.[11]

This complex data ecosystem has driven the massive take-up of readily available software applications (now universally just called apps) for mobile devices from which intelligence can be derived. The rapid adoption of social media (of which there are thousands of different variants available worldwide) has led to the creation of SOCMINT, or social media intelligence, as a distinct branch of analysis, including the application of computerised sentiment analysis.[12] A further relevant development has been the provision of cloud services, not just for easily accessible data storage but also to enable mobile devices to access very powerful software programs too large to fit on individual devices, such as search and inference engines able to recognize context and thus be faster and more efficient, translation to and from multiple languages and voice-activated inquiries. The benefits to the consumer are many – more appropriate responses to search engine requests, relevant "pop-up" advertisements on websites and apps, and free or cheap services. The private sector is thus an expert at harvesting, for its own commercial purposes, data on the internet usage of its customers, including data relevant to the suspects being investigated by intelligence and law enforcement authorities.

The World Wide Web has produced an explosion of open information of all kinds that can be browsed by any user. OSINT, or open-source intelligence, is another recent branch of intelligence analysis exploiting increasingly powerful search engines to locate and index information on web pages and to identify individuals from photographs and track the use of ships, aircraft, vehicles, premises, telephone, and fax numbers, all useful sources for investigations into criminal networks, including sanctions evasion. Now the world's information is online, potentially a few mouse clicks away, provided that the analyst has the specialist open-source skills and training to find it.

A further source for modern intelligence analysts is PROTINT, or data-protected personal information held on government databases such as vehicle records, passports, national insurance and immigration records, and private sector databases, such as bookings of airlines and hotel chains. Appropriate legal authority is in most Western nations needed in order to access such databases and in appropriate cases to have the digital access to allow data mining techniques to be applied. In the case of the UK, Parliament has agreed that the British security and intelligence agencies may hold copies of such bulk personal databases for use by analysts conducting investigations, but this requires renewable warrants and judicial oversight.[13] Such sources of supply of digital intelligence make an increasingly useful contribution to the intelligence jigsaw and to the painstaking analytic process of "discovery" of terrorist cells and criminal groups and the individuals involved in them.

The access and interpretation of digital intelligence are thus now a major analytic specialisation. After a terrorist attack, for example, analysts can try to establish the geolocation of suspected members of the gang and those who might have directed the attack or supported it – for example, whether they have used an internet mapping or other app to reconnoitre their target in the weeks before the attack, or whether there exists a pattern of mobile communications that could be used to uncover other terrorist plots.[14] Despite these opportunities for the authorities, the widespread availability of advice on how to avoid detection and surveillance makes the intelligence task increasingly challenging. This includes manuals that terrorist groups themselves have posted on the net.[15]

Into the future

All-source intelligence assessment in support of national security will continue to be essential given all the traditional foreign affairs and defence preoccupations with the activity of potentially hostile nations and regions of instability. At the same time, the more recent increase in demands for intelligence on major non-state threats to public safety will continue. This shift is described as moving from "the Secret State" typical of the Cold War period to "the Protecting State" of today, where the focus of national security concern is the direct security of the public, rather than that of the institutions of the state.[16] In recent decades countering the threat from Salafist-jihadist groups such as al-Qaeda and ISIS, and their associates and affiliates, has dominated Western intelligence communities. This has led to the development of new methods of analysis of digitised data and new forms of inter-agency analytic organisation such as the US National Counter-Terrorism Centre and the UK Joint Terrorism Centre and counterparts in many European nations. In addition to the major threat to the public from terrorism, we now have to add the threat of cyberattacks by hostile states or criminal groups, requiring specialist forensic cyber intelligence analysis. A further shift in analytic emphasis is under way, driven by the recognition that states can use cyberattacks on critical infrastructure[17] as part of subversive asymmetric campaigns (often called "hybrid" warfare) that also include covert information activity. An example from 2016 and 2017 is the Russian-backed attempts to influence elections in the United States and in Europe in directions perceived as favourable to Moscow. NATO and the EU have already backed the setting up in Helsinki of a European Centre of Excellence for Countering Hybrid Threats.[18] In addition, there is a growing interest in intelligence to support economic well-being, including anticipating threats to the availability of key scarce natural resource and identifying corruption and fraud and detection of market rigging by cyber criminals and hostile states.

It is inevitable that as technology advances, new sources will appear that will provide information for the analyst that can be turned into useable intelligence. Analysts will have to learn to understand sufficiently the technologies concerned to be able to judge the reliability of such sources and the biases that may be hidden in computerised analysis of data. As an example, artificial intelligence applied to facial recognition software, allied to high-resolution imaging from very small drones, may transform imagery for public protection. In the near future, digital "wearables" will also be popularised as consumer goods. An example is the digital bracelet or watch that takes pulse and heart rate measurements and links to the owner's mobile phone – and in the future possibly directly to the doctor's surgery to warn of impending trouble. A very wide range of other devices are now being made internet connectable, including domestic appliances and even children's toys. This is the so-called internet of things or, as it is being called, the Internet of Everything. Such devices increase the stock of information that might be relatable to an individual suspect and from which in some cases useful intelligence might be derived. However, they also increase the attack surface for those intent on cyber harm, and the analysts trying to track them will have to take such attack vectors into account.

Whether further technological developments, such as quantum computing, or other global upheaval such as might follow long-term climate changes, will result in a yet further level of intelligence analysis remains to be seen.

Notes

1 Ringu Tulku Rinpoch: *Living without Fear and Anger*. Oxford: Bodicharya, 2005.
2 Adapted from David Deutsch, *The Fabric of Reality*. London: Allen Lane, 1997, p. 60.
3 Charles F. Rocca Jr.: "Mathematics in the History of Cryptography", *Cryptologia*, Vol. 38, No. 3, 2014.
4 Carl von Clausewitz: *On War*. Princeton, NJ: Princeton University Press, 1989, p. 117.
5 NSA's SIGINT-strategy, published February 23, 2012, https://archive.org/stream/nsa-sigint-strategy-2012-2016/nsa-sigint-strategy-2012-2016_djvu.txt.
6 David Anderson: *A Question of Trust*. London: HMSO, 2015, pp. 133–140.
7 As described in the 2016 UK National Cyber Security Strategy, www.gov.uk/government/uploads/system/uploads/attachment_data/file/567242/national_cyber_security_strategy_2016.pdf.
8 Gordon Correra: "How France's TV5 Was Almost Destroyed by 'Russian Hackers'", *BBC*, October 10, 2016, www.bbc.co.uk/news/technology-37590375.
9 "Chasing Lazarus: A Hunt for the Infamous Hackers to Prevent Large Bank Robberies", *Kaspersky*, April 3, 2017, www.kaspersky.com/about/press-releases/2017_chasing-lazarus-a-hunt-for-the-infamous-hackers-to-prevent-large-bank-robberies.
10 The National Cyber Security Centre, www.ncsc.gov.uk.
11 "At First Cyber Meeting, China Claims OPM Hack Is 'Criminal Case'", *Ars Technica*, March 12, 2015, https://arstechnica.co.uk/tech-policy/2015/12/at-first-cyber-meeting-china-claims-opm-hack-is-criminal-case/.
12 David Omand, Jamie Bartlett, & Carl Miller: "Introducing Social Media Intelligence (SOCMINT)", *Intelligence and National Security*, Vol. 27, No. 6, 2012.
13 See, for example, the Regulation of Investigatory Powers Act, 2016, www.legislation.gov.uk/ukpga/2016/25/contents/enacted.
14 A series of real cases are described in the Report commissioned by the UK Parliament on the necessity for British agencies to have access to such bulk powers, David Anderson: "Report of the Bulk Powers Review", London: HMSO, Cm 9346, August 2016, Annexes 8–11.
15 Such as the online ISIS manual discovered by Dr Aaron Brantly of the West Point Combatting Terrorism Centre, www.wired.com/2015/11/isis-opsec-encryption-manuals-reveal-terrorist-group-security-protocols/.
16 See for example, Omand, *op. cit.*
17 Such as the case of 2017 Russian cyber-attacks on the Ukrainian electricity grid. See Andy Greenberg: "How an Entire Nation became Russia's Testlab for Cyber", *Wired Magazine*, June 20, 2017, www.wired.com/story/russian-hackers-attack-ukraine/.
18 "NATO Welcomes Opening of European Centre for Countering Hybrid Threats", *NATO*, April 11, 2017, www.nato.int/cps/en/natohq/news_143143.htm; and "EU Welcomes Establishment of the Finnish Centre of Excellence for Countering Hybrid Threats", *EU External Action*, April 11, 2017, https://eeas.europa.eu/headquarters/headquarters-homepage_en/24572/EU%20welcomes%20establishment%20of%20the%20Finnish%20Centre%20of%20Excellence%20for%20countering%20hybrid%20threats.

Further reading

Andrew, Christopher: *The Secret World: A History of Intelligence*. London: Allen Lane, 2018.

Richelson, Jeffrey T.: *A Century of Spies: Intelligence in the Twentieth Century*. New York and Oxford: Oxford University Press, 1995.

3 Intelligence as decision-making support

Espen Barth Eide

What characterises the threat environment in the digital age? How does this affect Norwegian foreign and security policy? And considering this, what is it like to be a decision-maker in the digital age, and how can intelligence be relevant decision-making support?

To answer the latter question first:

Intelligence is probably more relevant today than ever before in history. As Secretary of State and later Minister in both the Ministry of Foreign Affairs and Ministry of Defence for a total of ten years, I repeatedly experienced that the Intelligence Service provided invaluable support for acute events and crises – for example, after September 11, 2001, during the Georgia crisis of 2008, and throughout the terrorist attack in Amenas in 2013. Equally important was the Service's ongoing contribution to understanding the situation, both in its own neighbourhoods and when Norwegian soldiers operated under distant skies. The intelligence service provides not only unique information but also analysis of great benefit. As I will return to in this chapter, this part of intelligence support is becoming increasingly important. With news delivered at lightning speed and the ever-expanding ocean of information that characterises the digital age, the intelligence service helps national decision-makers uncover patterns and reduce the complexity of today's threat environment. Furthermore, the service often has a longer perspective than what a decision-maker manages to have in everyday life and can therefore alert to more subtle trends that it is critical to be aware of. In the digital age, "fake news" is also a growing problem, and the service plays an important role in validating information. The challenge of information overload is further reinforced by actors actively seeking to use the many opportunities that now exist to influence our thinking, by systematically influencing our understanding of what the world looks like. The distinction between true and false is being erased in the public domain. Among the most important tasks for the intelligence service in the years ahead will be to check the facts – that is, to be a validator for decision-makers.

What a minister or other decision-maker has of available intelligence will of course vary. Intelligence is first and foremost in support of the decision-makers who are responsible for national security, and in particular those related to defence and foreign policy. How much a decision-maker benefits from this intelligence also largely depends on her or his knowledge of the intelligence service itself.

Anyone who is going to use intelligence should also be aware of the opportunities and limitations inherent in this type of support and be able to ask the right questions. "As you ask, you get an answer", goes an old Norwegian saying. It also helps if you have at least a general understanding of the methods and sources of an intelligence service, including the specific methodological problems associated with intelligence assessments. On the other hand, it is important that the intelligence service also answers the questions that policymakers are not aware of and ask. And it is crucial that the service is able to disseminate this knowledge in a way that catches the attention of a minister in the midst of a busy workday, which is largely driven by the news' "24-hour cycle" and constant time pressure.

Threats in the digital age

If you take a long historical perspective, you can see that our experience with threats has at least had one stable feature: There has almost always been a certain advantage in being a defender rather than an attacker. Let's illustrate it this way: Up in his castle, sometime in the Middle Ages, the prince had a pretty good idea of who might be aiming for his head, and it was an advantage to be the biggest, strongest, and not least in a defender position. Whoever was inside the castle wall had an advantage over potential attackers. The attacker therefore had to compensate with more soldiers, better technology, and tactics, as well as seek to surprise. In more modern times, it was about defending one's own borders against invasion – and again, being able to prepare for this did at least give some gain over a possible invader. If you monitored the surroundings closely enough, you would also have a certain warning time before something bad happened. In the digital age, this is no longer as obvious, something I will return to later.

For states, the normal situation has been to not be under military attack. Norway has, for example, not been attacked militarily since 9 April 1940. The story of 9 April also clearly illustrates how this was an absolute breach of the normal state: Enemy warships sailed into Norwegian fjords, soldiers marched up Oslo's main street Karl Johan, and bombers flew over our homes. Within hours, the state went from peace to war. When, after five hard years, German forces returned the command to Norwegian soldiers at Akershus Castle on 8 May 1945, peace and normality were restored. Still, many probably think of war as a dichotomy: either it is peace or else there is war, and you know what is what. One set of rules applies in peace, another in war, one would like to think.

As shown in Chapter 1, it is debatable to what extent the world is actually in greater change today than it used to be, or whether we rather have the impression that everything is chaos as we learn about everything that is happening. What is indisputable is that developments within the so-called cyber domain are running at lightning speed. And this development has dramatic consequences for both the threat environment that Norwegian decision-makers are facing and our understanding of conflict and war. Somewhat exaggerated, one can say that in our cyber reality, you are lucky if you know that you are being attacked at the same time as it happens. As a rule, you only realise afterwards that you *have been* attacked. In the past, there was a clear violation of the normal state when a state was subjected to a hostile attack, and as a rule such an attack was unmistakably military in nature. The new norm is to be under *continuous* attack, at least in the cyber space, and that the attack does not necessarily happen with what we regard as military means or for that matter against military targets. NATO Secretary General Jens Stoltenberg points out that the alliance is under constant cyberattacks from Russia and other state actors. The alliance is exposed to as many as 500 known attacks every single month.[1] The same goes for the member states – and all other states around the globe. In this context, attacks in the digital space can be compared to background radiation: The radiation is there all the time, and the alarm goes off only if the radiation reaches a certain critical level.

In the digital age, it has become infinitely easier to attack an opponent than to be in a defender position. In the Middle Ages, one was relatively safe within thick castle walls, and an attacking army should preferably be larger, stronger, and better prepared than the defender. Today, technological developments have made society more vulnerable than ever before in history. The vulnerability is primarily related to critical infrastructure such as power supply and the telecommunications network. It will potentially have grave consequences for society if these types of infrastructure are affected by a serious cyberattack, for example that the authorities will no longer be able to maintain supplies of essential goods and services to the population.

When I, as Minister of Defence, established the Norwegian Cyber Defence in 2012, this was also a recognition that digital space today must be seen as a separate military domain, on par with land, sea, and air. At the NATO Summit in Warsaw in the summer of 2016, member states adopted the same for NATO. Secretary-General Stoltenberg even suggests that a particularly serious cyberattack could, under certain conditions, trigger NATO's Article Five, which says that an attack against one of the alliance's countries should mobilise all member states for joint military defence.[2]

Ever since the Napoleonic Wars, there has been a code of ethics between the states where a clear distinction has been drawn between war and peace, warring and non-warring. This was later formalised in humanitarian law. It is a good principle, which we should defend as far as we can – but for many players this distinction is about to be erased.

Simply put, the threat environment that Norway faces today is defined by two parallel global trends:

> The first trend is a continuing chaos that characterizes the international system. In several countries, especially in the Middle East, Africa, and Asia, state power has weathered for a number of years. In states such as Yemen, Somalia, Mali, and Afghanistan, the central government has significantly lost territorial control and monopoly of violence. Here, a vacuum of power has been created that is filled by non-state actors, including terrorists and criminals, which pose a threat far beyond the areas they control. An example is the so-called Islamic State, best known by the acronyms "ISIL" or "IS". At the

height of its power, this group controlled an area of Syria and Iraq the size of England, attracting tens of thousands of foreign warriors from virtually every part of the world – including around 100 Norwegian citizens. Digital tools contributed to the spread of the group's radical ideology, enabling powerful international mobilization of young people. In this context, the wave of terror that rolled across Europe shows a clear interaction between local conflicts far away from us and the threat environment here at home. Geographical distance does not protect as it once did in our globalized world.

Moreover, it is not only such groups that challenge the traditional monopoly of the state: Large companies are also increasingly acting autonomously from the territorial state, and they have even become important foreign policy players. Previously, the largest companies in the world were almost exclusively in the oil and energy sector, while today they are mainly in the technology sector. A few years ago, "BRICS" was on everyone's lips, referring to the presumably emerging countries of Brazil, Russia, India, China, and South Africa, while one today is far more concerned with the acronym "GAFA" referring to technology giants Google, Apple, Facebook, and Amazon. These companies have tremendous impact on the lives of people across the globe, and more or less live their own lives across national borders. This situation has given rise to cooperation between states to take back national sovereignty – primarily in connection with taxation of global corporations, but also to gain more control over what happens to people's personal data.[3]

The other major trend that defines the threat environment comes from what may be called the return of geopolitics: We again see an international system characterised by a lack of leadership and increasing rivalry between major powers. The United States is no longer the global hegemon as the country was in the wake of the Cold War. We have seen this trend for a long time, but it has become particularly evident under the Trump administration. The slogan "America first" signals that the United States should now focus on domestic needs and not take as much responsibility for the rest. The United States has announced that it will withdraw from several multilateral agreements and appears far less interested in taking on global leadership responsibilities. The United States has not thereby stopped engaging internationally – but today it is happening in a far more sporadic and casual way, rather than as an expression of some long-term strategy. One day, an immediate withdrawal from Syria is announced, the next day bombs are aimed at relatively symbolic targets, and then there is talk again of withdrawing.

In several regions, other major powers, such as China and Russia, seek to fill the power vacuum left by the United States. China is building up capabilities to be a "good #2" economically and militarily, seeking to challenge other countries' ability to define what is happening in China's neighbourhoods. Putin has stepped in to strengthen Russia's position in the troubled belt between west and east of Europe, something we clearly witnessed in Georgia and Ukraine, as well as securing strong influence in civil war-ravaged Syria and thereby securing its access to the Mediterranean. For decades, the United States has been the cornerstone of many states' defence and security policies – for European countries through NATO. In several NATO countries, it is now being asked whether Trump is a man who will fulfil the security guarantees provided in the event of a real crisis.

Implications for Norway

The threat environment that characterises the digital age is complex, often unclear, and rapidly changing. As we have already mentioned, the new normal state is to be constantly attacked in the digital space, and there is no longer an equally clear distinction between war and peace. This also means that it is very difficult for national decision-makers to know when a serious situation really arises. The sector principle – that is, the one in charge of a social sector in general also has it in crisis – is basically a good principle in terms of *preventing* and *preparing for* crises. But this principle is not necessarily as well-suited to *dealing with* complex crises, where different sectors are threatened simultaneously. On the contrary, the sector or subsidiarity principle can make it difficult for decision-makers to detect that Norway is facing a serious hostile attack. The sector principle means that the constitutional responsibility of the individual minister is also continued in a crisis. In other words, it is the individual ministries that are responsible for dealing with a crisis that affects their own area of responsibility and for coordinating with other ministries to ensure the necessary crisis management. It is only in the event of serious crises or disasters that the government as such is also involved in its handling.[4] For the authorities, it can be very difficult to see a possible connection between a major power failure in Nordland, failure of the telecommunications network in Western Norway, and that ambulances are suddenly not available in Eastern Norway, three situations that according to the sector principle should be handled by three different ministries and their underlying directorates. An adversary can therefore deliberately attack various sectors, for example to create confusion and paralyze critical community infrastructure to weaken the state's resistance to pressure or in the face of a major military attack.

In the digital age, Norwegian decision-makers must deal with the consequences of both the two trends I described here; thus, on the one hand, the chaos that characterises the international system and, on the other, increasing rivalry between major powers whose agenda occasionally runs counter to our national interests. Everything seems to be in movement these days.

Norway must now deal with a more interest-oriented world where liberal ideas are under pressure – also in the United States and in Europe. This may not be the world we want, but it is the reality; and we must deal with these changes in a realistic way.

Firstly, Norway's traditional partners are changing. The lighthouses that Norway has navigated safely in security and defence policy for decades, primarily the United States and the United Kingdom through NATO cooperation, are changing. Today, Norwegian authorities must rethink the notion of a predictable world organised by the United States, *Pax Americana*. A trend where the United States to a lesser extent plays the leadership role we became accustomed to in the decades following the Second World War has long been seen but has been greatly reinforced under President Trump. Trump has pulled the United States out of key international agreements such as the Paris climate agreement and the Trans-Pacific Partnership (TPP) trade agreement, and casted doubt on the United States' willingness to continue the North American Free Trade Agreement (NAFTA). The United Kingdom, which is a traditional key ally for Norway, is also changing. As a result of Brexit, Britain's international role has arguably weakened, and in the years to come, the country must redefine its relationship with the outside world.

Secondly, our powerful neighbour in the east, Russia, has dramatically changed. During his time in power, President Vladimir Putin has modernised and restructured the country's armed forces, which in turn has given Moscow both increased ability and confidence. In recent years, Putin's Russia has repeatedly demonstrated the will and ability to use these capabilities. Russia's annexation of Crimea in 2014, the subsequent "sneak-invasion" in eastern Ukraine, and Moscow's military intervention in support of Bashar al-Assad's regime in Syria are clear examples of the new confidence in Russian foreign and security policy. Norway has an important legacy here; we learned through even the coldest of the Cold War to balance firmness and clarity with the will to dialogue wherever possible. This stands by – but it is a major challenge for our leadership to strike the right balance in a time of major changes.

It is also in the interest of any Norwegian government to contribute to making the Atlantic as narrow as possible, politically speaking. However, the Norwegian authorities should no longer accept the role of the United States as a security guarantor as an eternal truth and should consequently look for additional partners in Europe, in addition to the transatlantic ties. Among our natural allies, it is primarily countries such as Germany, the Nordic countries, and the Netherlands, and with Macron, also France, that stand out. Germany is particularly important here. The Norwegian-German relations have often been about trade but may in the future be just as much about security and defence policy.

For many decades, the mantra, often proclaimed from the Parliament's pulpit, was that "Norwegian foreign and security policy is firm". Almost everyone sighed with relief. There was a considerable degree of national consensus around the major lines. For the Norwegian authorities, it was a value in itself to emphasise that the main lines would not change so that Norway was perceived as predictable by both our allies and Russia. In our days, Norwegian decision-makers have much greater freedom in the pursuit of foreign policy. For example, the experience of recent decades has shown that Norway is much freer than before to enter into cooperation with countries across the globe, or to engage in peace diplomacy in various conflicts. In other words, Norway has a *far greater* room to make its own considerations than before, and the fact that we do at times gives credibility to the world. The mastery of this art has also proven to make us more relevant to traditional partners. Managing such a policy, however, requires a great deal of creativity around which foreign policy arenas Norway should participate in and the procedures to be used to achieve foreign policy objectives – as well as good assessments of the consequences different road choices can be expected to have. Here too, the intelligence service's expertise can be of great use.

Intelligence as decision-making support

Now to the last question: What is it like to be a decision-maker in the digital age, and how can intelligence be relevant decision support?

First and foremost, everything is moving at a much higher pace. It is not so easy to substantiate empirically a claim that the number of decisions that must be made is increasing, while the time available before one has to decide is ever shorter. But as a minister and secretary of state, I have personally experienced that it is. However, I am not the first to point out that everything is going faster. Already well before the digital age, in the 1970s, the then Norwegian Foreign Minister Knut Frydenlund pointed out that the pace of politics had become so much higher than it had been during the time of Trygve Lie, who was Foreign Minister (in exile) and the UN's first General Secretary in the 1940s. And the pace of decision-makers began to seriously accelerate as the Internet spread from the early 2000s. Previously, as a minister, one could become aware of an issue before everyone else through the channels of her or his own ministry, but today this hardly ever happens. A wide range of newspapers, from the small Norwegian *Dagen* to *Rawalpindi News*, have probably reported on a matter before it reaches the table of a minister. In the digital age, information is available to everyone at all times. In the past, most people lived in a national newsroom. Today, everyone around the world is online, and in our own home, we can get real-time information directly from rural Afghanistan via smartphone, without any sort of filter. And there are many who go directly to the source to orient themselves. People have become less trusting in authorities, and they seek out information and arguments themselves to decide on different questions. Today, living in a global newsroom means that even a small, seemingly insignificant issue on the other side of the globe can suddenly end up being a hot political potato at home. In the digital age, it is increasingly difficult to keep your mouth shut and work quietly to resolve a matter, a hallmark of traditional intergovernmental diplomacy. Today, when an issue first becomes known in the news – and it happens very quickly – it is a short time before a government minister is demanded a public response, and the pressure from the media and the Parliament is often intense.

Now that the number of decisions needed to be made increases, the time available for a decision to be made decreases, and the fact that no processes can be kept hidden, makes it, in sum, terribly demanding to be a decision-maker in the digital age. This is not only my claim but also thoroughly documented by Nik Gowing and Chris Langdon in *Thinking the Unthinkable*.[5] In the book, which is based on interviews with 60 executives in private business, international organisations, and government, including myself, several leaders express concern that it is increasingly difficult to make well-thought-out, wise decisions in a world that is apparently more and more complex and ever-changing. Many carry a constant fear of being pushed to make decisions too quickly, and in the daily hamster wheel there is little time to think about the unthinkable. An inevitable consequence of everything going so fast that leaders do not have time to think is that they are constantly surprised by unexpected events. Few predicted the financial crisis of

2007, the Arab spring of 2011, or Russia's annexation of the Crimean Peninsula in 2014. This clearly illustrates that intelligence is more relevant today than ever before in history.

Firstly, in order to be confident of their own decisions in light of the challenges outlined, the intelligence service plays an important role as a trusted and close dialogue partner. Rather than "secrets" delivered in a sealed envelope, a digital-age decision-maker should be supported with good analysis: sober analyses of both what the world actually is and how it might come to be. As a decision-maker, I understand that the last thing is a lot to demand from an analyst, as this touches on the type of issues that are referred to in the intelligence literature as "mysteries". But that's exactly how intelligence can help a decision-maker to think of the unthinkable – and thus help reduce the risk of strategic shocks.

Today, as mentioned, the international landscape has become more confusing, while at the same time Norwegian decision-makers have far more leeway than before. This means that the scope of what one can do and what outcomes an action can have is greater than in a long time. Shifting Norwegian governments have had the ambition that Norway should "punch above its weight", which means to have a relevance in the international arena that exceeds the country's physical and economic size. To succeed in this, the Norwegian authorities must use "smart power", a type of strategy in international relations that is particularly linked to Professor Joseph S. Nye Jr., who heads the Kennedy School of Government at Harvard University. In a number of books, Nye argues that the cleverest strategy in international relations is to combine "hard" (military strength) and "soft" (alliances and partnerships and active participation in international institutions) means of power, with an emphasis on the latter.[6] While the traditional role of the intelligence service has been to play the one who warns of everything that can go wrong, the service in today's world can also help identify the room for action that those who design Norwegian security and foreign policy can use, as well as likely outcomes of various choices. Intelligence is thus a very useful tool in the toolbox of decision-makers seeking to use smart power. Before Norway entered the Security Council last time, which was in 2001, the government strengthened the liaison service between the Ministry of Foreign Affairs and the intelligence service precisely to support the Ministry of Foreign Affairs in this.

Secondly, the intelligence service makes an important contribution by reporting deviations from the "normal situation". As a minister, you maintain an understanding of the current situation through your own knowledge, network, and ministry. Every morning, as a minister, a meeting is held where your advisors present a situation update. In addition, a media update is provided, which is important as the daily agenda of a government minister is largely news driven. In the Ministry of Foreign Affairs, you always receive reports from the network of embassies and consulates, if there is something that requires special attention. In these morning meetings, however, it is not necessarily informed about the most important things that are happening in the world, as much of the attention will in practice be directed to what the media is recording right here and now. As a minister, secretary of state, or top official, the agenda is full at all times and the danger of *information overload* is constantly present. However, in a hectic and dynamic workday, the most important things can be those that do not happen. It is important not to forget this. One cannot stop worrying about potential threats simply because they have not materialised here and now. In this way, it is important that the intelligence service is not caught by the media's "24-hour wheel". In other words, the service must not be too concerned about reporting on current events but also keep a continuous focus on what can happen but has not yet happened. The intelligence service thus plays an important role in continuously monitoring the situation and reporting any deviations to the decision-makers.

As things move faster and more information becomes available, it is increasingly demanding to distinguish between what Nate Silver refers to as "the signal" and the "noise".[7] In what is, after all, still large amounts of normal situation, decision-makers need help to see the deviations. Warning, the traditional task of an intelligence service, has also become much more difficult in the digital age. Today, a military attack hardly starts with enemy soldiers and tanks rolling across the border from Russia. A far more likely scenario is that an attack begins with multiple sectors of society – for example, telecommunications, power grids, and gas production – being attacked at the same time by subtle non-military means combined with the spread of so-called "fake news". Such an attack is very difficult to detect. It is of critical national importance that the intelligence service continuously monitors the situation and notifies the decision-maker of any deviations from the normal picture. But at the same time, it is important that the service does not notify every minor deviation. If you give warnings too often, the result will easily be a "wolf-wolf effect" and the decision-maker will not eventually take the intelligence service's warnings seriously. At the same time, the warning time in today's threat environment has become very short, where hostile actors can launch rapid attacks and use a wide range of measures, and thus there is a considerable risk of not warning decision-makers in the case of deviations from the normal picture. In some situations and crises, intelligence reporting can have a de-scaling effect, by showing that what can look dramatic here and now is not in fact a major breach of what is considered as being the normal situation. This may be more important than ever in a time characterised by large amounts of inaccurate information.

Thirdly, I have personally experienced as a minister that the intelligence service can make a difference when a crisis arises. And in a globalised world, Norwegians and Norwegian interests can be affected anywhere and at any time. The terrorist attack on the gas facility In Amenas in Algeria in 2013, where five Norwegians were tragically killed, but where many were eventually also saved, is one clear example. On 16 January, the facility was occupied by a radical Islamist group that refers to itself as "The Masked Brigade", led by Mokhtar Belmokhtar. Several hundred workers from Algeria and eight other nations were taken hostage. During the dramatic days of the crisis, I, as foreign minister, experienced that national intelligence capacity was of crucial importance to me and the crisis staff in the Ministry of Foreign Affairs. Thanks to this support, we were able to follow the events at the In Amenas facility in near real time, which provided us with far better information than the one I perceived that even Algerian authorities had access to on their own.

This is just one example of a crisis where the intelligence service has provided important decision-making support.

Conclusion

Intelligence is more relevant than ever. It helps those who are navigating Norway in difficult times. Of course, the intelligence service competes with many other knowledge-producers for the attention of busy decision-makers, but it is my experience that the service is listened to. The great advantage of intelligence is that it is thoroughly processed, and the analyses are done by professionals whose sole task is to support you as a decision-maker.

In order to maintain its relevance, it is important that the intelligence service remains objective in its assessments and cannot be politicised, thus continuing to "speak truth to power". One last example: During the 2008 Georgia crisis, we, as Norwegian decision-makers, had a great benefit from the service's realistic assessments of the situation one was facing. The assessments surrounding the Georgia theatre were an important corrective to the reporting of some allies, where one could not easily distinguish between observable realities and attempts at influencing the understanding of the situation, and thus the political position, of the Norwegian government. In other words, the information was politicised, even the one that was shared confidentially between allies. Norwegian assessments were excellent at being objective and gave a good understanding of Moscow's actual intentions and capabilities. The way I experienced it, the intelligence service did not force its own opinions into the analyses but described the world as the service actually saw it. Then it was up to the politicians to translate these assessments into political action. It is critical that the service maintains this objectivity in its analyses.

Furthermore, the continued relevance of intelligence in decision-making requires a high understanding of the decision-makers' needs on the part of the intelligence service, as well as a high degree of "user expertise" among the decision-makers. User expertise is about understanding what the service can and cannot deliver, asking as precise questions as possible, and maintaining a close dialogue with the service. Arguably, not all decision-makers have a good enough understanding of what can be gained from the intelligence service. Therefore, for any incoming political leadership, expedition chiefs, chiefs of staff, and key advisors, it will be more than helpful to have a thorough introduction that clarifies the capabilities and limitations of the intelligence service. In such contexts, specific examples of what the service is capable of, and unable to contribute, should be given. Such an introduction could lead to increased and more targeted use of intelligence. The service, in turn, must have a good understanding of the decision-makers' workday, focus, and knowledge needs. Such understanding will help the service to disseminate its analyses in such a way that is of optimal benefit to decision-makers.

Undoubtedly, there is still a lot of truth in the old saying: "As you ask, you get an answer."

Notes

1 "Stoltenberg: NATO er under konstant dataangrep (Stoltenberg: NATO is under Constant Cyber Attacks)", *VG*, February 2, 2017, www.vg.no/nyheter/utenriks/nato/stoltenberg-nato-er-under-konstant-dataangrep/a/23924542/.
2 Ibid.
3 In 2017, Denmark even appointed the experienced diplomat Casper Klyng as its first ambassador to Silicon Valley, where several of the world's most important technology companies have their headquarters, Andreas Sandre: "Welcome to the Era of Tech Diplomacy", *Medium*, November 24, 2017, https://medium.com/digital-diplomacy/welcome-to-the-era-of-tech-diplomacy-2e174446d25.
4 For an account of the sectoral principle in Norway, see "Societal Safety: The Road to a Less Vulnerable Society", Meld. St. 17 (2001–2002), Ministry of Justice and Public Security, www.regjeringen.no/contentassets/ee63e1dd1a16409fa0bb737bfda9279a/no/pdfa/stm200120 020017000dddpdfa.pdf.
5 Nik Gowing & Chris Langdon: *Thinking the Unthinkable: A New Imperative for Leadership in the Digital Age*. Woodbridge, UK: John Catt Educational Ltd., 2018. For the background report on which the book is based, see https://adcforum.org/wp-content/uploads/2015/10/THINKING-THE-UNTHINKABLE-CHURCHILL-2015-REPORT.pdf.
6 Suzanne Nossel was the first to introduce the concept of "smart power" in an article published in March 2004 in the journal *Foreign Affairs*. Joseph S. Nye, Jr. further develops this concept in among others *The Future of Power*. New York: PublicAffairs, 2011.
7 Nate Silver: *The Signal and the Noise: Why So Many Predictions Fail – But Some Don't*. New York: Penguin Books, 2012.

Further reading

Gentry, John A., & Joseph S. Gordon: *Strategic Warning Intelligence: History, Challenges, and Prospects*. Washington, DC: Georgetown University Press, 2019, Chapter 10, pp. 201–214.
Gowing, Nik, & Chris Langdon: *Thinking the Unthinkable: A New Imperative for Leadership in the Digital Age*. Woodbridge, UK: John Catt Educational Ltd., 2018.
Hulnick, Arthur S.: "The Intelligence Producer – Policy Consumer Linkage: A Theoretical Approach", *Intelligence and National Security*, Vol. 1, No. 2, 1986, pp. 212–233.
Hulnick, Arthur S.: "Intelligence Producer – Consumer Relations in the Electronic Era", *International Journal of Intelligence and CounterIntelligence*, Vol. 24, No. 4, 2011, pp. 747–756, www.tandfonline.com/doi/abs/10.1080/08850607.2011.598812?journalCode=ujic20.
Lowenthal, Mark M.: "Chapter 27: The Policymaker-Intelligence Relationship", in Loch K. Johnson (ed.): *The Oxford Handbook of National Security Intelligence*. Oxford and New York: Oxford University Press, pp. 437–451.
Rovner, Joshua: *Fixing the Facts: National Security and the Politics of Intelligence*. Ithaca and London: Cornell University Press, 2011.

4   The necessity of experts

Stig Stenslie

What kind of knowledge should intelligence analysts have? Should they be among the best subject-matter experts of their generation, or should they be more, presumably, flexible generalists?

These are questions that occupy any intelligence service. The questions are far from new, but they have become more topical in recent years. The reason for this is that intelligence services provide support to an ever-widening range of decision-makers, at the same time as the list of top-priority intelligence requirements is becoming ever longer. As several of the book's authors have pointed out, in the digital age, national decision-makers sense that they are facing an increasingly complex and changing threat environment, and in order to provide relevant decision support, intelligence services must be able to familiarise themselves with ever-new geographical areas and topics. Hence, it is timely to ask what kind of knowledge intelligence analysts must possess in the digital age. As mentioned in the book's introductory chapter, it is they who have proclaimed the "death of the expert" – as everybody today can access all kinds of information with just a few clicks through Google and Wikipedia. Within the intelligence community, there has also been a tendency to downgrade experts in favour of generalists, or intelligence specialists. So-called structured analytic techniques (SAT) have been fronted as the way to the last – techniques that, somewhat caricatured, create "plug-and-play analysts" with the ability to analyse any requested issue.

In this chapter, I argue that SAT can be useful, and that the use of these can certainly contribute to better analysis. But at the same time, I warn against considering these somewhat simple techniques as a substitute for expertise in geographical areas and topics. In fact, in the digital age, with its complex and rapidly changing threat environment, the subject-matter expert is more needed than ever before.

A sham debate

Any discussion of analyst competence hardly escapes the so-called science versus art debate. This is among the debates that are being devoted most attention in the literature on intelligence. At the core of the battle is the question of whether intelligence analysis is, in essence, an "art", based on experience, subjective, and intuitive judgements, or a "science", which must be based on structured, systematic methods of analysis.[1] In line with the argument earlier, the chapter argues that intelligence analysis should be both. Thus, the debate is characterised by being a sham debate.

Science

Already in the wake of the Second World War, US intelligence researchers like Sherman Kent emphasised the importance of putting scientific methods ahead of intuition.[2] Kent believed that intelligence analysis had to take the step from art – where the practitioner had learned his work through experience – to a modern profession – where the practitioner is educated in the scientific methods of his field and uses these in his practical work as an analyst. To realise this goal, Kent thought it was necessary to develop a distinct professional literature and establish distinct educational programmes to train intelligence analysts.[3] The CIA listened to Kent's advice and in 1955 established an academic journal, *Studies in Intelligence*, and in 1974 the Center for the Study of Intelligence. Several others shared Kent's view of the need to professionalise the intelligence corps. Among these were Washington Patt and "R.A. Random". The latter, who wrote under a synonym in the mentioned CIA journal, went so far as to claim that if analysts denied scientific methods in favour of intuition they would

> reject rationality and scientific principle as a basis for practice, and substitute intuitive guesses and unanalyzed conjectures.[4]

However, it was not until the 1990s that the ideas of professionalisation and the use of scientific methods seriously accelerated within the intelligence community.[5] It was at this time that the US intelligence services began systematically to use "alternative analysis". This is a set of techniques intended to help an analyst think outside their own preconceived notions and the precursor to structured analysis techniques. In the aftermath of the Cold War, there was a generational shift in the US intelligence services, and during the 1990s, US intelligence agencies recruited many new analysts. A large proportion of these were young people without higher education. They had to be schooled. Accordingly, in 1999, Mary McCarthy, then senior intelligence officer on the staff of the National Security Council, urged the intelligence community to develop "social science for dummies".[6] The answer was structured analytical techniques, within the intelligence community best known under the acronym "SAT". These techniques have been largely developed by former CIA analysts Richards J. Heuer Jr. and Randolph H. Pherson.[7] The "SAT Bible" itself is the book *Structured Analytic Techniques for Intelligence Analysis*, which today is the core curriculum of virtually every SAT introductory course.[8]

In the wake of September 11, 2001, US intelligence agencies recruited a large number of analysts. Many of the analysts lacked higher education. The services at this time came under harsh criticism from politicians and the public for not being able to warn about the terrorist attacks, despite the fact that there was information gathered indicating an imminent attack. Lack of analysts and analytical creativity was identified by investigation committees as the main reason for the intelligence failure. In addition, the subsequent military operations in Afghanistan and Iraq, respectively, helped further increase the need for intelligence, including clever analysts. In response to these challenges, then President George W. Bush Jr. ordered the services to double the number of analysts.[9] This resulted in a new wave of young and uneducated women and men rolling into the secret services, and they were given basic courses in critical thinking and various analytical techniques to become quickly operational.[10] SAT was a perfect fit for this purpose. In 2007, US authorities adopted so-called analytical standards, which were mainly based on specific analytical techniques and tools that were easy to teach and understand. Those who completed training in these techniques became certified intelligence analysts.[11] SAT, the idea of analytical standards and educational programmes that led to the certification of analysts, was soon adopted by other Western security and intelligence services. In the private business sector too, SAT became fashionable. Soon a consultancy industry emerged offering SAT training.[12]

Today, intelligence services attach great importance to the use of SAT. The techniques are intended to "promote rigorous analysis, lessen the risk of intelligence failure, and make analysts' reasoning more transparent to consumers".[13] Heuer and Pherson point out that intelligence failures like 9/11 are often the result of preconceived notions, bias, which are often the result of intuitive thinking. SAT is an alternative way of thinking, which is intended to help reduce the importance of bias. The techniques are thus intended to help the analyst to think outside the box.[14] While traditional intelligence analysis based on intuition is essentially an individual exercise, the duo Heuer and Pherson emphasise that intelligence analysis based on SAT should be a process involving a team of analysts. This will further reduce the risk of conventional thinking among analysts.[15]

Professor Richard K. Betts, at Columbia University, for his part, emphasises the importance of SAT to make intelligence analyses more transparent to customers. He points out that policymakers often do not see the relevance of intelligence analysis because they believe that analysts are less experienced and have less knowledge than themselves. Betts believes this underpins the importance of using SAT. While a customer is unlikely to take analysts using their own judgement seriously, she or he is far more likely to listen to assessments derived from a methodically well-founded analysis.[16]

Info box 4.1 Typology of SAT techniques

The literature describes several hundred more or less different structured analysis techniques. In an unclassified guide for intelligence analysts published by US authorities, SAT is classified into three main categories. These are techniques that any analyst who has completed courses in SAT is expected to know.[17]

The first category is *Diagnostic Techniques*, whose purpose is to make assumptions and logical arguments more transparent.

* Key-Assumptions Check" is among these techniques. The technique is used in the initial phase of an analytical process and involves listing

and evaluating various factors that are taken for granted before conducting an analysis. Clarifying such assumptions, which the analyst can base her or his conclusions on, consciously or unconsciously, can help to avoid an analysis based on incorrect assumptions.

- "Quality of Information Check" is a key task for any analyst throughout the analysis process and involves assessing the validity and reliability of the information that underlies the analysis. It is important to identify what one knows and what one does not know in order to provide precise information needs to the collection disciplines and to make it clear to the customer how much emphasis should be placed on the analysis. Furthermore, the technique can help reveal attempts by an opponent on deception.
- "Indicators or Signposts of Change" is a technique that involves an analyst periodically reviewing a list of observed events or trends, with the goal of being able to notify if unexpected changes occur. Warning analysis is a core task for any intelligence service.
- "Analysis of Competing Hypotheses" is a technique in which an analyst identifies a set of alternative explanations (hypotheses) and then seeks to find evidence that denies, rather than confirms, the various hypotheses.[18]

The second category contains *Contrarian Techniques*, which aim to challenge one established, prevailing thinking.

- "Devil's Advocacy" is among these techniques. It is a known phenomenon that even the best analyst, or even a whole team of analysts, from time to time "falls in love" with one explanation. This can make the analyst overlook information that does not support this specific explanation, which poses a significant risk of intelligence failure. The technique is to challenge a single established truth or consensus by seeking to substantiate an alternative explanation.
- "Team A/Team B" is a similar technique. The difference from the previous technique is that it recognises that there are several different perspectives. The technique involves putting two (or more) teams of analysts against each other and allowing them to argue for two different points of view or competing hypotheses. When there are conflicting views among analysts, the Team A/Team B technique can help the analysts involved better see each other's points. This can help to reduce friction and narrow the gap between analysts' positions. In addition, the technique can make it clear to the customer that there are different views among the analysts, a fact that does not appear when an intelligence service presents one assessment. By providing information and arguments that are intended to support the various positions openly, the customer gets a better starting point for forming her or his own opinion.
- "High-Impact/Low-Probability Analysis" is a technique that focuses on a seemingly unlikely event, which will have major political consequences should it occur. The fact that something has a low probability means that

analysts often do not take the time to think through the potential effects if the unthinkable should actually happen, something the technique can remedy. Likewise, the technique can help the customer make contingency plans in the unlikely event that the unthinkable should occur.

- "What If? Analysis" assumes, unlike the previous technique, that an event of potential (negative or positive) effect has already happened. The focus is on explaining how this could occur, rather than assessing probability and effect.[19]

The third and final category includes *Imaginative Thinking Techniques*, which aim to nurture new perspectives, knowledge, and alternative scenarios.

- "Brainstorming" is one such technique and involves a group of analysts thinking together to generate new perspectives. A prerequisite for success is to cultivate a climate where everyone feels safe enough to present their ideas without inhibitions.
- "Outside-In Thinking" is used to identify the full range of factors and trends that indirectly affect a phenomenon. This technique is particularly useful for an analyst in charge of a particular geographic area and can help her or him to establish an overview of all relevant variables that should be included in an analysis.
- "Red Team Analysis" is a technique for predicting the behaviour of an actor, individual or group, by trying to recreate how they will think in a given situation. It is a known cause of intelligence failure that analysts tend to see a foreign actor as their own mirror image, thus assigning their own motives, values, and understanding to the object of analysis. The analyst will thus assume that a "rational" actor will do exactly the same thing she or he herself/himself had done in the face of certain threats or opportunities. However, history shows that foreign leaders often act completely unforeseen, due to different cultural, structural, and personal conditions. To succeed with this technique, it is required that the analysts who are part of the "red team" have in-depth knowledge of both the actors and the environment in which they operate – including language and culture.
- "Alternative Futures Analysis" involves systematically exploring different ways in which the situation can develop. Describing different futures, or scenarios, is a particularly useful technique in questions that are so complex and uncertain that it makes little sense to consider just one outcome.[20]

Art

Contrary to those who argue that intelligence analysis should be more scientific, there are several who believe that this type of activity is to be considered an art. They believe that analysis should be an inductive process based on education, experience, and instinct. As an artist, a good analyst uses creativity and imagination. This approach to intelligence analysis has arguably always been, and still is, the prevailing approach among analysts.

In the nineteenth century, the German military strategist Karl von Clausewitz emphasised that intelligence analysis must rest on a combination of knowledge and intuition: "Many intelligence reports in war are contradictory; even more are false, and most are uncertain." To separate facts and fiction, Clausewitz argued that an officer "must possess a standard of judgement", which could only be gained from "knowledge of men and affairs and from common sense". Moreover, an officer's judgement "should be guided by the laws of probability".[21]

The authors of the much-cited *Butler Report*, which investigated the intelligence on Iraq's alleged weapons of mass destruction programme, which played a key role in the British government's decision to invade Iraq (as part of the US-led coalition) in 2003, emphasised that intelligence is an art by opening the report with the aforementioned Clausewitz quote.[22] Mark M. Lowenthal, a professor at Johns Hopkins University and former assistant director of CIA's Central Intelligence for Analysis and Production, argues that intelligence analysis is, and will always remain, a form of art and can never become a science:

> Intelligence is not and never will be a science and anyone who tries to promote it will be doing our profession a grave disservice. . . . If we start equating intelligence to a science the unrealistic expectations will only go up. Intelligence is an art. It is an intellectual activity. An art.[23]

Those who believe that intelligence analysis is an art generally support their view by pointing out that analysts typically seek to answer questions that are so complex that the application of structured analysis techniques is of little help. In complex questions, the analyst considers countless variables. The task is complicated by the fact that, in addition to the known variables, there are also several relevant variables unknown to the analyst. The analyst's task is further distorted by the fact that the "target", that is, the actor who is the subject of analysis, often seeks to hide important information or even attempts to obscure its capabilities and intentions by deliberately disseminating misleading information. When the variables and information bases are so unclear, the use of SAT is arguably *pseudo-science* rather than science. The techniques and assessments may seem reliable to the customer, but in reality they do not hold water.[24]

Those who maintain that intelligence analysis is an art believe that the best analysts are looking for patterns and rely on their own intuition. Robert D. Folker Jr. considers this type of approach as a form of unstructured analysis. Intuition is a sensation of the analyst, and she or he is not necessarily able to explain in concrete terms how one has concluded or to present data supporting the conclusion. SAT can easily be learned. Intuition, on the other hand, cannot be learned. Intuition comes with experience.[25] One problem with this understanding is that a similarity is drawn between intuition and the absence of structure. Intuition-based analysis can also be structured, especially when conducted by highly trained analysts. But the structure is not necessarily visible to an outsider. Folker himself realises this and has moderated his original definition. According to him, the real difference between the two different analytical approaches is that intuition is an invisible analytical process while the structured approach is a visible process.[26]

Both

The art versus science debate has been raging for several years, and as shown the fronts are steep. But as mentioned earlier, this is a sham debate. It is wrong to set up intuitive and scientific methods as opposites, as a good analyst must be able to combine both.[27] This is not unique to the intelligence profession. Stephen Marrin, a former CIA analyst and now a pioneer in the field of intelligence studies, compares intelligence analysis with various other similar activities. He particularly emphasises medicine as a model for how one can integrate both art and science into a single profession. Marrin believes that an intelligence analyst, like a doctor, must combine science and art in his practice. When a doctor reasons for a diagnosis, she or he uses scientific knowledge of medicine, anatomy, and physiology. In addition, a physician with longer experience will meet the patient as an artist. Based on experience and instinct, the doctor will be able to clarify the diagnosis by distinguishing classic symptoms of one condition from abnormal symptoms indicating another condition.[28]

Better analysis, but hardly used

Despite the fact that intelligence services are increasingly emphasising SAT, it is little known to what extent these techniques are used in daily work and whether they actually contribute to better analyses.[29] To answer these questions, I conducted a survey that sought to shed light on a sample of intelligence analysts' practical experiences with using SAT. The sample consisted of analysts who have completed basic education in SAT at the Norwegian Defence Intelligence University College. Questions were sent to 91 analysts, 45 of whom responded. This gives a response rate of 49 per cent. Although the sample is limited, the survey provides a certain basis for answering the questions. In order to clarify some of the questions that were asked, in-depth interviews were conducted with a selection of respondents after the survey. In addition, managers of intelligence analysis teams were interviewed to include their views on the use of SAT.

Of my respondents, 42 per cent say that SAT largely contributes to improving the quality of the analyses, while 49 per cent state that these techniques have such an effect to some extent. Thus, more than 90 per cent see a positive correlation between the quality of the analysis and the use of SAT. The use of the techniques helps to improve the quality of the analyses by reducing preconceived notions, opening up new perspectives, and leading to more precise or "correct" assessments. Only a small proportion of the respondents believe that SAT to a limited extent, or not at all, contributes positively to the quality of the analysis work. In other words, an overwhelming majority of respondents believe that the techniques actually contribute to improving the quality of the analyses they produce, a finding that points in the same direction as the conclusions of other studies.[30] Stephen J. Coulthart, as an example, finds in a similar survey based on a selection of analysts at the US State Department's Bureau of Intelligence and Research that 80 per cent of respondents believe that SAT improves the quality of analyses to a large (17 per cent) or some (63 per cent) degree.[31]

Following the survey, managers of analysis teams were asked to report on their personal experiences with using SAT. In these interviews, it appears that managers to a lesser extent than analysts believe that these techniques pave the way for better products. A key point that nevertheless emerged in these interviews is that the use of SAT helps to make the process of quality assurance of analysts' assessments easier. Intelligence services, unlike academia, can to a very limited extent use external peer review, and the services must thus rely on good internal mechanisms for quality assurance of products. According to a team manager:

> SAT contributes to making intelligence products more transparent, which makes it easier to critically evaluate the premises on which the conclusions are based. It is more difficult to assess the quality of an analysis based on implicit assumptions.[32]

On the other hand, 55 per cent of respondents in the survey stated that they rarely use SAT and 5 per cent that they never use these techniques. Forty per cent stated that they use SAT frequently, while no one responded that they always use these techniques. The most frequently used techniques are Key-Assumptions Check, Quality of Information Check, Brainstorming, Indicators or Signposts of Change, and Devil's Advocacy. Other techniques such as Analysis of Competing Hypotheses, Team A/Team B Analysis, Red Team Analysis, and Alternative Futures Analysis are used to a small extent. Thus, the intelligence analysts surveyed use SAT to a very limited extent in their practical work. This is despite the fact that all respondents have completed SAT courses and belong to an organisation that invests a lot of time and resources in training analysts in these techniques.

Also, these findings coincide with other studies which show that intelligence analysts use SAT to a limited extent.[33] Coulthart found in his study that as many as 46 per cent of those surveyed rarely use SAT and that 33 per cent never use these techniques.[34] He included in his sample also analysts who had not completed education in SAT, while my study only included those who have completed such a course. This probably helps explain the relatively lower use of SAT among analysts within the agency that Coulthart studied. Furthermore, my study shows that simple techniques are used to a much greater extent than those that are more complex and require a greater degree of teamwork among analysts. For example, as many as 78 per cent use Brainstorming, while only 3 per cent use Team A/Team B Analysis – which is a central technique in SAT literature. This finding coincides with Robert D. Folker Jr.'s observation that the most complex structured analysis techniques are used to a lesser extent within US intelligence services.[35]

It is an obvious paradox that the respondents in the survey express themselves positively on the quality gains associated with SAT but that few actually use these techniques. The survey reveals two main reasons for the latter: The first is that SAT techniques are too time consuming. Of the respondents, 46 percent state this reason for not using the techniques in the last 12 months. No intelligence analyst who has experienced the demands of the digital age for *speed* should be surprised by this finding, and in the academic literature, many authors also point to time pressure as a major reason why analysts use SAT to a small degree.[36] Among these are Folker, who believes that time constraints inevitably foster the intuitive approach to analysis, and that "[u]nder the accelerating pressures of time, intelligence analysts feel that structured analytical approaches are too cumbersome".[37]

The other main reason why respondents state that they do not use SAT is that these techniques are of little help in solving the set of tasks one is set to work on. Fifty per cent highlight this justification. In the wake of the survey, follow-up interviews were conducted with some of the respondents who stated that SAT did not fit in with their tasks in order to gain a better understanding of why they thought there was a discrepancy between tasks and techniques. Several analysts believe that methodological principles and theoretical perspectives learned through higher degree studies in subjects such as political science are more relevant than the use of SAT. One respondent who was particularly critical of SAT stated:

> SAT can easily become a methodical obsession rather than useful analytical tools. Systematic and structured analytical thinking forms the basis for all serious study programs. "Devil's Advocacy" is a catchy name, but being critical of one's views is something a first-year student learns at university – or even before that.[38]

In his study, Coulthart finds no correlation between time spent and the use of SAT.[39] He, on the other hand, highlights analysts' perception of SAT as a key variable with regard to the use of these techniques.[40] Analysts' attitudes towards the techniques reflect both the culture within an intelligence service and the managers' knowledge of and views of SAT. In my follow-up interviews, few of the respondents commented critically on the use of these techniques as such, and an overwhelming majority believe that the techniques contribute to better analyses. This indicates that my respondents do not have a negative view of SAT. At the same time, 38 per cent state that the nearest manager facilitates the use of SAT to a small extent, and some of the interviewed team managers see little relevance in the use of the techniques. This finding suggests that managers' attitudes may have an impact on the use of SAT. While Coulthart identifies lack of teaching as a major reason why analysts do not use SAT, only 12 per cent of respondents in my study report inadequate training as a reason why the techniques are not used.

No substitute for expertise

In the SAT literature, the central authors are careful to emphasise that these techniques are intended to support the intelligence analyst. In addition to being familiar with these techniques, she or he must also be subject-matter experts with solid education from the sciences, area and language studies. Thus, SAT is not sufficient. According to Heuer and Pherson:

> Analytic methods are important, but method alone is far from sufficient to ensure analytic accuracy or value. Method must be combined with substantive expertise and an inquiring and imaginative mind.[41]

Despite these authors' emphasis on the importance of subject-matter expertise, there are also those inside the intelligence community who believe it is sufficient for an analyst to master SAT. They present SAT as techniques that enable an analyst to solve virtually any question, and the importance of subject-matter expertise is under-communicated. John A. Gentry points at such attitudes within the US intelligence services.[42] In light of this, it is symptomatic that these services have given less and less priority to the recruitment and retention of expert analysts since the 1990s.[43] One indication of this trend is that within the US intelligence services there is a rapidly declining proportion of analysts holding a doctorate. During the Cold War, on the other hand, analysts immersed themselves in the systems of the Soviet Union and China for many years or even a whole career, becoming experts who could compare themselves with the most skilled specialists in academia.[44]

The reasons why the expert analyst appears to be on his way out of US intelligence services are complex. Firstly, since the end of the Cold War, there has not been one major enemy, and the threat picture is rapidly changing. Intelligence services must today address questions about far more countries and regions, and non-governmental as well as state actors, than before. This means that the services find it opportune to hire and train flexible generalist analysts. Secondly, the development is a result of US intelligence services in the wake of 9/11, as well as subsequent military operations in Afghanistan and Iraq, quickly hiring an army of new analysts. Rather than taking the time to zoom in on the university and research environments for experts, one chose to go for low-hanging fruits. As mentioned, SAT was a presumptively suitable means of rapidly operating the army of new, young, and inexperienced analysts. Thirdly, it cannot be ruled out that anti-academic sentiments within the intelligence services also underlie this development. Several authors argue that there are such tendencies within the US intelligence services.[45] According to Richard L. Russel, many managers within the US intelligence community have a dislike for subject-matter experts: "Few of the DI's (Directorate of Intelligence) managers have ever written a book or even devote significant attention to reading them."[46]

The SAT literature further underscores the need for these types of techniques with references to research by renowned American psychologist Philip E. Tetlock.

Based on years of studies of "experts'" ability to predict the future, Tetlock concludes that professors, leading bureaucrats, journalists, and other experts' future analyses are less precise than the guesses of the "man in the street".[47] An important reason for this is that experts often find it difficult to change their assessment of a situation in the face of radical changes or paradigm shifts, a phenomenon known as the "paradox of expertise". Experts are good at explaining why things are as they are but poor at predicting the future. They will often draw on historical lessons – but history rarely repeats itself. In a summary of Tetlock's research, Louis Menand concludes that "[experts] are poorer forecasters than dart-throwing monkeys".[48] Are we to believe the research of Tetlock, intelligence analysts, who are experts in their respective fields, are probably no better suited to making predictions than amateurs and dart-throwing monkeys. As previously mentioned, research suggests that SAT helps intelligence analysts become more creative in their assessments and thus may provide better predictions about the future. But emphasising this point too much is problematic – as intelligence analysis is not a guessing contest. As Thomas Fingar points out: "Prediction is not – and should not be – the goal of strategic analysis."[49] Rather than estimates of the future, policymakers need intelligence analysts who can contribute to better understanding of drivers and context. In this way, the analyst must have in-depth knowledge of her or his area of responsibility.

Furthermore, there are problems associated with the SAT vocabulary. It is misleading to refer to SAT as "science". This implies that those who do not use SAT work "unscientifically". The reality is sometimes the opposite. The analyses of an analyst with a higher degree in, for example, social science are likely to be more scientific than those of an analyst with only lower-level education and SAT courses, as the former's analyses will rest on solid theoretical and methodological insight. Rather, SAT is surrounded by an aura of *pseudo-science*. A social scientist with a doctorate will find a crash-course in SAT as little scientific as an experienced doctor will perceive a beginner's course in first aid. Similarly, it is problematic to associate the word "structured" with SAT. This implies that those who do not use SAT work "unstructured", which is not necessarily the case. With many years of training in research methodology and theory, there comes an ability to approach questions in a structured way, although the methodological and theoretical basis is not necessarily explicitly stated in the analysis. In continuation of this, it is problematic to imply that those who don't work with structured analytical techniques rather base their assessments on "intuition", a term that has a strong association to the, at least in intelligence circles, not so flattering term "gut feeling". Analyses that are not SAT-based can be just as methodologically well-founded as long as they are conducted by experts trained in the methods and theories of social sciences, area and language studies. Both current and basic intelligence work requires in-depth expert knowledge, but especially the latter type analysis – which is often highly complicated – requires solid training and expertise.

To explain the need for experts, it is relevant to highlight *garbage in, garbage out*, a data-processing term. The term refers to the phenomenon in informatics or information and communication technology that computers, because they use only logical processes, will process all kinds of data with which they are fed, including incorrect or irrelevant data (*garbage in*), and they will then deliver inaccurate, or outright inaccurate, results (*garbage out*). Likewise, there is a danger that intelligence analysts using structured analytical techniques, without having sufficient area and/or thematic knowledge, will produce inaccurate analyses. Thus, *garbage in, garbage out*.

Robert Jervis identifies a lack of in-depth knowledge of foreign countries and regions as a key weakness of today's US intelligence community – which at worst could be a source of intelligence failure:

> The IC (intelligence community) needs much greater competence in foreign languages, cultures, and histories. This means allowing some analysts to focus on a country or a region for extended periods of time, and perhaps for an entire career. . . . During the Cold War it (the intelligence community) cultivated specialists on the USSR and PRC who could hold their own with those in the universities, but this is no longer true because of the lack of a single adversary and the value placed on flexible generalists. Few analysts have research training or doctorates or can tap into the scholarly community.[50]

Much more is required of an analyst than the ability to read classified reporting and write summaries. Intelligence services must still have a broad repertoire of expert analysts – the "academic nerds", recruited from the best research and university institutions. My conclusion is neither unique nor new but reflects precisely what Sherman Kent spoke of decades back in time:

> In a sense, intelligence organizations must be not a little like a large university faculty. They must have the people to whom research and rigorous thought are the breath of life, and they must accordingly have tolerance for the queer bird and the eccentric with a unique talent. They must guarantee a sort of academic freedom of inquiry and must fight off those who derogate such freedom by pointing to its occasional crackpot finding.[51]

Conclusion

The need for intelligence as a decision-making support in ever-new areas makes it an urgent task to bridge the gap between "art" and "science". Intelligence analysts need to acquire relevant methods which can help reduce bias and make the assessments more transparent and thus easier to test. Based on my findings, although few use these techniques, most analysts think that SAT bring analyses in the right direction. The reason for this paradox is complex, but one important reason is that the focus on current intelligence and scarce deadlines leaves little room for the use of SAT. Although these techniques are important tools, they should never be a substitute for subject-matter expertise. Any intelligence service still depends on experts, that is, those with solid knowledge in foreign languages, cultures, history, and other relevant topics. An expert in Chinese politics and language has the best conditions to easily acquire SAT, but one cannot understand China based on a two-week crash-course in SAT. In other words, SAT is a useful support tool if these techniques are used by analysts with in-depth specialist knowledge. If not, the end result will be *garbage in, garbage out.*

Notes

1 Robert D. Folker Jr.: "Intelligence Analysis in Theater Joint Intelligence Centers: An Experiment in Applying Structured Methods", Occasional Paper No. 7, Center for Strategic Intelligence Research. Joint Military Intelligence College, 2000, p. 6, https://fas.org/irp/eprint/folker.pdf.

2 Sherman Kent: *Strategic Intelligence for American World Policy.* Princeton, NJ: Princeton University Press, 1949, p. 175.

3 Sherman Kent: "The Need for an Intelligence Literature", *Studies in Intelligence*, Vol. 1, No. September 1, 1955, pp. 1–8.

4 R.A. Random: "Intelligence as a Science", *Studies in Intelligence*, Vol. 2, No. 2, 1958, pp. 77–78.

5 Richards J. Heuer Jr. & Randolph H. Pherson: *Structured Analytic Techniques for Intelligence Analysis.* Washington, DC: CQ Press, 2010, pp. 8–10.

6 Stephen Marrin: *Improving Intelligence Analysis: Bridging the Gap Between Scholarship and Practice.* Abingdon, UK: Routledge, 2011, p. 31.

7 For some key contributions on SAT, see Katherine Hibbs Pherson & Randolph H. Pherson: *Critical Thinking for Strategic Intelligence.* Washington, DC: CQ Press, 2013; Randolph H. Pherson & Sarah Miller Beebe: *Cases in Intelligence Analysis: Structured Analytic Techniques in Action.* Washington, DC: CQ Press, 2011; Heuer & Pherson, *op. cit.*; and Richards J. Heuer Jr.: *Psychology of Intelligence Analysis.* Washington, DC: CIA's Center for the Study of Intelligence, 1999.

8 Heuer & Pherson, *op. cit.*

9 Walter Pincus: "Bush Orders the CIA to Hire More Spies", *The Washington Post*, November 24, 2004, p. A4.

10 John A. Gentry: "The 'Professionalization' of Intelligence Analysis: A Skeptical Perspective", *International Journal of Intelligence and Counter Intelligence*, Vol. 29, No. 4, 2016, p. 648.

11 For analytical standards and certification requirements, see American Board for Certification in Homeland Security, www.abchs.com/about/boards/abia/.

12 For the Pherson Associates website, see LLC, www.pherson.org/.

13 Stephen Artner, Richard S. Girven, & James B. Bruce: "Assessing the Value of Structured Analytic Techniques in the U.S. Intelligence Community", RAND Corporation, 2016, p. 2, www.rand.org/content/dam/rand/pubs/research_reports/RR1400/RR1408/RAND_RR1408.pdf.

14 Heuer & Pherson, *op. cit.*, pp. 4–7.

15 *Ibid.*, pp. 7–8.

16 Richard K. Betts: "Intelligence Warning: Old Problems, New Agendas", *Parameters*, Vol. 28, No. 1, 1998, p. 33.

17 U.S. Government: "A Tradecraft Primer, Structured Analytic Techniques for Improving Intelligence Analysis", March 2009, p. 5, www.cia.gov/library/center-for-the-study-of-intelligence/csi-publications/books-and-monographs/Tradecraft%20Primer-apr09.pdf.

18 *Ibid.*, s. 7–15.

19 *Ibid.*, pp. 17–25.

20 *Ibid.*, pp. 27–36.

21 Karl von Clausewitz, quoted in Reed R. Prost: "Clausewitz on Intelligence", in Roger Z. George & Robert D. Kline (eds.): *Intelligence and National Security, Strategists: Enduring Issues and Challenges*. Oxford: Rowman and Littlefield, 2006, p. 3.

22 "Review of Intelligence on Weapons of Mass Destruction", London: The House of Commons, 2004, p. 7, https://fas.org/irp/world/uk/butler071404.pdf.

23 Quote borrowed from, Stephen Marrin: "Is Intelligence Analysis and Art or a Science?", *International Journal of Intelligence and Counter Intelligence*, Vol. 25, No. 3, 2012, p. 533, www.tandfonline.com/doi/pdf/10.1080/08850607.2012.678690.

24 Folker, *op. cit.*

25 *Ibid.*, p. 14.

26 Robert Folker quoted in, Stephen Marrin: "Intelligence Analysis: Structured Methods or Intuition?", *American Intelligence Journal*, Vol. 25, No. 1, 2007, p. 8.

27 Other authors have also come to the same conclusion, for example Folker, *op. cit.*; Julian Richards: *The Art and Science of Intelligence Analysis*. Oxford and New York: Oxford University Press, 2010; and Marrin: "Is Intelligence Analysis and Art or a Science?", *op. cit.*

28 Marrin: *Improving Intelligence Analysis . . .*, *op. cit.*, pp. 99–126; Stephen Marrin & Jonathan Clemente: "Improving Intelligence Analysis by Looking to the Medical Profession", *International Journal of Intelligence and Counter Intelligence*, Vol. 18, No. 4, Winter 2005–06, pp. 707–729; and Stephen Marrin & Jonathan Clemente: "Modeling an Intelligence Analysis Profession on Medicine", *International Journal of Intelligence and Counter Intelligence*, Vol. 19, No. 4, Winter 2006–07, pp. 642–665.

29 At the time of writing, there are only two studies that have systematically investigated the practical use of SAT: Stephen J. Coulthart: "Why Do Analysts Use Structured Analytic Techniques? An In-depth Study of an American Intelligence Agency", *Intelligence and National Security*, Vol. 31, No. 7, 2016, pp. 933–948, www.tandfonline.com/doi/abs/10.1080/02684527.2016.1140327; and Artner, Girven, & Bruce, *op. cit.*

30 Coulthart, *op. cit.*; Artner, Girven, & Bruce, *op. cit.*; and Folker, *op. cit.*

31 Coulthart, *op. cit.*, p. 942.

32 Interview, Oslo, June 7, 2017.

33 See, Coulthart, *op. cit.*; and Folker, *op. cit.*, pp. 11–12.

34 Coulthart, *op. cit.*, p. 940.

35 Folker, *op. cit.*, p. 8.

36 See, as examples, Folker, *op. cit.*; Arthur S. Hulnick: *Fixing the Spy Machine: Preparing American Intelligence for the Twenty-First Century*. Westport, CT: Praeger, 1999, p. 53; and Rob Johnston: *Analytic Culture in the U.S. Intelligence Community: An Ethnographic Study*. Washington, DC: Center for the Study of Intelligence, 2005, p. 15.

37 Folker, *op. cit.*, p. 14.

38 Interview, Oslo, May 30, 2017.

39 Coulthart, *op. cit.*, pp. 943–944.

40 *Ibid.*, pp. 942–943.

41 Heuer & Pherson, *op. cit.*, p. 7.

42 Gentry, *op. cit.*

43 See, among others, Gentry, *op. cit.*; Mark M. Lowenthal: "Is the US Intelligence Community Anti-intellectual?", in Isabelle Duyvesteyn, Ben de Jong, & Joop van Reijn (eds.): *The Future of Intelligence: Challenges in the 21st Century*. London and New York: Routledge, 2014, pp. 39–46; Robert Jervis: *Why Intelligence Fails: Lessons from the Iranian Revolution and the Iraq War*. New York: Cornell University Press, 2010, p. 195; and Richard L. Russel: *Sharpening Strategic Intelligence: Why the CIA Gets It Wrong and What Needs to Be Done to Get It Right?* New York: Cambridge University Press, 2007, pp. 119–148.

44 Jervis, *op. cit.*, p, 195; and Russel, *op. cit.*, p. 123.

45 Gentry, *op. cit.*; Lowenthal, *op. cit.*; and Russel, *op. cit.*

46 Russel, *op. cit.*, p. 126.
47 Philip E. Tetlock & Dan Gardner: *Superforecasting: The Art and Science of Prediction.* New York: Crown, 2015; and Philip E. Tetlock: *Expert Political Judgment: How Good Is It? How Can We Know?* Princeton, NJ: Princeton University Press, 2005.
48 Louis Menand: "Everybody's an Expert: Putting Predictions to Test", *The New Yorker,* December 5, 2005, www.newyorker.com/magazine/2005/12/05/everybodys-an-expert.
49 Thomas Fingar: *Reducing Uncertainty: Intelligence Analysis and National Security.* Stanford, CA: Stanford University Press, 2011, p. 53.
50 Jervis, *op. cit.*, p. 195.
51 Kent: *Strategic Intelligence for American World Policy, op. cit.*, p. 74.

Further reading

Artner, Stephen, Rich Girven, & James Bruce: "Assessing the Value of Structured Analytic Techniques in the U.S. Intelligence Community", *RAND Corporation*, 2016, www.rand. org/pubs/research_reports/RR1408.html.
Coulthart, Stephen: "Why Do Analysts Use Structured Analytic Techniques? An In-depth Study of an American Intelligence Agency", *Intelligence and National Security*, Vol. 31, No. 7, 2016, pp. 933–948.
Gentry, John A.: "The 'Professionalization' of Intelligence Analysis: A Skeptical Perspective", *International Journal of Intelligence and CounterIntelligence*, Vol. 29, No. 4, 2016, pp. 643–676.
Heuer Jr., Richards J., & Randolph H. Pherson: *Structured Analytic Techniques for Intelligence Analysis*. Washington, DC: CQ Press, 2010
Julian Richards: *The Art and Science of Intelligence Analysis*. Oxford and New York: Oxford University Press, 2010.
Marrin, Stephen: "Is Intelligence Analysis and Art or a Science?", *International Journal of Intelligence and CounterIntelligence*, Vol. 25, No. 3, 2012, pp. 529–545, www.tandfonline. com/doi/pdf/10.1080/08850607.2012.678690.

5   Open-source and social media intelligence

Bjørnar Sverdrup-Thygeson and
Vegard Engesæth

The digital era entails two interrelated tectonic changes to the world of intelligence analysis, one of quantity and one of quality. Firstly, the information revolution entails a massive increase in available open-source material, and second, this information deluge is in large parts driven by interpersonal and social processes bleeding into the open domain at an unprecedented scale. This transformation in the field of open-source intelligence, OSINT, is thus amplified by the advent of the new field of social media intelligence, SOCMINT. The immense range of datapoints becoming accessible for an analyst was a revolution that happened suddenly and without precedence, and as such it has taken the intelligence community a while to utilise it effectively. In the early years, the absence of an effective apparatus for making use of this digitally driven revolution contributed to a number of intelligence failures and opportunities missed, most notably the "Arab Spring". This revolution does, however, also open up a range of opportunities for more sophisticated and cost-effective intelligence analysis. However, this paradigm shift of information necessitates a methodological change from one of addressing the traditional intelligence issue of dealing with information scarcity to one of analysing intelligence under conditions of information excess.

The digital age has entailed an unprecedented deluge of information, a lot of it emanating from social interactions in a novel digital social media sphere.[1] Former GCHQ director Sir David Omand and his colleagues presented SOCMINT as the latest member of the intelligence family in a 2012 article, noting: "We live in the age of social media. Facebook, Twitter, Google and LinkedIn are all examples of the rapid transfer of people's lives – interactions, identities, arguments and views – onto a new kind of public and private sphere; a vast digital social commons".[2] In Chapter 2, Sir David Omand examines in greater detail how this trait of modern intelligence fits into the broader historical development of the in the intelligence services. This transfer is happening on an unprecedented scale. On Facebook alone, 250 million photos are added per day, as are 200 million tweets on Twitter.[3] That was in 2012. Only a few years later Twitter reported that the number of tweets per day had increased to 500 million.[4] A fundamental issue at hand is that whereas the amount of available information has been increasing at an exponential pace, human cognitive capacity has stayed hardwired at the same level. This – so to speak – Malthusian information trap has only recently been established as a concern for intelligence analysis, having for centuries had the paucity of information as their overriding concern.

Reflecting the title of this book, it is worth noting that already in 2001, a previous book, *Intelligence Services in the Information Age*, discussed how the new, information-rich world with its unprecedented volumes of information available at unprecedented speeds entailed an entirely new arena for intelligence services.[5] In the two following decades these issues have only grown acutely more important, due to the two earlier mentioned developments which will be treated in this chapter: firstly, the exponential increase in the amount of readily available information; secondly, the advent of the social media revolution – in which the general population turned from primarily being a consumer of web-based information to a producer of such.

> Hundreds of millions of people are, each minute, creating and consuming an untold amount of digital content in an online world that is not truly bound by terrestrial laws. . . . [Making] it possible for almost everybody to own, develop and disseminate real-time content without having to rely on intermediaries.[6]

In this new digital age, then, a near-instant flow of news comes from millions of accounts of large social media-driven platforms, often in near real-time. However, as, for example, Eric Schmidt and Jared Cohen point out; "[this] will expand the scope of coverage, but probably reduce the quality on a net level".[7] An often-used example of this effect is the IT consultant in Abbottabad, who unwittingly live-tweeted what would only later be clear was the top secret raid on Osama bin Laden's compound.[8] This event demonstrates not only the pervasiveness of information through new social media channels but also some of the problematic issues embedded in it, namely how the information expressed is often bereft of analysis, insight, and context. As Espen Barth Eide and Lars Haugom examine in-depth in Chapters 3 and 8, respectively, of this volume, the speed of these new data flows simultaneously poses a distinct added layer of difficulty, as policymakers are forced to react to ever shorter news cycles. This creates pressure on intelligence analysts to produce analyses faster, at the danger of debilitating trade-offs with analytical depth – in order to stay competitive with rapid, but unverified, online news sources.[9] More data, in other words, is not necessarily better as far as analysis goes. It may even make good analysis more difficult. How, then, to best approach this brave new world of information?

OSINT revolution

The vast new expanse of OSINT information amounts to a revolution in intelligence affairs. This is because, contrary to public perception and to a certain extent the view of some intelligence professionals, open-source information is now crucial to the intelligence analysis project. Since OSINT is a recent member of the intelligence family, there is still some debate on how to define the discipline.[10] However, a commonly accepted definition is based on US Intelligence

Community Directive 301,[11] describing it as "insight gleaned from publicly available information that anyone can access by overt, non-clandestine or non-secret means to satisfy an intelligence requirement".[12] A key point of the information acquisition process in OSINT is that the information is only acquired second-hand,[13] which makes the vetting process of establishing the trustworthiness of the information all the more important.[14] As such, the large-scale change created by big data and social media analysis is not a sideshow for intelligence analysis but goes to the heart of the task of a multi-source analyst.

This reflects an already ongoing revolution, where the role of OSINT for the intelligence community has been revolutionised, in lockstep with the rapid growth in the volume and composition of OSINT itself. Former senior US intelligence official Mark Lowenthal quotes a senior intelligence official estimating that at the height of the Cold War, around 20 per cent of the information collected on the Soviet Union was from open sources.[15] Following the end of the Cold War, there were a number of initiatives pushing for further integration of OSINT sources in intelligence analysis.[16] As the US Aspin-Brown Commission concluded in 1996: "A greater effort also should be made to harness the vast universe of information now available from open sources."[17] At times, this has come up against surprising resistance:

> Despite all of the lip service given to the importance of OSINT, there remains an in-grained IC [intelligence community] prejudice . . . against open sources. There will always be IC officials, and some of their policy customers, who believe that the greater the difficulty involved in collecting the intelligence, the better the intelligence has to be.[18]

However, the change in the information landscape was such that OSINT forged ahead to a preeminent position for intelligence analysts. Estimates of the prevalence of OSINT in forming the background for intelligence analysis is no longer counted in the low 20 per cent but constitutes the overwhelming majority of the information intake.

> OSINT is the lifeblood of intelligence. Statistics vary, but most seem to agree that OSINT makes up 70–80 per cent of the United States intelligence database. Since the end of the Cold War, and the opening up of many closed countries, even that estimate may be too low.[19]

Indeed, some experts assume that in this new networked era, the OSINT proportion of intelligence collection may approach 95 per cent.[20] This increased proportion of OSINT sources in the collection and analysis processes also ripples through to the decision-making level. "One senior military intelligence officer recently commented that while in the 1990s classified information was eighty percent of what he used to make decisions, today it is under ten percent."[21]

Not only has open-source information become massively more important for intelligence analysis, the nature of OSINT itself has also gone through unprecedented changes. Publicly available information is multiplying, and being digitised, at a revolutionary rate.

> By some estimates, the amount of data stored on earth doubles every two years, meaning that humankind will produce as much data in the next 24 months as it has throughout its entire history so far. Intelligence agencies have always had to find needles in haystacks. Today, the haystacks are growing exponentially.[22]

In addition to the increase in the volume of information, its nature is also rapidly changing – as the digitisation of the world's available information is a key precondition for all forms of "Big Data" analysis. Whereas only a quarter of the world's stored information was digital in the year 2000, this had risen to beyond 98 per cent in 2013.[23] This ever-expanding haystack is causing concern about how it may challenge the community's ability to produce good analyses. As summarised by Phil Nolan in a somewhat downbeat note:

> Analysts are losing the war against volume. The next huge "big mistake' won't come from a failure to connect the dots, but instead from missing dots buried in a mountain of noise. . . . In the past decade, this classified flood has been doubled by a tsunami of "open source" information (OSINT) – unclassified, publicly available information from publications, blogs, You-Tube videos, Twitter feeds, and so on.[24]

This "information tsunami" has, however, also engendered entirely new possibilities for insight, and novel forms of intelligence collection and analysis. Chief among these is the intelligence analysis of social media (SOCMINT). Not only is this new information stream one of the main contributors to the flow of new datapoints, it also has a number of distinct traits that sets it apart from traditional OSINT sources, opening up both a wealth of new possibilities and a set of fundamental ethical and practical challenges.

Social media intelligence

Over the past ten years, the emergence of social media has had a profound impact on how we interact online and what information we share. Combined with a rapid increase in connectivity across the world, this is creating a massive expansion of information and information sources. As noted by some observers, this is turning people across the world into both conscious and un-knowing intelligence collectors.[25] "When Russia invaded eastern Ukraine in 2014, the most compelling evidence came from timestamped photos taken by Russian soldiers and posted on social media, showing tank transporters and Ukrainian highway signs in the background."[26] Social media feeds are now a natural feature of military commands, corporate operations centres, and news rooms. SOCMINT has likewise become a valuable source of information for intelligences services. In the following, this chapter will explore what SOCMINT is, how it may be used, the technical, methodological and analytical challenges involved, as well as ethical considerations associated with using social media for intelligence purposes.

As noted earlier, the term social media intelligence and the acronym SOCMINT was first developed by Sir David Omand et al. in their 2012 article outlining what they saw as a burgeoning new field within open-source intelligence (OSINT). By that time, social media had already grown to be an important and natural part of life in many countries across the world, and their value as a source of information was therefore increasingly recognised by police services, media organisations, and intelligence services. The 2011 "Arab Spring" protest, where the use of Twitter played an important role in mobilising and organising protesters, was a turning point for how social media came to be viewed as a tool for social change as well as a source of information about public opinion, social movements, and emerging incidents. Since then, the social media landscape has grown massively both in scope and in complexity. The proliferation of social media usage across the globe is one of the main reasons for the huge increase in global data generation. Creating content is cheap and the amount of data available is increasing exponentially.[27] At the same time, the number of social media platforms is increasing, and social media trends are changing at a greater pace.

The social media revolution has come alongside a significant increase in connectivity. Traditional internet connectivity is still low in many parts of the world, but mobile data coverage is growing rapidly. Combined with lower prices of mobile phones this is contributing to a much greater geographic distribution of social media usage. This also creates a much greater geographic reach of SOCMINT compared to traditional OSINT.[28] The potential for SOCMINT has thus increased greatly. However, the same developments are challenging security and intelligences services when it comes to efficiently and effectively using SOCMINT. As we will show in the following, these features combined entail that SOCMINT will require strong analytical tools in order to make full use of the information available.

SOCMINT opportunities

From an intelligence analysis point of view, SOCMINT has two main uses: providing early warning and providing an additional source of information in intelligence analyses. Moreover, SOCMINT may also serve as a valuable resource in target search and collection for collection disciplines. Mapping networks and identifying persons of interest through social media are obviously well-established methods for intelligence and security services.[29]

A distinguishing feature of SOCMINT is the ability to monitor emerging incidents and developments in real time. As noted earlier, social media users sharing their content online in reality become intelligence collectors who provide real-time on-the-ground information.[30] This can obviously be of great value for current intelligence work and crisis management. Because so much of social media activity now takes place on mobile devices, and because such devices have become much more readily available, geolocation data has become an important component of SOCMINT. This makes it possible, for instance, to identify where specific pictures have been taken, and to correlate SOCMINT with other open-source or classified information. Beyond the obvious focus of social media platforms for SOCMINT, another important feature is how complex analytical tools play a crucial part in successfully exploiting the data.

Big data analytics

A key challenge for SOCMINT is the ability to mine data from an extremely large dataset in order to offer meaningful analysis.[31] This is a challenge that is beyond the capabilities of human analysts. Even if the human brain likely still works faster than the fastest supercomputer, the ability to structure and process vast amounts of information and turn it into useful intelligence requires the use of sophisticated data processing analytical tools.[32] Social media analytics is of course a key part of the business model of the companies behind the many applications of the social media sphere. As the saying goes, when a product is available for free, the user becomes the product. Understanding user behaviour and preferences in order to market these as products towards a broad section of companies and organisations has proven a profitable business model.

There are also a great number of companies whose focus is to offer monitoring and analytics services of social media. Kevjn Lim notes that "social media applications have melded into a 'vast digital commons' capable of facilitating complex analysis of sentiments, semantics, clusters and networks".[33] In addition to the business sector, a whole range of actors utilises various means of crowdsourcing intelligence. The renowned investigative journalism website *Bellingcat*, draws upon the combination of a dispersed network of personnel, amateur volunteers, and information from a wide array of open sources to develop sophisticated intelligence reports.[34]

Analysts can, of course, make use of social media without sophisticated tools, to help find relevant sources and content, and glean some insight into developing events and how certain issues are being discussed. However, without analytical tools aiding the analysis and providing a broader dataset, such analyses will be of limited value, other than perhaps as starting points for further research and investigation. Software like *Dataminr* provide media organisations, businesses, and the public sector with the ability to monitor and analyse Twitter and certain other social media platforms. Other programmes such as *Recorded Future* and *Palantir* also offer tools to monitor open-source web intelligence. In the US intelligence community, a number of different analytics or metrics software are in use, such as "Visible: Socializing the Enterprise", *Geofeedia*, the CIA's Open-Source Indicators, and the Department of Defense Information Volume and Velocity programme.[35] The CIA-affiliated venture-capital firm *In-Q-Tel* has also provided capital to many start-up companies in this field.[36]

The utility of SOCMINT is therefore closely tied to developments in big data analytics and the use of artificial intelligence and machine learning technology to collect, structure, and process great amounts of data. Using big data analytics, SOCMINT may provide a way to inform strategic intelligence. The advances in natural language processing (NLP) and image recognition technology have been a crucially important factor in this development. One of the greatest challenges with big data, which also applies to social media data, is how to collate and process data from different sources, and in different formats.[37] This applies in particular to unstructured data – for instance, images, text, and audio. Such unstructured data provides little additional information – for example, how various pieces of data relate to each other. NLP and image recognition can help extract insight and analytical value from such unstructured datasets. As such they have become an important factor of Big Data analytics in SOCMINT.

One example is the Integrated Crisis Early Warning System (ICEWS), an OSINT solution maintained by Lockheed Martin, which is a tool to extract event data automatically from news reports.[38] The tool itself is a natural language analysis engine, but importantly it extracts structured information such as entities, relationships, events from text. Other similar tools, also based on NLP technology, map the intensity of social media interactions. There are broad commercial uses for NLP in SOCMINT, not least when it comes to gauging consumer sentiments towards products and services. Free tools are also available online, such as the website Social Mention, a social media search and analysis platform that draws together social media mentions of products, companies, or issues.[39]

The emergence of these analytical tools and techniques enhances the value of SOCMINT for researchers and analysts. Applied with care and being mindful of the shortcomings (discussed later), SOCMINT can give useful and real-time information regarding political, economic, and social developments. Combined with other intelligence information, this can be a powerful tool for analysts. The real-time aspect of social media also makes it possible to detect and provide early warning of developing events, ranging from public protest to natural disasters. There are also a number of ongoing efforts to utilise various large datasets in order to take analysis beyond the near simultaneous, that is, to predict occurrences before they happen.[40] However, these have so far tended to run into difficulties. One of the most prominent, and best funded, examples of these, Google's Flu Trends initiative, shut down after a few years after a row of persistent prediction failings.[41]

SOCMINT challenges

For all its promises, then, SOCMINT also has several challenges. For researchers and intelligence analysts alike, it is important to be aware of the shortcomings and pitfalls in order to avoid flawed analyses. One of the most obvious drawbacks of SOCMINT is how social media users may represent only a certain sociodemographic segment within society. This may also apply within the group of social media users, for instance when it comes to the use of specific hashtags.[42] A related category of bias that also should be considered, is the "astroturf"-effect, the extent to which one may overly conflate digital events with real-world actions, particularly as large social-media networks of actors expressing certain opinions may turn out to be a shell network of fake online personas rather than an organic movement.[43] This selection bias in the data could lead to skewed analyses and flawed conclusions, if not taken into account and corrected for.

The various solutions that employ NLP and other technologies are useful tools in SOCMINT. Indeed, they are necessary in order to fully exploit social media information and analyse large datasets. However, such technologies are not without their challenges. Building algorithms that interpret intention and meaning from unstructured data is challenging. Some studies show that the accuracy of sentiment analysis tools is low, and that they struggle with interpreting meaning and not just counting instances.[44] There are a number of reasons why it has proven difficult to utilise this information overload. Prime among these are the still robust challenges entailed by the fact that humans at the core communicate different than machines. Languages reflecting centuries of often unspoken assumptions are not easily captured in binary bits. For instance, substantial difficulties remain, not least related to language traditions where context is more implicit, and as such more difficult for machine learning to access and express.[45] Strides are being made, though, demonstrated vividly in Google Translate's rapidly improving ability to translate between different languages, as well as the latest advances in GPT-3.[46] This demonstrates that the field is evolving rapidly, and as more advanced machine learning techniques are developed.[47]

Another problem is how to correct for bias in the analytical models. Through machine learning, the algorithms used in SOCMINT tools are increasingly automatically created and trained. As Brantly notes:

> Algorithms that are predicated on biases within learning structures are self-reinforcing and will produce progressively less accurate analysis. Whereas, a human analyst can correct for bias between analyses automated learning algorithms absent oversight and corrective adjustments might result in increasingly significant error.[48]

While one can expect tools to improve, it will require continued attention from developers and users alike. At the same time, the sophistication of deepfake technology is increasing rapidly and becoming readily available. This creates an additional layer of challenges when it comes to separating the real from the spurious, and requires new solutions to counter effectively.[49] For analysts, all these aspects mean that it is crucial to maintain a good understanding of how SOCMINT analysis tools collect and analyse data.[50]

A shifting social media landscape

Social media usage has changed considerably over the years since they first emerged in the mid-2000s. Not only has overall usage increased enormously, but the plethora of different applications available means that social media consumption is now spread across a much higher number of platforms. Facebook and

YouTube have remained the largest in monthly average users, but since the early 2010s the number of social media platforms has increased substantially, and the number of users of these has grown. This development has also led to significant variations between age segments, with younger users starting use new platforms more quickly. Likewise, in many countries this has led to a drop-in use of the biggest platforms among the younger age groups.[51] The pluralisation in social media applications is accentuated further because of the development of a more geographically diversified "splinternet", where platforms such as Weibo is dominant within China, but largely absent outside of the country.

Three trends are discernible when it comes to social media use. For one, video content is increasing, and this is happening across platforms. Related to that, ephemeral content, such as time-limited video stories, is becoming much more prevalent. A third development is how platforms where group membership is a major component is growing (e.g. WhatsApp and WeChat). Both the higher number of platforms being used and the way they function pose challenges for effective use in a SOCMINT context. The move towards more video across platforms, increases the amount of unstructured data which may be harder to analyse. At the same time, the trend of more ephemeral content reduces the availability of data to structure and analyse.

Ethics

To an extent, the value of SOCMINT is based on novel behaviour and norms entailing that people are engaged *en masse* in what would earlier have been considered "oversharing" of their personal lives. Considering the ethical implications therefore takes on extra importance. The move towards platforms based around group membership adds to this complexity and poses additional questions as to what should be considered open source. Kira Vrist Rønn argues in Chapter 11, and elsewhere with Sille Obelitz Søe, that the notion that social media platforms are open is problematic.[52] In their foundational discussion of SOCMINT, Sir David Omand et al. argue that it is necessary to distinguish between open-source, non-intrusive SOCMINT, and closed-source, intrusive SOCMINT.[53] Furthermore, they argue that for SOCMINT to be considered open-source, "it should not be able to identify individuals, [nor] be used as a means of criminal investigation, or puncture wishes of the user".[54] Kira Vrist Rønn and Sille Obelitz Søe argue that even this may be a difficult standard to meet because of the dual nature of social media platforms: They feel private to the users, but they are in fact public spaces. In reality, this makes social media platforms grey zones when it comes to making use of the information they contain.[55]

The social media trends described earlier push move more of the social media behaviour into forms and fora where the expectation of privacy may be greater. For SOCMINT practitioners this means putting forward well considered and sufficiently argued cases for why and how to conduct the collection. An adaptation of Omand's five principles for the intelligence community has been suggested for SOCMINT:

1   There must be sufficient, sustainable cause.
2   There must be integrity of motive.
3   The methods used must be proportionate and necessary.
4   There must be right authority, validated by external oversight.
5   Recourse to secret intelligence must be a last resort if more open sources can be used. (Applying this principle to SOCMINT, less intrusive forms should be preferred to more intrusive covert forms.)[56]

This set of principles is a useful framework but still requires intelligence services to make difficult judgement calls – particularly because of the rapid changes within the social media sphere.

The future of SOCMINT and OSINT

Despite the challenges and potential shortcomings, SOCMINT presents opportunities for intelligence services, particularly when it comes to early warning, strategic analysis and horizon scanning. The same applies to OSINT more broadly. Importantly though, the social media revolution and data explosion does not do away with human analysts. In line with Stig Stenslie's arguments in Chapter 4, it rather increases the need for subject-matter expertise and analytical rigour.

Analytical tools

As we have touched upon earlier, the successful utilisation of SOCMINT for analysis and early warning requires the use of sophisticated analytical tools and the incorporation of machine learning technology. As has been pointed out by Adam Schiff, in the Congress report taking stock of the US intelligence community: "Intelligence agencies must do a better job of adapting to the sheer amount of open-source data available to them. . . . That means properly utilising artificial intelligence and machine learning to analyse data to find what we need to make decisions quickly."[57] The traditional way of regarding OSINT as the most "democratic" intelligence discipline, based on the fact that it "requires no advanced technology"[58] is thus being challenged. In fact, the torrent of OSINT and SOCMINT sources will increasingly demand some level of advanced technology in order to provide an edge in analysing the overflowing amounts of information.

As Lars Haugom, Cato Yaakov Hemmingby, and Tore Pedersen discuss in Chapter 6, artificial intelligence and machine learning offer many possibilities for intelligence analysis. Solutions that automate collecting and systematising information can enhance analytical work by providing a wider range of data inputs and increasing contextual awareness for the analyst. However, human analysts are still necessary to form hypotheses and theories and to generate answers to complex issues,[59] the point being: "If the technology does not produce intelligence that analysts can use, it is pointless. Technology for the sake of technology is a waste."[60]

However, the need for advanced tools also highlights another important issue, namely the ability of intelligence services to keep up with technological development within the social media ecosystem. This requires a willingness to test and evaluate new tools continuously, and to be able to implement solutions rapidly. Doing so will be challenging for intelligence services, which in many respects may not have acquisition processes and organisational capabilities suited to the task.[61] With some notable exceptions, the majority of advanced SOCMINT solutions and tools are being developed by commercial enterprises. For intelligence services to employ SOCMINT efficiently and effectively, closer collaboration with commercial entities and academia is necessary. At the same time intelligence services need to build and maintain internal digital capabilities in this area.

Analytical frameworks

In order to draw value from the information revolution, however, not only the software, but also their human operators need to be sophisticated. Even if Big Data tools may be able to provide insights on correlations, strategic trends and anomalies, they are still not able to provide insights into causation, i.e. why these correlations are happening.[62] As Aaron Brantly notes:

> The notion that large volumes of data in some way presupposes omniscience is false. Correlation is not a substitute for rigorous scientific method and robust causal models predicated on thoughtfully informed hypotheses. While human analysts make use of structured analytic techniques to minimize biases, the underlying attributes of data analysis for intelligence is likely to reside in robust theory.[63]

As Stig Stenslie discusses in depth in Chapter 4, this speaks to the importance of training analysts in the use of solid knowledge-frameworks and in-depth cultural understanding. To this point it is also necessary to better bridge certain old divisions in the epistemic community, in order to best utilise the influx of large-scale digitised information by combining methodological insights from the humanities and social science with those of computer science:

> Those disciplines best equipped to understand and explain human behaviour – the social and behavioural sciences, political science, psephology, anthropology and social psychology – have not kept pace in relating this insight to the big-data approaches necessary to understand social media. Conversely, these very same big-data approaches that form the backbone of current SOCMINT capabilities have not used sociology to employ the measurements and statistics they use to the task of meaningfully interpreting human behaviour.[64]

It also highlights the need for developing analysts' skill sets when it comes to where and how to search, particularly since useful information tends to be harder to find and exists in many different languages. As we have pointed out earlier, data appears less in text form, and increasingly in photo and in particular, video formats. The increasingly personal, and less formal nature of information found in the SOCMINT domain, further accentuates the necessity for analysts to be well versed in local languages and customs, and the dense intertextual web of their perspectives, narratives, and priorities.[65] It has also been argued that future IC analysts should look to the realm of open information not just as a source for data-points but also, and more systematically than is already the case, as a source for readily analysed data.[66] However, this is an approach that carries a number of distinct challenges in itself, in terms of validation and openness.

Going forward, the emphasis should be on finding the best possible way for analysts and digital tools to work together in order to harness the novel information flows. The matter of cost-effectiveness is a point that comes even more to the fore in terms of automating certain processes. In order for the analyst to be able to spend the majority of her time on those areas where the human mind synergises most efficiently with that of the machine. This, then reflects the call for a more "analyst-centric" approach to intelligence as, in Alan Dupont's words:

> The traditional intelligence cycle clearly has less explanatory and organisa-
> tional utility in the post-Cold War world. The discrete functionality implied in
> the separation of the intelligence process into collection, collation, analysis and
> dissemination reflects the concepts, practice and organisational dynamics of an
> earlier era. What will distinguish the successful practitioners of twenty-first-
> century intelligence is the ability to fuse and integrate all elements of the process
> to provide seamless support for policymakers and operational commanders.[67]

Christopher Eldridge, Christopher Hobbs, and Matthew Moran have suggested the following distinct areas wherein software tools can contribute to this:[68]

- Continuous collection based on targeted searches with refined data scrapers.
- Indexing and tagging of sources and content.
- Identifying and visualising relationships between entities across information sources and direct attention to correlation patterns.
- Exploratory searching to give analysts a sense of information potentially available compared with information currently used in analyses.
- Automated categorisation based on content, sourcing, language style.

Decoding, interpreting and contextualising such information, and in the next turn using it to make nuanced analyses and judgements are still beyond even the most sophisticated software and speaks to the need for human analysts in the process.[69] Indeed, the quantity of available information combined with new tools for harnessing them, should be a cause for an increase, rather than a decrease in the relative number of analysts.[70]

Conclusion

The increased importance of OSINT and SOCMINT for intelligence analysts is a natural consequence of the digital era that has entailed an exponential growth in information. The rise of social media has further contributed to this increase in both volume and geographical scope, as incremental progress in the smartphone area, de facto, puts powerful handheld computers in the hands of a steadily widening circle of the human population.[71] However, even with the help of the advances in computing power, a key challenge has been that the information load has tended to keep abreast of the intelligence analysts' abilities to process it.

As the world of chess long used to be the main symbolic battleground for the battle between human and machine minds – where the human brain famously lost in 1997 – it is worth noting the development of chess teams consisting of teams of humans and computers together – a development often termed under the headline "Joint Cognitive System".[72] This allows for computers to play on their "strengths", and this will further enable analysts to focus on those areas in which they hold both absolute and comparative advantages over the machines.

Clint Watts notes in his book on world politics and social media that "the world was a better place before social media"[73] However one may feel about it, social media is now an unavoidable part of modern life. As such, SOCMINT also clearly offers government agencies a significant additional avenue to understanding political, economic and societal developments. The insights that may be gleaned from SOCMINT can provide important intelligence that should be integrated into analysis on a number of issues. SOCMINT can also be an important tool for providing early warning of developing incidents, such as violent protests, terrorist attacks, or natural disasters and accidents.

However, it is also worth noting that SOCMINT is no panacea that will provide deep insights that are otherwise unavailable. The increase in sensors alone does not replace the need for theory, subject-matter expertise and thorough analysis. For all the reasons we have listed earlier, processing and analysis capability, the quality of the analytical tools, access to a continuously growing set of social media platforms, as well as a selection bias in terms of who uses social media, SOCMINT should be used with care and be subject to the same rigorous source critique as other intelligence disciplines.

In order to best complement automated processes, the key focus for the analyst should be to double down on internalising rich contextual knowledge, drawing on the field of humanities, as well as analytical training and source critique. "With the world awash in a sea of information the task of the intelligence analyst is growing daily more difficult, and mastery of the art of assessment will be an even more indispensable component of tomorrow's knowledge edge."[74] On this basis, then, one should proceed to integrate these hallmarks of systematic social enquiry as a solid foundation for bridging over to the field of quantitative analytics, in order to be able to creatively shape analytical frameworks salient for the pursuit of knowledge in the context of the digital age.

We thus return to the central premise of this book, namely that the digitalisation of our societies, the explosion in open-source information and the attendant information overload problem, in fact underscores the importance of placing the analysis at the core of the intelligence mission.

Notes

1 Nate Silver: *The Signal and the Noise: Why So Many Predictions Fail-but Some Don't.* London: Penguin, 2012, p. 9.
2 Sir David Omand, Jamie Bartlett, & Carl Miller: "Introducing Social Media Intelligence (SOCMINT)", *Intelligence and National Security*, Vol. 27, No. 6, December 1, 2012, p. 803.
3 *Ibid.*, p. 803.
4 Alexei Oreskovic: "Here's Another Area Where Twitter Appears to Have Stalled: Tweets per Day", *Business Insider*, accessed November 15, 2020, www.businessinsider. in/heres-another-area-where-twitter-appears-to-have-stalled-tweets-per-day/ articleshow/47684428.cms.
5 Michael Herman: *Intelligence Services in the Information Age: Theory and Practice.* Cass Series – Studies in Intelligence. London and Portland, OR: F. Cass, 2001, p. ix.
6 Eric Schmidt & Jared Cohen: *The New Digital Age: Reshaping the Future of People, Nations and Business* London: Alfred A. Knopf, 2013, pp. 3–4.
7 *Ibid.*, p. 49.
8 *Ibid.*, pp. 47–49.
9 Amy Zegart & Michael Morell: "Spies, Lies, and Algorithms", *Foreign Affairs*, Vol. 98, No. 3, May 2019, p. 92.
10 H. Akın Ünver: "Digital Open Source Intelligence and International Security: A Primer", *Centre for Economics and Foreign Policy Studies*, 2018, p. 2.
11 US National Open Source Enterprise: "Intelligence Community Directive Number 301", July 11, 2006, https://fas.org/irp/dni/icd/icd-301.pdf.
12 James J. Wirtz & Jon J. Rosenwasser: "From Combined Arms to Combined Intelligence: Philosophy, Doctrine and Operations", *Intelligence and National Security*, Vol. 25, No. 6, December 1, 2010, p. 736.
13 *Ibid.*
14 Eliot A. Jardines: "Open Source Intelligence", in Mark M. Lowenthal & Robert M. Clark (eds.): *The Five Disciplines of Intelligence Collection*, 1st edition. Thousand Oaks, CA: CQ Press, 2015, p. 5–6.
15 Mark M. Lowenthal: "Open Source Intelligence: New Myths, New Realities", *Defense Daily Network Special Reports*, November 5, 1998, p. 1.
16 Bowman H. Miller: "Open Source Intelligence (OSINT): An Oxymoron?", *International Journal of Intelligence and CounterIntelligence*, Vol. 31, No. 4, October 2, 2018, p. 705.
17 "Preparing for the 21st Century – An Appraisal of U.S. Intelligence: Report of the Commission on the Roles and Capabilities of the United States Intelligence Community 1 March 1996", *American Intelligence Journal*, Vol. 16, No. 2/3, 1995, p. xxi.
18 Lowenthal, *op. cit.*, p. 2.
19 Arthur S. Hulnick: "The Downside of Open Source Intelligence", *International Journal of Intelligence and CounterIntelligence*, Vol. 15, No. 4, November 2002, p. 566.
20 Loch K. Johnson, Loch J. Johnson, & James J. Wirtz: *Intelligence and National Security: The Secret World of Spies: An Anthology.* Oxford: Oxford University Press, 2008, p. 44.
21 Phil Nolan: "A Curator Approach to Intelligence Analysis", *International Journal of Intelligence and CounterIntelligence*, Vol. 25, No. 4, December 1, 2012, p. 787.
22 Zegart & Morell, *op. cit.*, p. 91.
23 Kevjn Lim: "Big Data and Strategic Intelligence", *Intelligence and National Security*, Vol. 31, No. 4, June 6, 2016, p. 622.
24 Nolan, *op. cit.*, p. 786.
25 Zegart & Morell, *op. cit.*, p. 90.
26 *Ibid.*
27 *Ibid.*, p. 91.

28 Rose Bernard et al.: "Intelligence and Global Health: Assessing the Role of Open Source and Social Media Intelligence Analysis in Infectious Disease Outbreaks", *Journal of Public Health*, Vol. 26, No. 5, October 2018, p. 510.
29 Robert Dover: "SOCMINT: A Shifting Balance of Opportunity", *Intelligence and National Security*, Vol. 35, No. 2, February 23, 2020, p. 225.
30 Greg Slabodkin: "GEOINT Tradecraft: 'Human Geography' – 'Defense Systems'", *Defense Systems*, October 29, 2013, https://defensesystems.com/articles/2013/10/29/geoint-human-geography.aspx.
31 Michael Hastings: "Automated Analytics. Natural Language Processing in Social Media Intelligence", *Marine Corps Gazette*, n.d., p. 18.
32 Aaron Brantly: "When Everything Becomes Intelligence: Machine Learning and the Connected World", *Intelligence and National Security*, Vol. 33, June 7, 2018, p. 562.
33 Lim, *op. cit.*, p. 629.
34 Ünver, *op. cit.*, pp. 15–16.
35 Lim, *op. cit.*, p. 630.
36 Zegart & Morell, *op. cit.*, p. 92.
37 Burgert Senekal & Eduan Kotzé: "Open Source Intelligence (OSINT) for Conflict Monitoring in Contemporary South Africa: Challenges and Opportunities in a Big Data Context", *African Security Review*, Vol. 28, No. 1, January 2, 2019, p. 22.
38 *Ibid.*
39 Helen Kennedy: "Perspectives on Sentiment Analysis", *Journal of Broadcasting & Electronic Media*, Vol. 56, No. 4, October 2012, p. 436.
40 Kira Radinsky & Eric Horvitz: "Mining the Web to Predict Future Events", in *Proceedings of the Sixth ACM International Conference on Web Search and Data Mining – WSDM '13* (The Sixth ACM International Conference, Rome, Italy: ACM Press, 2013), 255, https://doi.org/10.1145/2433396.2433431; and Julian Tsz Kin Chan & Weifeng Zhong: "Reading China: Predicting Policy Change with Machine Learning", *SSRN Electronic Journal*, 2018, https://doi.org/10.2139/ssrn.3275687.
41 Christopher Eldridge, Christopher Hobbs, & Matthew Moran: "Fusing Algorithms and Analysts: Open-Source Intelligence in the Age of 'Big Data'", *Intelligence and National Security*, Vol. 33, No. 3, April 16, 2018, p. 397.
42 Lim, *op. cit.*, p. 630.
43 Schmidt & Cohen, *op. cit.*, pp. 127–28.
44 Kennedy, *op. cit.*, p. 437.
45 Jardines, *op. cit.*, p. 23.
46 GPT-3: Generative Pre-trained Transformer 3; an automated language model that uses deep learning to produce human-like text.
47 John Thornhill: "Is AI Finally Closing in on Human Intelligence?", *Financial Times*, November 12, 2020, www.ft.com/content/512cef1d-233b-4dd8-96a4-0af07bb9ff60.
48 Brantly, *op. cit.*, p. 568.
49 Zegart & Morell, *op. cit.*, p. 90; and Will Knight: "The AI Company Helping the Pentagon Assess Disinfo Campaigns", *Wired*, accessed November 10, 2020, www.wired.com/story/ai-helping-pentagon-assess-disinfo-campaigns/.
50 Brantly, *op. cit.*, p. 568.
51 Esteban Ortiz-Ospina: "The Rise of Social Media", *Our World in Data*, accessed November 15, 2020, https://ourworldindata.org/rise-of-social-media.
52 Kira Vrist Rønn & Sille O. Søe: "Is Social Media Intelligence Private? Privacy in Public and the Nature of Social Media Intelligence", *Intelligence and National Security*, Vol. 34, No. 3, 2019, pp. 362–378.
53 Omand, Bartlett, & Miller, *op. cit.*, p. 820.
54 *Ibid.*
55 Rønn & Søe, *op. cit.*, p. 366.
56 Omand, Bartlett, & Miller, *op. cit.*, pp. 820–22.

57 Adam Schiff: "The U.S. Intelligence Community Is Not Prepared for the China Threat", *Foreign Affairs*, October 7, 2020, www.foreignaffairs.com/articles/united-states/2020-09-30/us-intelligence-community-not-prepared-china-threat.
58 Lowenthal & Clark, *op. cit.*, p. 1.
59 Eldridge, Hobbs, & Moran, *op. cit.*, p. 396.
60 Lowenthal, *op. cit.*, p. 2.
61 Zegart & Morell, *op. cit.*, p. 92.
62 Eldridge, Hobbs, & Moran, *op. cit.*, p. 397.
63 Brantly, *op. cit.*
64 Omand, Bartlett, & Miller, *op. cit.*, p. 816.
65 Miller, *op. cit.*, p. 709.
66 Nolan, *op. cit.*, pp. 786–87.
67 Alan Dupont: "Intelligence for the Twenty-First Century", *Intelligence and National Security*, Vol. 18, No. 4, December 1, 2003, p. 34.
68 Eldridge, Hobbs, & Moran, *op. cit.*, p. 400.
69 *Ibid.*, p. 392.
70 Neil Couch & Bill Robins: "Big Data for Defence and Security", *Core*, 2013, pp. 9–10, https://core.ac.uk/display/30675953; and Eldridge, Hobbs, & Moran, *op. cit.*, p. 398.
71 Jardines, *op. cit.*, p. 13.
72 Eldridge, Hobbs, & Moran, *op. cit.*, p. 399.
73 Clint Watts: *Messing with the Enemy: Surviving in a Social Media World of Hackers, Terrorists, Russians, and Fake News*. New York: HarperCollins Publishers, 2019.
74 Dupont, *op. cit.*, p. 22.

Further reading

Brantly, Aaron: "When Everything Becomes Intelligence: Machine Learning and the Connected World", *Intelligence and National Security*, Vol. 33, June 7, 2018, pp. 562–573.
Dover, Robert: "SOCMINT: A Shifting Balance of Opportunity", *Intelligence and National Security*, Vol. 35, No. 2, February 23, 2020, pp. 216–232.
Eldridge, Christopher, Christopher Hobbs, & Matthew Moran: "Fusing Algorithms and Analysts: Open-Source Intelligence in the Age of 'Big Data'", *Intelligence and National Security*, Vol. 33, No. 3, April 16, 2018, pp. 391–406.
Omand, Sir David, Jamie Bartlett, & Carl Miller: "Introducing Social Media Intelligence (SOCMINT)", *Intelligence and National Security* Vol. 27, No. 6, December 1, 2012, pp. 801–823.
Zegart, Amy, & Michael Morell: "Spies, Lies, and Algorithms", *Foreign Affairs*, vol. 98, no. 3, May 2019, pp. 85–96, www.foreignaffairs.com/articles/2019-04-16/spies-lies-and-algorithms.

6 Analysing with artificial intelligence

Lars Haugom, Cato Yaakov Hemmingby, and Tore Pedersen

In the satire puppet movie *Team America: World Police* from 2004, the global task force Team America bases its operations entirely on intelligence from the computer I.N.T.E.L.L.I.G.E.N.C.E. This high-tech wonder tells the task force where international terrorists are located and supports their operations as they set out to neutralise the bad guys. However, the machine is not without flaws, and when it makes mistakes it is addressed as "Bad I.N.T.E.L.L.I.G.E.N.C.E." by the team. When Team America's HQ is bombed and the computer incapacitated, things go bad for the team. Without the technological supremacy I.N.T.E.L.L.I.G.E.N.C.E. provides, the force becomes an easy prey for North Korea's leader, who is planning a cunning attack on the United States in order to achieve world rule.[1]

In 2004, it seemed quite unlikely that a computer could take over almost all tasks intelligence services have – from data collection and analysis to operational support. Today, the picture is less clear. In high-tech communities there is considerable optimism regarding the future use of so-called artificial intelligence (AI). An astonishing development in this area has led to expectations that computers – by means of instructions for assignments or algorithms – in a few decades will be able to carry out many tasks more effectively than the human brain. This development has major implications for knowledge-based enterprises. The digital age is marked by a growing amount of information and a more complex worldview – real or imaginary – that journalists, researchers, analysts, and other professionals relying on knowledge must relate to. If computer programs are able to gather, analyse, and communicate analysis just as good as or even better than human beings, it is also likely that the technology will be utilised for these purposes. Within banking and finance, such programs are already used to a great extent. Assessing loan applications and providing investment advice can now be done without involving people. Within several professions, such as journalism, medicine, and law, it seems likely that in the future the task of professionals will be to monitor and perform quality control rather than carrying out the tasks themselves. This can to a certain extent be compared to the introduction of robots and other advanced machines in industry. Machines can now carry out production that previously required a number of workers along an assembly line, with just a few people monitoring the process. The machines of today can do the job just as well or even better than workers in previous times.

This chapter is on the use of artificial intelligence in intelligence analysis. More specifically, it seeks to show how the evolution of artificial intelligence can be developed and designed so that the human brain and machine processes can complement each other. The key to understanding such complementarity is primarily to ascertain what we humans are particularly good at and with what we are not so successful. This must be held up against which tasks machine algorithms are extraordinarily good at and which tasks they do not perform very well. In this chapter we will argue that intelligence analysis is an area where people and machines can "cooperate" in order to arrive at timely, relevant, and trustworthy results, and then communicate these results to decision-makers. It is highly likely that technology based on artificial intelligence will become an increasingly important and highly necessary tool for intelligence analysts. At the same time, it is not likely that this technology will fully replace human analysts – neither when it comes to production nor communication of intelligence. Technology based on artificial intelligence is consecutively implemented by intelligence and security services and is part of their strategy for meeting the challenges of the digital age. Publicly available information on how this technology is used by intelligence and security services is negligible, primarily because such information could reveal something about the services' capabilities and capacities. We have therefore had to base this chapter on empirical data from more open organisations. That said, empirical findings indicate quite clearly what kind of tasks artificial intelligence is particularly useful for and hence how technology will affect the relationship between man and machine in the field of intelligence analysis.

The first section of this chapter is about the basic differences between human intelligence and thinking on the one hand and artificial intelligence on the other. The second section deals with how and why this technology is considered suitable for intelligence analysis and, by extension, the future relevance and role of the analyst in the intelligence process.

Brain versus algorithms

In daily speech, we equate intelligence[2] with being clever, but intelligence is more complex than that. Intelligence can, for example, mean to be good at something in different ways, like having an above-average ability to understand languages or numbers. Intelligence can also be related to the ability to think logically, regardless of languages and numbers. Social skills, or the ability to understand other people's emotions, may also be characterised as intelligence.[3] These latter forms of intelligence are often described as social intelligence and emotional intelligence. They are typically included in the concept of intelligence because understanding social interaction and assessing other people's emotions are important for problem-solving.

Intelligence may be defined as the ability to achieve complex objectives.[4] In reality, it is a concept constructed for describing and measuring people's ability to solve various types of problems. How intelligent we are depends on how we view intelligence. Do we view intelligence as an "overarching" ability that helps us solve all kinds of problems, or are we talking about verbal intelligence and numeric intelligence? Alternatively, are we concerned with social interaction, as in the ability to detect and assess the signals that people are sending out and then interact with these people in an expedient manner?

If we were to compare human intelligence with the phenomenon of artificial intelligence, it does not make much sense to take this traditional understanding of intelligence as our starting point. Because intelligent systems are not intelligent in the same way as human beings,[5] it is more meaningful to start with human cognition, perception, and thinking and then compare this set-up with the algorithmic processing of the machine.

One criterion for people to gain knowledge is the ability to conclude correctly – that is, the ability to reason logically and make an inference via different premises to a valid conclusion.[6] If the premises are true and the reasoning follows logical criteria, the conclusion will also be true. Another criterion is the ability to generalise from single observations to a "rule".[7] If a phenomenon has always repeated itself under certain conditions, we may have reason to assume that the phenomenon will repeat itself under the same conditions in the future too. The challenge here, however, is that initially we must be able to identify the conditions and then must understand which other conditions might lead to irregularities. It will not get easier if we have limited time at our disposal. If the complexity increases, too, this is an additional challenge. In such cases, it might be appropriate to get help from artificial intelligence. Since artificial intelligence usually works faster and is able to process considerably larger volumes of information than human beings can, it makes a good ally when we set out to solve complex problems within a short time frame.

Artificial intelligence

Artificial intelligence is not entirely a new phenomenon. One of the pioneers in this area was the British mathematician Alan Turing, who is best known for his pivotal role in cracking Germany's Enigma-code during the Second World War. In the early 1950s, before the term "artificial intelligence" was even coined, Turing posed the question: "Are machines able to think?" In order to answer this question, he defined a test, which later became known as the Turing test: If a person repeatedly asks a question to another person and a machine at the same time, and the questioner is not able to distinguish between which answers are given by the human and the machine, then we can say that the machine is thinking.

Turing inspired generations of researchers to try to build a computer that passes his test, but for a long time machines and software limited how far artificial intelligence could be developed. Only in recent years has research in this field come far enough that it makes sense to talk about machines that can execute specific tasks just as good – or better – than human beings.

Modern computers have sufficient speed and capacity to handle the large volumes of data required for machines to be able to "learn". In addition, digitalisation has considerably improved the access to large datasets. Today, machines can access billions of examples that may be used in a learning process, not just a few hundred. Research on artificial intelligence has also developed from a focus on general problem-solving towards solving very specific problems within limited areas, like face recognition. Last, but not least, research efforts have been directed towards teaching machines to think like machines, not as human beings. For example, it is not necessary for a machine to know what a football match is in order to identify pictures of football matches. The machine only needs access to a high number of pictures from football matches in order to learn that a certain composition of people, places, and things, in the form of dots in the picture, with a high degree of certainty is equal to the term "football match".

What we call intelligent machines may be simple, meaning that they relate to predefined algorithms and never deviate from these algorithms when they process information. The machine carries out the same task every time and always correctly – if it is programmed correctly. In contrast, a faulty or incorrectly programmed machine will produce unreliable results. However, machines can also be complex. This means that they can not only perform simple tasks like sorting persons in a dataset according to age but also conduct advanced operations such as manoeuvring a car through traffic. In order to handle such tasks, the machine must be allowed to be partially autonomous, meaning self-controlled. The machine is pre-programmed with algorithms allowing it to interact with the surroundings, and because of this interaction, the machine can adjust its algorithms or make new ones according to what it has "learned" from these surroundings. This is what we today understand as artificial intelligence.

Machines with autonomous and complex algorithms are particularly well-suited to sort through large volumes of data, also when the data are unstructured. The ability to understand natural language or photos are examples of how complex machines can handle unstructured data. IBM's Watson is one example of a machine that can find answers in a huge amount of unstructured information, if there are answers to be found. In other words, the machine will find the needle in the haystack, if the needle exists, and Watson can process the whole haystack. Watson was, for example, superior in outsmarting ordinary participants in the game Jeopardy where solutions existed in the enormous data volume Watson had access to. In contrast, the machine experienced considerable problems in finding the right answer when the solution was not part of the data volume but was located outside of it.[8]

Machines with autonomous and complex algorithms are also used to predict how natural or societal phenomena will evolve. Google Flu Trends (GFT),[9] developed to predict the spread of influenza, is a good example. From the start, GFT was calibrated for flu reported to doctors and national health registers. At the same time, the system was fed data from Google search engines mapping when people were browsing for flu symptoms. From the outset, the system made good predictions for the geographical proliferation of flu, but after a while, the quality of predictions declined. GFT predicted a more substantial spread of flu than what turned out to be the case. The reason for this was that the system was not able to determine when people had the flu, and when they were worried about their health without actually having the illness.

In other words, artificial intelligence has obvious limitations compared to the cognitive abilities of human beings – at least where the technology stands today. At the same time, it cannot be denied that artificial intelligence is able to handle a considerably larger amount of information than human beings and that the bulk of information can be processed infinitely much faster than humans are capable of. Additionally, developments in this area are moving fast and are expected to do so for many years to come – that is, unless the technology encounters serious obstacles that we are not able to foresee today.

Today, artificial intelligence is synonymous with what is called artificial "narrow" intelligence, meaning machine intelligence that is equal to or surpasses human intelligence for *specific* tasks. IBM Watson is a prominent example. The next big step in the field is expected to be artificial *general* intelligence, meaning machine intelligence that is equal to human intelligence for *all* tasks, and artificial *super* intelligence with machines that are capable of conducting all tasks better than human beings.[10] It is particularly this last step that has led to dystopia and doomsday prophecies about a future where machines take over the world.

Experts in the field disagree about how fast this development will and can go. Estimates regarding when artificial general intelligence will be implemented vary with more than 50 years, from 2022 to 2075,[11] and the debate on the introduction of artificial super intelligence is very much on whether this will take place in this century or not.[12]

The use of artificial intelligence

Artificial intelligence is already a part of our digital daily life, even though we do not reflect much on it. When Netflix recommends a new TV series, or Amazon suggests a new book, it is done by means of artificial intelligence. A software program compares our previous choices with the choices made by millions of other users all over the world. The program then establishes a profile for each user, compares the profile with other profiles in the system, and through this finds out what we are likely to be interested in and want to watch. Functions like face recognition and machine translation are also built on artificial intelligence, where the picture or linguistic term we search for is matched with available online data. Increasingly, we are also using voice-activated services like Siri from Apple, Microsoft's Cortana, and Google Now. By recognising soundwaves, the meaning of words, and sentence structure, these programs can present proposed solutions to the users. The technology has also begun to make its way into a number of service industries. In December 2017, the airline SAS announced that it would soon introduce a computer software named Turi that finds flights and can make reservations for travellers. Based on oral or written statements like "next flight to Paris" or "Stockholm London tomorrow", Turi will provide you with the relevant flight details and thereafter both make a booking and send the travel details to your e-mail or Facebook account.[13]

Even the law enforcement sector is being automated by means of artificial intelligence in a number of countries. Discussions on automated police force often make us think about movies like Robocop, where we encounter a fully automated and effective law enforcement based on artificial intelligence and advanced mechanics.[14] Even though a robotised police force remains a futuristic vision, several countries are in the process of testing solutions in this field. In 2017, the Dubai police introduced a robot that can serve the public.[15] The US car manufacturer Ford conducts research on automated police cars, which with the help of artificial intelligence and other technologies are supposed to function without human drivers.[16] Intelligent systems shall be able to place the patrol vehicle in an ideal position to catch traffic offenders.

Artificial intelligence in intelligence analysis

In intelligence analysis, technology based on artificial intelligence is also increasingly used. There are at least five good reasons for this development. Artificial intelligence can make it easier to (1) find relevant information and structure it, (2) make more accurate predictions, (3) prevent unwanted incidents, (4) cooperate internally and across intelligence communities, and (5) communicate intelligence in a more effective way. Next, we take a closer look on each of these points.

Finding and structuring relevant information

The first and perhaps most important reason for the use of artificial intelligence in intelligence analysis is that such systems can make it far easier for the analyst to handle a growing ocean of information, retrieve what is relevant, and get this information presented in a structured manner.

Identifying the distinct or particular (anomaly detection) is probably the most significant challenge that artificial intelligence can assist the analyst within this context. In addition to this comes the challenge of sorting and comparing unclassified and classified information – which in many cases is growing due to an increased capacity in information gathering. One of the main points made in the official 9/11 commission report after the terrorist attacks in the United States on September 11, 2001, was that information indicating an attack did exist, but a lack of analyst capacity and limited information sharing between services prevented an assessment of much of this information.

Information overview has also become more complex with new sources like social media and the Internet. This challenge has only mounted since the 9/11 commission presented its report in 2004, partly because of an increasing amount of fake news and disinformation that an analyst must relate to. The question is therefore whether the analysts of tomorrow will be able to confront the new information reality without using technology based on artificial intelligence, which, in addition to search for information, is also capable of disclosing false information and establishing correlations between large bulks of disparate data from a range of different types of sources.

Analysts in the intelligence and security services are already using software based on artificial intelligence in order to find and structure relevant information.

Search engines for different online platforms and more specialised tools used to detect correlations in a complex world are all built on what is called the "narrow" artificial intelligence (narrow AI). IBM's Analyst Notebook, visualising correlations and patterns of data, is a good example of such tools. Furthermore, new and more advanced programs are gradually being introduced. The advantage with these programs is that they can function as a shared information and production platform for different parts of a service and are in a straightforward way able to show what information exists about a given subject within the organisation at all times. The systems delivered by American Palantir Technologies represent one example of such programs.[17]

This type of technology can clearly help solve many of the challenges faced by intelligence and security services in Western countries. Several such challenges are well presented in a research note from the UK. The paper, which is based on interviews of 25 individuals from police, academia, and technical-related institutions, points to several limitations regarding how British police make use of existing data today. The fragmentation of databases and applications hampers efficiency, and there are still many units that cannot communicate effectively with each other. Data analysis is still to a large degree done manually, also in areas where software can do the job just as well and faster than human beings. There is also a lack of advanced tools that can search in and structure large volumes of unstructured data – including pictures and video material. Hence, analysts are not able to exploit the full potential of the information to which they have access.[18]

For the police, artificial intelligence has a substantial potential for operational policing. Obviously, operational tools like photo and video gear, eavesdropping equipment, and tracking devices all become more advanced. More interesting is how technology based on artificial intelligence makes it possible to combine different sensors and systems in order to achieve a better situational picture, rapid warning, or a more certain confirmation of a person's identity. As such, there is considerable potential in the use of artificial intelligence in prevention, investigations, and evidence gathering.

Regarding the two latter types of activity, the Norwegian National Criminal Investigation Service (KRIPOS) has carried out a joint project with the Netherlands Forensic Institute. The project, called "The Glove", is about developing a digital forensic tool that can do a quick analysis of large amounts of data and make the information easily accessible to investigators. Another example is from the Norwegian Customs, which in 2017 signed a contract with Palantir Technologies in order to systemise data in a more efficient manner.[19] The Norwegian Police Directorate has also cooperated with the same company in developing the so-called Gotham-solution – a system that enables the police to sort, analyse, and connect large amounts of information from several data sources and registers.[20] Furthermore, through international agreements Norwegian police have been given search access in a number of partner countries' respective DNA and fingerprint databases, as well as vehicle registers. This means, for example, that the 400,000 fingerprints in the Norwegian police register are supplemented with several millions more from partner countries. By using the new technology searches in these databases can be conducted in seconds or minutes. Hence, the police do not only get access to new types of information of considerable importance in combating transnational crime and terrorism but also benefit from improved and more efficient working processes.

Making more accurate predictions

The second reason why technology based on artificial intelligence is implemented in intelligence analysis is that it makes it easier for the analyst to make predictions. The development of predictions is a central part of intelligence analysis. This task has not become easier in a world that is becoming more complex and where conditions may rapidly change. The contribution of artificial intelligence here is primarily to find correlations between a large number of factors in time and space and to indicate an expected development based on the correlations. This is a task where machine intelligence is superior to human intelligence by far.

According to Andrew Hellman, head of CIA's Directorate for Digital Innovation, the use of advanced algorithms and analysis techniques has made the CIA considerably better at predicting incidents around the globe, ranging from illegal money transactions to the flow of extremists and political unrest. Machine learning on large amounts of data from both classified and unclassified sources has allegedly enabled analysts to identify correlation between disparate data and to use these correlations to substantiate predictions. According to Hellman, the new technology has in some cases enabled the CIA to foresee political unrest five to six days before it actually broke out.[21] Exactly which type of political unrest the technology managed to predict, and in how many cases the new technology was unable to predict unrest, Hellman said nothing about. Hence, we know little about how trustworthy or reliable CIA's machine-generated predictions really are with the use of current technology.

Artificial intelligence has also been used in order to predict future operations by the Islamic State (ISIL) in Iraq. In 2015, a group of researchers analysed 2,200 ISIL-related military-type incidents. The goal was to derive correlations and "rules" for ISIL attacks with vehicle-borne improvised explosive devices (VBIED) and indirect fire weapons. According to the research group, it was possible to model ISIL' behaviour, identify priority targets, and expose strong correlations in the organisations' military tactics by using algorithms on the dataset. For example, they found that an increase in the use of VBIEDs in Baghdad often preceded ISIL' attacks on cities in northern Iraq, suggesting that ISIL used attacks in Baghdad to distract the Iraqi security forces from targets north in the country.[22] However, as in the example with the CIA here, we know little about how strong correlations the machine intelligence was able to establish for the research group. For example: How often were car bomb attacks in Baghdad *not* followed by attacks in the north?

It is also likely that artificial intelligence will be of considerable importance for so-called predictive policing.[23] Predictive policing is not new in itself if this means that the police shall be one step ahead of the criminals. Over the last decades, police in a number of countries have systematically used strategic analysis and various tools for mapping crime in order to deliver a focused effort against specific challenges. Finally, for the last few years, we have seen several examples of police using advanced high-tech computer software to handle a fast-growing flow of information and predict developments in specific areas of crime.

The term "predictive police work" is today used specifically for processes that include the use of computer software with artificial intelligence. One example is Crime Pattern Analysis, which is used to find correlation between factors that affect criminal activity, such as time of day, geographical areas, victim characteristics, and *modus operandi*.[24]

For several years, the Los Angeles Police Department (LAPD) has used a system called PredPol.[25] The main purpose of this system is to stay ahead of and disrupt criminal offences. In an operations room criminal analysts and technicians work side by side with access to many types of technology and multiple sources. Offences are continuously registered and algorithm-based data analysis is done in order to identify specific challenges. Updated information can then be transferred from the operations' room to police patrols in the district. The police in Kent (UK) have also used PredPol, but as a somewhat wider tool and in a coordinated effort with social workers and others involved in crime prevention. In addition, the system has been used to identify where police patrols should be sent to at different times of the day.[26]

Unsurprisingly, the effect of PredPol and similar systems is disputed. While the software producer and LAPD argue that the system is providing good results, critical voices call for independent research before any conclusions are made in this matter. There are also claims of embedded biases in PredPol linked to factors such as race, ethnicity, and area of residence, with the result that a number of people unrelated to any crime come to the attention of the police.[27] Consequently, the use of artificial intelligence in police work brings a number of judicial questions to the fore, particularly if the technology is used in surveillance of individuals. Here the technical possibilities provided by artificial intelligence can come into conflict with the right to privacy and other basic human rights.

Preventing unwanted events

This brings us to the third reason why artificial intelligence is well-suited for intelligence analysis, namely that the technology can be used to prevent unwanted events. Technology based on artificial intelligence can, for example, be used to uncover peoples' behaviour online and thus identify users who potentially are involved in, or wish to commit, criminal acts. This type of computer software can therefore be put to broader use – from counterterrorism to preventing sexual abuse of children.

Attempts have been made to prevent recruitment to the ISIL by means of artificial intelligence. In 2016, Google's parent company Alphabet initiated a project with this objective. Through what they called *Alphabet Jigsaw's Redirection Method*, the company tried to alter the intentions of potential jihadists browsing for ISIL material online. In addition to finding material published by ISIL, users were directed to sites that countered their presumed ideology and worldview. According to Google, this project achieved surprisingly good results. Over a ten-month period, more than 300,000 users browsing ISIL-related subjects were presented for anti-ISIL material on YouTube. These users clicked on anti-ISIL links and spent more time on anti-ISIL channels on YouTube than the average Google user.[28]

As with several previous examples in this chapter, we do not have an independent assessment of how successful Google's project really was. For example, to what degree can the number of visits from users to a website tell us anything about their political views? Moreover, if the users change their behaviour due to the content they are presented with, how lasting will such a change be? The mapping of and attempt to change online behaviour can also be ethically worrisome if the computer software is unable to distinguish between potential extremists and those who visit such sites due to professional interest or mere curiosity.

On the other hand, it is not hard to imagine how Google's project could be developed further by intelligence and security services to identify possible recruits to extremist organisations and then try to turn them by using online information and more direct approaches, such as preventive visits and conversations to dissuade.

Cooperating across institutional divides

A fourth argument is that new technology makes it easier to cooperate across institutional divides, within the intelligence services, between different national services, and across borders. Running systems on shared platforms where analysts and collectors in the same service, or in different services, can work together on a joint product is an important objective of this development. Another is technology that makes it easier to share classified information between services. Both these technological developments promote cooperation between units in intelligence communities. At a time with a more complex threat environment, increased intelligence cooperation has become more important than ever for securing the continued timeliness and relevance of intelligence services. Technology based on artificial intelligence can make intelligence cooperation more extensive, speed up the distribution of intelligence information, and potentially increase the quality of intelligence products by larger information inflows and more contributors.

A continuous challenge in intelligence cooperation is that information to be shared is classified and therefore must be encrypted before being transferred from one service to another. In other words, data are coded so they become impossible to read for outsiders. The data must first be encrypted by the sender and decrypted by the receiver before the content can be used or processed. Likewise, any response passing the other way must be encrypted and decrypted before the receiver can make use of it. Technologically, it has not been possible to make changes to data once they are encrypted. This represents a technological bottleneck if intelligence analysts in different organisations are to work together – that is, unless they have access to and work on shared computer servers. Moreover, the process with encryption and decryption always entails a risk that the content will be compromised.

To resolve this problem, Microsoft has developed a technology it calls Crypto Nets. According to the company, this technology makes it possible to work with encrypted content without decrypting it first, because computers can "learn" to read encrypted material directly. The technology will make it possible for different users to work on the same encrypted information but without risking that the content is compromised after decryption.[29] So far this technology has been intended for the health sector, where exchange of confidential patient information between different units represents a challenge. The potential for intelligence services is also substantial. Technologies like Crypto Nets can, for example, enable allies or partner services to share and work together on large amounts of information and data but without the substantial risk of compromising classified material in the process. It is particularly within the analysis of transnational threats, such as the proliferation of weapons of mass destruction (WMD), terrorism, and organised crime, that this type of technology will be especially valuable. It allows extensive analysis cooperation between intelligence and security services, police and customs, in different countries affected by the threat.

Streamlining intelligence communication

The fifth and last argument is that artificial intelligence can automate parts of intelligence communication and thereby streamline this task for the analyst. Communicating intelligence to decision-makers through reports, briefings, and updates is time-consuming for the analyst. Moreover, it is likely that time spent on preparing intelligence products will increase in the digital age, not least because multimedia platforms make it possible to keep the decision-makers almost continuously updated. Lars Haugom elaborates more on this point in Chapter 8 in this volume. Technology that makes it possible to leave parts of the communication of intelligence to computer software can save time for the analyst so she or he can focus more on analysis itself and on complex questions that require more interpretative intelligence products and closer interaction with decision-makers.

New systems based on artificial intelligence not only are able to understand written and spoken human language (Natural Language Understanding – NLU) but can also make themselves understood by using human language (Natural Language Generation – NLG). Advanced NLG-systems like Narrative Science Quill are both capable of examining all the facts they have access to, establishing what shall be included in a report or note and then transforming this into a language that is understandable and tailored for a specific audience. In finance, such systems have already been implemented, for example in the analysis of expected future profit in private companies.[30] In intelligence analysis the same type of systems can be used for reports produced in a fixed format, where most of the work is to report change over time according to a given set of indicators. A prerequisite is of course that systems are able to generate products that are understandable and precise enough to function as decision support.

By making parts of the intelligence production more efficient and freeing up time for the analyst, technology based on artificial intelligence can also be regarded as a resource-saving tool. Intelligence and security services all over the world are growing steadily as new and transboundary threats surface in the shape of terrorism, hybrid warfare, or threats against vulnerable networks and infrastructure. A more complex threat environment demands that intelligence services employ an adequate number of analysts with the right competence, enabling these services to understand and assess both new and more "traditional" threats. If more of today's tasks for the analyst can be carried out by computer software, this may serve to limit the number of analysts needed, even if the total portfolio of the service is increasing in total. It may also make it possible for analysts to focus on tasks that computer software is not able to handle.

Algorithms over brain?

When witnessing the rapid technological development within artificial intelligence, the question becomes whether this technology will fully replace the analyst in the future, or if such systems will continue to be advanced tools for the analyst. Based on what we know about artificial intelligence today and the expected development in this area, our conclusion is that machines will not be able to fully replace the intelligence analyst. Machines will gradually be able to carry out many of the tasks currently done by the analyst but will not make the analyst superfluous.

The most important reason for this is that technology is far superior to human beings in certain areas but not in others. Machines are, for example, superior when it comes to searching through large bulks of information quickly and producing a (relatively) trustworthy result. Human beings, in contrast, can be hindered by certain mental "pitfalls" when examining large and complex bulks of information quickly – at least when this information is new and they lack experience on the subject at hand. Such obstacles may produce a less trustworthy, or in the worst case an unreliable, result.

On the other hand, human beings have their strength in fantasy and in the ability to imagine things that have not even taken place and of which there is no exact memory in the brain. This ability enables human beings to test different scenarios and courses of action and imagine their outcome in a meaningful way – in interaction with both oneself and other people. It is, for example, possible to imagine that we perform a certain act even though we have no previous experience or memory of having performed the act. Likewise, it is possible for a human being to imagine various types of acts or events, likely and unlikely. It is also, for example, possible to imagine opening the door at home to find that a celebrity has come to visit, even if such an event has not taken place and is not likely to ever happen. A parallel in intelligence analysis is the encouragement to "think the unthinkable": Imagining a development or situation that is based on historical experience seems rather unlikely but still represents a possible outcome. Machines do not have the ability to such fanciful and creative thinking, no matter how "intelligent" they are supposed to be.

If machines are to take over many of the tasks currently undertaken by analysts, there will also be a pressing need to secure human overview and control of the intelligence process. According to Allan Dafoe of the University of Oxford, there are two aspects to the question of human overview: the first is AI safety, which focuses on the technical questions of how AI systems are built and applied; the second is AI governance, which focuses on the institutions and contexts in which AI is built and used.[31]

The possibility for system failure is always present, and the consequences of system failure will just get bigger if machines are to take over some or many of the analysts' present tasks. Prerequisites for implementing artificial intelligence in intelligence analysis must therefore be that machines do what they are supposed to do, that they do not do anything they are not supposed to do, that they do not represent a security risk, and that they are under proper control. In the literature on artificial intelligence, these prerequisites are described as verification, validation, security, and control.[32]

Info box 6.1 Safety prerequisites for implementing artificial intelligence

Verification means that we must make sure that the computer software fully satisfies all the expected requirements – in other words, the software actually is able to carry out those tasks that we want it to. In critical sectors of society, such as power supply and transportation, a lack of verification may lead to catastrophic results as technology is increasingly taking over more and more in the running of systems. In intelligence analysis the consequences of a lack of verification will normally be less severe than in critical infrastructure. However, it is not very effective to apply computer software that can both analyse data and communicate results if the finished intelligence product contains substantial flaws and omissions.

Validation means that we must ensure that the computer software does not perform other tasks than what we want it to do and that it produces valid results. Investment companies have, for example, suffered great financial losses because machine intelligence could not predict unusual changes or movements in the stock market. In intelligence analysis we can imagine similar situations where machine intelligence is capable of detecting and analysing expected patterns in the activity of states and groups but does not register occurrences where something totally new or unexpected is taking place.

Security means that in addition to ensuring ourselves that the computer software is functioning correctly and delivers valid results, we must make sure that it does not cause damage. When it comes to artificial intelligence, it is often robots and their ability to hurt people physically that are highlighted. The use of artificial intelligence in intelligence analysis raises another issue, namely that of malware. A software program consists of line-by-line source code that it is difficult to fully control. With the introduction of artificial intelligence, it will be increasingly challenging to ensure that there is no "backdoor" in a program that can enable external actors to monitor, and potentially also control, the intelligence process. If machines subsequently take over more and more of the process, from analysing data to writing and communication of reports, such "backdoors" can provide hostile powers with valuable insights into priorities and assessments, and an excellent opportunity to influence national decision-makers. Security in this context must include clearance of both the software itself and the company producing it, as well as a vetting process for personnel involved in software development and implementation. Furthermore, there must be effective diagnosing tools for detecting potential "backdoors" and Trojan horses hidden in the program. Even though the intelligence analyst will not have a direct part in this type of preventive security work, she or he will be well placed to detect irregularities in what the program produces.

Control, meaning *human* control, is a fourth prerequisite for the implementation of artificial intelligence. The example of driverless cars is often used to illustrate that artificial intelligence must operate under human control if accidents are to be avoided. Even though driverless cars allegedly have better accident statistics than cars driven by humans, we cannot be certain that what the program perceives from the car's sensors is being interpreted correctly. It is therefore necessary that the person in the driver's seat can intervene and override the program if an accident is about to happen. In intelligence analysis it is equally necessary that a human analyst controls the results that software programs arrive at and that these results are presented correctly in products communicated to decision-makers.

The second and potentially more challenging aspect of human overview is AI governance, which on a general level seeks to maximise the odds that people building and using advanced AI do so in a way that benefits humanity.[33] Transferred to the field of intelligence analysis, AI governance would seek to ensure that AI is applied in a responsible way that does not compromise the core values and accountability of intelligence organisations.

The question of AI governance is in many ways a continuation of the human-centred debate on technological innovation, rooted in the idea that machines make calculations and humans make judgements.[34] In the human-centred school of thought there is a pronounced unease at the idea of innovation to the point where there is no difference between humans and machines and between human thinking and machine thinking.[35] Similar to this perspective, Jonathan Zitrain, professor of law and computer science at Harvard University, warns that the development of AI entails a shift of reasoning and judgement away from people. According to Zitrain, this can be good as it frees up time for other pursuits and deeper undertakings. However, it is also profoundly worrisome because it decouples big decisions from human understanding and accountability.[36] Furthermore, as pointed out by Karamit S. Gill, editor of the *AI & Society* journal, despite access to abundant data and faster computers, human judgement cannot easily be turned into algorithms. Gill here refers to a point that was also discussed earlier in this chapter, namely that "human judgement is about the process of finding a coherence among often conflicting and yet creative possibilities that cannot be reduced to calculation. . . . Still, turning judgement into an algorithm is a dominant focus in AI-research".[37]

One obvious hazard of this development is spelt out by Joi Ito, a former professor at Massachusetts Institute for Technology (MIT). To the extent that machines can replicate human intelligence, they can also replicate human stupidity. Algorithms are written by humans and can therefore propagate the same biases that are prevalent in society, perpetuating them "in the guise of "smart machines".[38] This challenge is compounded by the fact that the writing of algorithms is seldom an open and transparent activity. In most cases algorithms are made and protected by software developers keen to preserve their position in a highly competitive market.

Against this background, good governance in applying AI to intelligence analysis should entail on the one hand measures to ensure that human judgement prevails in the analytical process and on the other safeguards against possible biases in the algorithms of AI systems. The first point would ensure a continued central role for the human analyst in intelligence analysis. The latter point would probably require intelligence services to employ experts who can work closely with software developers in applying AI systems to the intelligence process.

Keeping the preconditions of AI safety and AI governance in mind, the main task of intelligence analysts in the future may be to control the analytical process and the quality of products, making sure that the technology generates correct and valid results rather than doing analysis themselves. This would most certainly entail a change in the role of the analyst, but would not result in the analyst becoming superfluous as a result of technological development.

Conclusion

Considering what we now know about the strengths and weaknesses of human beings and machines, there is not necessarily a competition between brain and algorithms. On the contrary, technological development makes it possible for machines to handle heavy and resource- and time-demanding tasks and to communicate certain types of intelligence products to decision-makers. The analysts can for their part focus on the work that machines are unable or unsuitable for, including to ensure that the results machines arrive at are correct and relevant for the decision-makers. If, for example, it is necessary to find a very specific type of information in a large and complex amount of information, machines can do this task tirelessly and without becoming exhausted. When the information is found, however, and it is necessary to analyse and communicate the meaning of it, the human analyst will still have a role that machines cannot be given. Machine algorithms can clearly support human judgement but not replace it. The same applies to contact with the customers of intelligence. Probably, machines will increasingly be able to both produce and communicate intelligence faster than what the analysts are able to, and this will contribute to the intelligence services' continued timeliness and relevance. However, when it comes to reliability, technology will not be able to replace human interaction and dialogue between the intelligence expert and decision-maker. Here, even I.N.T.E.L.L.I.G.E.N.C.E. in the movie Team America cannot compete with the human analyst, regardless of how good intelligence the machine is able to provide.

Notes

1 *Team America: World Police*, 2004, www.imdb.com/title/tt0372588/.
2 Robert J. Sternberg: "The Concept of Intelligence", in Robert J. Sternberg (ed.): *Handbook of Intelligence*. Cambridge: Cambridge University Press, 2000, pp. 3–15.
3 John D. Mayer & Peter Salovey: "The Intelligence of Emotional Intelligence", *Intelligence*, Vol. 17, No. 6, 1993, pp. 433–442.
4 Max Tegmark: *Life 3.0. Being Human in the Age of Artificial Intelligence*, Kindle edition. New York: Alfred A. Knopf, 2017, Loc. 921.
5 Nick Bostrom: *Superintelligence: Paths, Dangers, Strategies*. Oxford: Oxford University Press, 2014.
6 Walter Schaeken et al. (eds.): *Deductive Reasoning and Strategies*. Mahwah, NJ: Lawrence Erlbaum Associates, 1999.
7 Brett K. Hayes: "The Development of Inductive Reasoning", *Inductive Reasoning*, January 2007, pp. 25–54.
8 David Ferrucci et al.: "Watson: Beyond Jeopardy!", *Artificial Intelligence*, Nos. 199–200, 2013, pp. 93–105.
9 David Lazer et al.: "The Parable of Google Flu: Traps in Big Data Analysis", *Science*, Vol. 343, No. 6176, 2014, pp. 1203–1205.
10 Stephan De Spiegeleire, Matthijs Maas, & Tim Sweijs: "Artificial Intelligence and the Future of Defense: Strategic Implications for Small- and Medium-Sized Force Providers", *The Hague Center for Strategic Studies*, 2017, p. 30, https://hcss.nl/sites/default/files/files/reports/Artificial%20 Intelligence%20and%20the%20Future%20of%20Defense.pdf.
11 *Ibid.*, p. 51.
12 Tegmark, *op. cit.*, Loc. 615–622.
13 Judi Lembke: "Your Personal Travel Agency" (in Norwegian), *Scandinavian Traveler*, December 28, 2017, https://scandinaviantraveler.com/no/fly/ditt-personlige-reisebyra.
14 Bernard Marr: "How Robots, IoT and Artificial Intelligence are Transforming the Police", *Forbes*, September 19, 2017, www.forbes.com/sites/bernardmarr/2017/09/19/how-robots-iot-and- artificial-intelligence-are-transforming-the-police/#741a1c3e5d61.
15 "Robocop Joins Dubai Police to Fight Real Life Crime", *Reuters*, July 1, 2017, www.reuters.com/ article/us-emirates-robocop/robocop-joins-dubai-police-to-fight-real-life-crime-idUSKBN18S4K8.
16 "Robocopcar Could Catch Crooks All By Itself", *The Times*, January 30, 2018, www. thetimes. co.uk/article/robocop-car-that-could-catch-crooks-all-by-itself-l95frwb7z.
17 Marius Jørgenrud: "Secretive Palantir Starts Up in Norway" (in Norwegian), *Digi.no*, February 14, 2017, www.digi.no/artikler/hemmelighetsfulle-palantir-starter-opp-i-norge/37658.
18 Alexander Babuta: "Big Data and Policing. An Assessment of Law Enforcement Requirements, Expectations and Priorities", RUSI Occasional Paper, September 6, 2017, https://rusi.org/publication/occasional-papers/big-data-and-policing-assessment-law-enforcement-requirements.
19 Stig Øyvann: "The Norwegian Data Protection Authority (Datatilsynet) Is Taking a Closer Look at Norwegian Customs" (in Norwegian), *Computerworld*, January 29, 2018, www.cw.no/artikkel/datatilsynet/datatilsynet-ser-naermere-pa-tolletaten.
20 Hibba Sarmadawy: "Now the Norwegian Police Can Search Directly in the FBI's Database" (in Norwegian), *VG*, June 11, 2017, www.vg.no/nyheter/innenriks/personvern/naa-kan-norsk-politi-soeke-direkte-i-fbis-database/a/24012847/.
21 Frank Konkel: "The CIA Says It Can Predict Social Unrest as Early as 3 to 5 Days Out", *Defense One*, October 4, 2016, www.defenseone.com/technology/2016/10/cia-says-it-can-predict-social- unrest-early-3–5-days-out/132121/.
22 Andrew Stanton et al.: "Mining for Causal Relationships: A Data-driven Study of the Islamic State", *arXiv.org*, August 5, 2015, https://arxiv.org/abs/1508.01192.

23 For a good definition of this term, see Jerry H. Ratcliffe: *Intelligence-Led Policing*. London: Routledge, 2016, p. 151.
24 John Buckley: *Managing Intelligence*. Boca Raton: CRC Press, 2014.
25 "Predicting Crime, LAPD-style", *The Guardian*, June 25, 2014, www.theguardian.com/ cities/2014/jun/25/predicting-crime-lapd-los-angeles-police-data-analysis-algorithm-minority-report.
26 "How Technology Is Allowing Police to Predict Where and When Crime Will Happen", *The Independent*, October 7, 2017, www.independent.co.uk/news/uk/home-news/police-big-data- technology-predict-crime-hotspot-mapping-rusi-report-research-minority-report-a7963706.html.
27 See for example Jerry H. Ratcliffe: *Intelligence-Led Policing*. London: Routledge, 2016, pp. 151–152; Kristian Lum & William Isaac: "To Predict and Serve", *Significance Magazine*, Vol. 13, No. 5, October 2016, https://rss.onlinelibrary.wiley.com/doi/full/10.1111/j.1740-9713.2016.00960.x.
28 Andy Greenberg: "Google's Clever Plan to Stop Aspiring ISIS Recruits", *WIRED*, September 7, 2016, www.wired.com/2016/09/googles-clever-plan-stop-aspiring-isis-recruits.
29 Tom Simonite: "A Cloud That Can't Leak. Researchers at Microsoft Have Built a Virtual Vault that Could Work on Medical Data Without Ever Decrypting It", *MIT Technology Review*, August 8, 2011, www.technologyreview.com/s/424942/a-cloud-that-cant-leak/.
30 Kristian Hammond: *Practical Artificial Intelligence for Dummies*. Hoboken, NJ: John Wiley & Sons, 2015.
31 Alan Dafoe: "AI Governance: A Research Agenda", Centre for the Governance of AI, Future of Humanity Institute, University of Oxford, 2018, p. 6, www.fhi.ox.ac.uk/wp-content/uploads/GovAI-Agenda.pdf.
32 Tegmark, *op. cit.*, Loc. 1726–1931.
33 Dafoe, *op. cit.*
34 See for example Howard Rosenbrock: *Machines with a Purpose*. Oxford: Oxford University Press, 1990; Mike Cooley: *Architect or Bee? The Human Price of Technology*. London: Hogarth Press, 1987; and Joseph Weizenbaum: *Computer Power and Human Reason: From Judgment to Calculation*. New York: W.H. Freeman and Company, 1976.
35 Karamjit S. Gill: "Uncommon Voices of AI", *AI&Socitey*, No. 32, 2017, p. 482.
36 "MIT Media Lab to Participate in $27 Million Initiative on AI Ethics and Governance", *Robotics@MIT*, https://robotics.mit.edu/mit-media-lab-participate-27-million-initiative-ai-ethics-and-governance.
37 Gill, *op. cit.*, p. 479.
38 Jai Ito: "Well-Intentioned Uses of Technology Can Go Wrong", *The New York Times*, December 5, 2016, www.nytimes.com/roomfordebate/2016/12/05/is-artificial-intelligence-taking-over-our-lives/well-intentioned-uses-of-technology-can-go-wrong.

Further reading

Bostrom, Nick: *Superintelligence: Paths, Dangers, Strategies*. Oxford: Oxford University Press, 2014.
De Spiegeleire, Stephan, Matthijs Maas, & Tim Sweijs: "Artificial Intelligence and the Future of Defense. Strategic Implications for Small- and Medium-Sized Force Providers", *The Hague Center for Strategic Studies*, 2017, https://hcss.nl/sites/default/files/files/reports/Artificial%20Intelligence%20and%20the%20Future%20of%20Defense.pdf
Hammond, Kristian: *Practical Artificial Intelligence for Dummies*. Hoboken, NJ: John Wiley & Sons, 2015.
Ratcliffe, Jerry H.: *Intelligence-Led Policing*. London: Routledge, 2016.
Tegmark, Max: *Life 3.0. Being Human in the Age of Artificial Intelligence*. New York: Alfred A. Knopf, 2017.

7 Warning of hybrid threats

Patrick Cullen and Njord Wegge

With Russia's annexation of Crimea in 2014 the West was caught by surprise. Within a few days, events on the ground demonstrated how a highly sophisticated state actor was able to execute complex strategies and operations that effectively and illegally changed the borders in Europe.[1] The Russian operations in Crimea and Eastern Ukraine have often been labelled "hybrid warfare", as in many ways it operates between regular warfare and politics. "Operations in the grey zone between peace and war" is another frequently used and partly overlapping definition.[2] The incidents in Crimea can also be interpreted as a wakeup call to the West, as it illuminated a lack of capacity of Western intelligence services to detect operations of a hybrid nature at an early stage.

In this chapter we ask how the intelligence analyst should meet the developing threats from hybrid warfare and explore how new methods for early warning could be developed. Do intelligence analysts simply need a new and more diverse set of indicators to watch, or do the challenges posed by hybrid warfare require a different kind of solution?

To this end, we apply the concepts of "monitoring" known unknowns versus "discovering" unknown unknowns and explore how this distinction can help us conceptualise the different challenges for detecting hybrid warfare. Specifically, we try to illuminate why the future of early warning might require us to think of creative alternatives to early warning indicator watch lists. This analytical structure is then applied to four real-world examples of current attempts by military and intelligence services to experiment with new ways to detect hybrid warfare at an early stage.

Hybrid warfare

Hybrid warfare is very hard to define, and no authoritative definition exists.[3] In this context the most common objection to modern definitions of "hybrid-ness" is the view that hybrid warfare is not new in the history of warfare.[4] Since the core of hybrid warfare includes looking for the unexpected, mapping and exploiting weaknesses of the enemy across all the different sectors in society, and inflicting pain on an opponent often without using lethal power – for example, by using propaganda, deception, or an information campaign exploiting existing tensions in society – some reasonable arguments can be made supporting the view that "there is nothing new" in hybrid warfare.

Since this chapter investigates warning intelligence pertaining to hybrid warfare, there is a need to briefly encounter the definitional debate. An investigation into the conceptual evolution of the term "hybrid warfare" shows that the term has been used as far back as in 2002 in a study of the war in Chechnya.[5] Nevertheless, a more relevant starting point for what has become the current definitional debate is the work of Frank Hoffman, a retired US Marine and now a military scholar at the National Defence University in Washington, DC. Building on the National Defence Strategy of 2005, Hoffman pointed out that even though US defence planning was developing well to meet a large variety of new challenges, stretching from traditional and irregular threats to terrorists and criminal networks, there was a tendency to think of these threats separately. He argued that "these may no longer be separate threats or modes of war", pointing out how the characteristics of war and peace have become blurred.[6] Hoffmann defined hybrid warfare as "any adversary that simultaneously and adaptively employs a fused mix of conventional weapons, irregular tactics, terrorism, and criminal behaviour in the battlespace to obtain their political objectives".[7] He was heavily influenced by how Hezbollah had been able to present a difficult and persistent threat to Israel over time, particularly by its ability to pose a mixed irregular and conventional military threat and inflict considerable damage on Israel in the conflict in 2006. This war occurred after rockets were fired into Israel by Hezbollah forces in Lebanon, leading to massive Israeli retaliation from the air, followed by a ground invasion of southern parts of Lebanon. The conflict led to massive collateral damage in Lebanon and illustrated the difficulties an overwhelmingly stronger state actor could face when opposed with demanding non-state adversary applying hybrid warfare.

As Frank Hoffman often is regarded as one of the, if not *the* most, prominent academic authors addressing the challenges and tactics of hybrid warfare, the definition here can be characterised as an early authoritative attempt to describe the phenomena. Nevertheless, Hoffman's definition was soon criticised for being too focused on non-state actors and for over-emphasising the material and kinetic aspects of power at the cost of the cognitive dimension.[8] Another crucial characteristic of what was generally referred to with the term hybrid warfare was the multisectoral nature of the threat. The military battle space did not need to be at centre stage. Instead, more or less all the instruments of power within society – military, political, economic, civil, informational (MPECI) – could potentially be used in hybrid operations, and all sectors of society – political, military, economic, social, infrastructure, and information (PMESII) – could be on the receiving end of an attack.[9]

Much of this newer, broader, and alternative European understanding of hybrid warfare is reflected in the ongoing Counter-Hybrid Warfare program in the US-led Multinational Capability Development Campaign (MCDC). MCDC is an unclassified civil-military project that has been running in two-year cycles since 2013 and provides a platform for collaborative, joint, multinational concept and capability development. The project does not develop physical military capabilities, but rather it stimulates doctrinal development where civilian experts and military personnel meet in a non-classified setting to discuss how to respond to current and future security challenges. In the 2015–2016 cycle of the project, researchers from more than a dozen participating states were tasked with finding ways to counter hybrid warfare. However, when being asked by decision-makers to come up with solutions and identify ways to counter this threat, the researchers naturally also encountered the problem of defining the phenomena. After a long debate, the counter-hybrid warfare researchers ultimately decided to *describe* rather than define the phenomena of hybrid warfare.[10] Through reviewing the latest academic literature and empirical evidence on hybrid warfare, the MCDC researchers established a baseline understanding of the contested term, describing it as "the synchronized use of multiple instruments of power tailored to specific vulnerabilities across the full spectrum of societal functions to achieve synergistic effects".[11]

This description of hybrid warfare is further elaborated:

> The relative novelty of hybrid warfare lays in the ability of an actor to synchronize multiple instruments of power simultaneously and intentionally exploit creativity, ambiguity, non-linearity and the cognitive elements of warfare . . . (it is) . . . typically tailored to remain below the obvious detection and response thresholds, and often relies on the speed, volume, and ubiquity of digital technology that characterizes the present information age.[12]

The baseline assessment hence cleared up important parts of the conceptual confusion regarding what should be included as hybrid warfare, essentially establishing a common language for the concept within the MCDC community.

The description of the characteristics of hybrid warfare fits well into the overall topic of this volume and its focus on intelligence analysis in the digital age. As modern societies' dependence on digital technology is stronger and more intertwined than ever before, one can also observe that the scale of the digital vulnerability represents something new – not least as it can include almost all aspects of the civil society at once. In this context one could point out how the cyberattack on Estonia in 2007, crashing almost the entire internet infrastructure of the country for three days, demonstrated the vulnerability of advanced modern societies to cyberattacks. The Estonian case is often referred to as a standard example of hybrid warfare in the cyber domain.[13]

Hybrid warfare and early warning intelligence

The recent Russian covert and overt actions in Crimea and Eastern Ukraine have led to a revival of interest in warning intelligence among Western intelligence agencies. Taken by surprise one day in late February 2014, the world woke up watching polite, uniformed, and armed men, with no insignia, taking control of strategic places in Crimea, including communication masts, broadcasting studios, key roads, and military facilities, without having to resort to the use of violence.[14]

Through applying a combination of Spetsnaz – special operation forces – and information operations, Russia quickly established a new situation on the ground. The physical takeover of the peninsula was accompanied by coordinated dissemination of pro-Russian narratives, primarily in the Russian-speaking population in Ukraine and Russia, seeking to legitimate the actions.[15] A few weeks later, Russia attempted to give the illegal and de facto annexation of the peninsula a gloss of democratic legitimacy through a rushed referendum, resulting in an overwhelming majority voting for reunification with Russia.[16] This was a result deemed void by Western commentators.[17] The Russian hybrid operation in Crimea was followed by a related campaign in Eastern Ukraine. Under the cover of supporting local pro-Kremlin separatist groups in Donetsk and Luhansk, Russian special forces and some elements from regular units appeared in Eastern Ukraine. These forces, which allegedly were on vacation, were part of a massive political, diplomatic, and information campaign exploiting vulnerabilities such as ethnic, religious, and social tensions in Ukraine.[18] This operation also established a new situation on the ground, depriving Kiev of control in the eastern parts of the country. However, the operation as such ran into greater problems than what was encountered in Crimea, effectively triggering a Ukrainian counter-mobilisation.

The Crimea event highlighted the problem of early warning in the days of elusive hybrid warfare, making the Russian operation in Crimea, and its continuing campaigns in Eastern Ukraine, the new "standard reference" of what was meant with hybrid warfare, even though the term continues to be disputed.[19] The elusive, quick, non-violent, and highly effective Russian operation in Crimea established new facts on the ground. The subtle and sophisticated "shock success" of the anonymous green men surprised political decision-makers in Europe and the United States, and made it obvious that sufficient warning had not taken place on behalf of the Western intelligence services.[20] Or, in the words of the US Senate Intelligence Committee Chairwoman, Dianne Feinstein: "We have to better deploy our resources . . . it should not be possible for Russia to walk in and take over the Crimea and it's a done deal by the time we know about it" (Politico 2014).[21]

Warning intelligence

Warning intelligence is defined by the US Department of Defence as "(t)hose intelligence activities intended to detect and report time sensitive intelligence information on foreign developments that forewarn of hostile actions or intention against United States entities, partners, or interests".[22] Traditionally, an important part of warning intelligence has been conducted with "indicator based methods" at centre stage.[23] The method was developed during the Cold War to warn NATO about whether or not the Soviet Union was preparing an attack on any member of the alliance.[24] With this method, key indicators are identified and then monitored over time, enabling the analyst to establish a baseline of what "normal" activities, events, or operations look like. Indications and warning intelligence are hence focused on detecting relevant changes in the operational status of the opponent. These are changes that ideally can provide intelligence analysts and decision-makers with an alert – or early warning – if potential unwanted activity is being observed.[25]

In practice, the method is based on putting together long and detailed indicator lists where an analyst carefully watches developments on several variables thought of as being important, as they might reveal insight to whether the enemy state is preparing an attack or other types of serious and harmful activities. According to former senior intelligence analyst for the US Defense Intelligence Agency, Cynthia Grabo, analysts would typically draw on three types of knowledge when compiling the indicator lists: "logic or long-time historical precedent; specific knowledge of the military doctrine or practices of the nation or nations concerned; and the lessons learned from the behavior of that nation or nations during a recent war or international crisis".[26]

Through watching developments on the selected indicators, the intelligence analyst could assess and separate routine events, such as maintenance, training, and exercises, from suspicious activities or anomalies that could be preparations for an attack.[27] By doing this detailed work over time, earlier findings and time data could also be compared with potential incremental changes "in the search for evidence of a gradual change in readiness that might constitute a pattern of denial and deception intended to lull an observer into a false sense of security that was intended to bolster a clandestine movement toward generated alert".[28] Hence, by using this method systematically and over time, the analyst could improve the quality of assessments, giving better-funded suggestions of the most probable course of action to come, as well as a qualified assessment of potential intentions of the adversary.[29]

Watching and reporting on indicators usually require familiarity of cultural and local issues, as well as in-depth knowledge of the field and context in which the indicators are found.[30] With a skilled country expert watching a crucial set of indicators, the report from the analyst can in some instances contribute to significantly improve the accuracy of the bigger, multi-source picture being reported.[31] At the same time, it can be argued that the use of indicators tends to discourage creativity by the analyst, where the information sought for comes from a rigid watch list of predetermined indicators for warning, which are in turn fitted into prior established categories and conflict scenarios.[32]

Grabo writes in the original 1970s draft from her classic work on warning intelligence:

> For various reasons, some obvious and some less well-recognized, the collection and analysis of military data or indications is the predominant element in warning. By far the greater number of items or indicator lists deal with military, or military-related, activities. By far the greater portion of the collection effort, and particularly the most expensive collection, is devoted to obtaining data on the military strengths, capabilities and activities of enemy and potential enemy forces.[33]

This quote illustrates well the traditional focus in early warning intelligence: the monitoring of military capabilities and activities related to the military sphere.

While it is still important to watch issues like the location and readiness of military weapon systems, status of military support chains, activities on military communication platforms, or whether soldiers are withheld on exercises, the threat from hybrid warfare considerably expands what should be regarded as relevant information. This problem of what should or should not be regarded as relevant information relates to the old intelligence challenge of sorting out relevant "signals" from "noise", meaning sorting out the few pieces of intelligence-relevant information from large amounts of collected data.[34] Given the operational emphasis in hybrid warfare on elusiveness, the creation and exploitation of ambiguity, and the use of non-military instruments of power to attack across all of society, one can argue that distinguishing noise from signals has become even harder with the threat from hybrid warfare. Nevertheless, while indicator-based collection might have limitations when seeking to monitor non-traditional targets in the post-Cold War security environment, exemplified by the 9/11 terrorist attack on the United States, intelligence scholars have made good arguments for its continued relevance in the face of such untraditional threats, if modified and updated to address these new threats.[35]

Going into the unknown

The new challenges posed by hybrid warfare underscore that there is a need to develop our ability to think creatively about the expanded set of non-military tools and targets involved in an attack. This fact can dramatically expand the horizon the warning analyst needs to watch. In the following section we will address the problem hybrid warfare presents to the warning analyst. As mentioned earlier in this chapter, hybrid warfare is "the synchronized use of multiple instruments of power tailored to specific vulnerabilities across the full spectrum of societal functions to achieve synergistic effects". Since hybrid warfare can potentially include many different ways and means of attack, and can target all aspects of society, the potential risk of information overload for the analyst stands out as one of the major problems.[36] In addition, even if systems able to handle the collection of very large amounts of data were developed, how to detect creative or even unique hybrid attacks at their very early stages remains a major challenge for the intelligence analyst, since the potential scenarios essentially are limitless.

One way to try and overcome this problem of identifying activity that may be related to a hybrid warfare campaign is to establish a baseline understanding of what is "normal" in a given context and then to investigate deviations from this "normal" to see if these anomalies may be evidence of a concealed hybrid attack.[37] However, as many states for years have experienced malign activities in the form of hacking, sabotage, information campaigns with "fake news", and so forth, actually establishing a baseline of "normal" across all sectors of the society is a difficult challenge.[38]

On a more general level, a key question for improving the ability of intelligence services to warn of hybrid attacks is whether we need more data, or if we need new and better ideas. This is a crucial question to ask, even though the answer might be affirmative on both dimensions. Moreover, the issue is new in neither social science nor the intelligence community. It has been raised before as an issue of self-examination in response to other failures to foresee events. The most prominent example is perhaps the intelligence community's failure to predict the collapse of the Soviet empire and the end of the Cold War.

The failure to foresee the end of the Cold War gave a key impetus to important paradigmatic developments within the academic field of international relations, such as the rising popularity and scholarly application of post-positivist methodological approaches like "constructivism."[39] Was the failure to foresee the collapse of the Soviet Union before it actually happened due to a lack of updated, accurate data, or was it rather a consequence of lacking imagination? In addressing the social reality as constructed, emphasising the explanatory power of ideas, at the cost of material factors, the new "non-rationalist" research paradigm gave rise to new ways of viewing processes in international politics.

In the crisis management literature, the same problem of lack of methods to generate new ideas and thinking around the unexpected has been raised.[40] Recent research in this field emphasises that it is indeed impossible to foresee all potential crises, "even if we had all the potential resources and expertise at our disposal."[41] Complexity and chaos theories add to this complexity, arguing that "in many cases, systems have non-linear dynamics where the behaviour of the system is not causally deterministic, but rather random, and where the randomness is caused by the exponential growth of errors and uncertainties."[42] While the crisis management literature differs substantially from research into the problem of hybrid warfare – most strikingly by the absence of a malign actor behind the crisis event – some of the problems related to how to provide warning before an event occurs at the "receiving end" are quite similar.

One way to logically structure our thinking about warning intelligence for hybrid warfare is to differentiate potential future hybrid attacks into two separate categories of "known unknowns" and "unknown unknowns". Known unknowns refer to risks related to hybrid warfare that we know we may be unaware of, such as the possibility of a future cyberattack against a known, or yet to be discovered, vulnerability to an electrical grid. However, risk related to hybrid attacks may also exist where we are not even aware of its nature, our vulnerability to it, or even of our own ignorance to the threat. This is the field of "unknown unknowns", where only the imagination and capabilities of the hybrid threat represent the limits.

A useful way of developing this thinking about known unknowns and unknown unknowns from a hybrid warfare warning intelligence perspective is to differentiate *monitoring* from *discovery*.[43] Monitoring involves a process of scanning the environment for known unknowns – usually with the aid of indicators – to look for a set of preconceived information about possible hybrid warfare attacks that one knows that one does not know. For instance, hybrid warfare may occasionally create questions for intelligence analysts that involve a set of known unknowns related to whether an election is being targeted by adversary information operations. Discovery, on the other hand, involves an attempt to manage the problem of unknown unknowns. This process involves capturing and then correctly interpreting information related to a potential harmful adversarial action that has not been anticipated or imagined by the analyst. This type of information is not amenable to a monitoring methodology built upon "perceiving what we expect to perceive"[44] via either pattern recognition or the use of indicator lists precisely because the analyst has never seen this pattern before and is not equipped with an indicator list for a type of attack that has never occurred before (or perhaps never even imagined). In other words, she or he cannot know in advance what she or he is looking for.

When studies of hybrid warfare refer to the adversarial use of creative and ambiguous tools and means, the manipulation of cognition and detection thresholds, and the unpredictable appearance of a specific hybrid warfare campaign, they are beginning to sketch how hybrid warfare early warning intelligence necessarily involves grappling with this problem of "discovery". Importantly, the practice of discovering unknown unknowns need not sit in opposition to practices of monitoring per se, but as we will argue here, it does require a different type of monitoring that moves beyond watching preconceived indicators. Instead, it must focus on detecting anomalies and developing practical techniques to recognise previously unseen patterns.

The following four sections examine some of the current efforts being made to provide early warning for hybrid warfare in both homeland security and overseas/deployed contexts. Dividing these methods into two *ideal type* categories to highlight their differences, the first two sections discuss experimental concepts being developed to treat hybrid warfare as a known unknown to be *monitored* in each context. The latter two sections discuss experimental attempts being made to treat hybrid warfare as an unknown unknown and a problem to be *discovered* in each context.

Known unknown part I: widening the lens

Hybrid threat actors pose not only military but crucially also non-military challenges to national security. There is also growing international concern that hybrid warfare may coordinate use of military and non-military instruments of power to attack various vulnerabilities of a state across the whole of its society. Unsurprisingly, this understanding of hybrid warfare has thus created a need to "widen the lens" of the warning intelligence analyst's gaze to address the expanding number of tools, and the greater number of targets, available to adversaries using hybrid warfare. In the field of warning intelligence, this is driving a requirement to create new indicators to monitor vulnerabilities within one's own society to identify signals of active or imminent hybrid warfare operations. It is also driving a specific requirement to identify indicators for hybrid warfare beyond the traditional military sphere and towards the creation of new indicators involving the use of non-military and non-kinetic tools. In practice, hybrid warfare has thus pushed some military organisations involved in national defence towards pragmatically experimenting with new ways to adopt traditional Cold War–era warning methodologies and techniques to meet the new warning challenges hybrid warfare creates in non-military spaces. The Austrian military, for example, is currently experimenting with adapting a Center of Gravity (CoG) methodology familiar to NATO and many military organisations as an early warning tool capable of dealing with the problem posed by hybrid warfare.[45]

Although there is no single CoG method, in its essence it is a traditional military planning tool used to organise anticipatory thinking about the potential military actions of an adversary. It does this by looking for causal connections between an adversary's assumed objectives, capabilities, requirements, and the potential effects of these actions on one's own critical vulnerabilities.[46] Once a warning analyst completes this CoG analysis, it is the intelligence officer's job to "learn the procedures, find the network (both the attacker network and one's own target network to be defended), define the sensors spectrum, and launch the sensors"[47] that would facilitate early warning. In simplified terms, the CoG approach requires the warning analyst to creatively think how an adversary might attack one's own weaknesses, then identify in the real world which adversary actors could accomplish this task, and then figure out and implement practical ways (e.g. using human intelligence or financial intelligence) to anticipate such an attack.

Whereas during the Cold War the Austrian Army used CoG analysis to focus on how to understand and anticipate purely *military* threats, today the Austrian Army is experimenting with ways to apply CoG methodologies to anticipate synchronised military and non-military means of attack across a much wider set of critical vulnerabilities in Austrian society – for example, to provide warning for hybrid warfare.[48] To date, Austrian CoG analyses of hybrid warfare scenarios have indicated that "most of the attacks will take place in 'non-military fields'".[49] As a result, much of their applied CoG process of (1) identifying (non-military) national critical vulnerabilities; (2) linking them to assumptions or hypotheses of adversary objectives and (non-military) capabilities; and then (3) developing new warning indicators linking the two is now being actively experimented with by the Austrian Army in novel ways outside of the military domain (such as the economic realm). Applying the CoG approach in this way essentially tries to shrink the spaces where surprise can occur, by expanding *monitoring* activity to include a wider set of domains, potential targets, and means of attack.

This CoG approach also attempts to limit where true *discovery* of an unknown unknown is required of the analyst, by expanding monitoring activity to include a wider set of potential targets, ways, and means of attack. This includes non-military tools that have already been hypothesised by the warning analyst in this updated CoG process. In this sense, CoG is not a *discovery* tool. Instead, it is a tool for monitoring known unknowns by creating templates of anticipated adversary behaviour. Warning analysts can then deliberately scan the environment for observations matching a previously manufactured list of warning indicators derived from the CoG process. Furthermore, these a priori models of expected adversarial behaviour need not be the product of pure creative thinking but also may be based on observations of previous hybrid attacks.

Two further points of interest stand out from the Austrian experience in expanding CoG methods in this way. Firstly, while the military can assist with "widening the aperture" of a state's warning intelligence gaze by providing useful tools to various ministries so they can monitor their sectors for early signals of hybrid warfare, usefully applying these tools will require the political buy-in of these civilian government actors to accept military assistance. Achieving this may be politically or even legally sensitive and not always a simple task. Moreover, for the CoG methodology to create new non-military indicators of hybrid warfare across all sectors of society, it will also require the active participation of the civilians with the subject-matter expertise within the various ministries (and ideally private sector expertise) to usefully apply their practical knowledge to the CoG method. For example, while the Austrian Army can "deliver and explain" the CoG methodology to the Austrian Finance Ministry, the implementation of the CoG process in the finance sector would require ministerial subject-matter expertise to be involved. The Austrian military does not have the necessary knowledge of the finance sector to recommend such non-military sector-specific solutions. While the realities of hybrid warfare may require these steps to be taken, defence and intelligence organisations must also be sensitive to limiting the impact and costs imposed on various agencies by creating this kind of expanded early warning requirement and capability.

Known unknown part II: moving indicators to the left

Beyond the problem of needing to "widen the aperture" discussed earlier, a second problem of developing adequate warning intelligence for hybrid warfare can be seen in calls from within the US Special Operations Community for the need to create early warning indicators applicable to threats developing in the "grey zone".[50] According to Hal Brands,

> *gray zone* conflict is best understood as an activity that is coercive and aggressive in nature, but that is deliberately designed to remain below the threshold of conventional military conflict and open interstate war . . . *gray zone* challenges, in other words, are ambiguous and usually of incremental aggression.[51]

"Grey zone" conflict – which is understood as an aspect of hybrid warfare in this chapter – remains an unresolved problem for the warning intelligence officer because these types of challenges have traditionally not been considered as severe enough security threats to warrant the monitoring attention of the intelligence community.[52]

Visualised along a left-to-right spectrum of activity, where peace exists at the extreme left-end of spectrum and conventional or nuclear warfare exists on the extreme right-end of the spectrum, adequate warning for hybrid warfare requires warning intelligence officers to make a "shift to the left" to create indicators for the hybrid warfare security problem. This is precisely what US Army Special Operations Command (USASOC) meant when it called for a need "to perceive indications of challenges, threats, and opportunities for non-standard campaigns that state and non-state actors are pursuing on the left side of the operational spectrum".[53] From this perspective, despite its strategic intent to operate below the threshold of a conventional shooting war, hybrid warfare is a form of strategic competition being pursued by revisionist powers looking to alter the international status quo, and this "requires that we develop indicators and warning to assess, sort, form responses, and rescale security challenges much earlier in their development and risk profiles".[54] For USASOC, hybrid warfare creates challenges for warning intelligence precisely because it requires the intelligence analyst to create and monitor indicators for security challenges that were previously considered too minor or insignificant to even be considered relevant or too underdeveloped to be monitored.

The role that the US special operations community sees for itself in the realm of intelligence collection for hybrid warfare is also interesting for the intelligence analyst because it points in the direction of closer collaboration between these two actors. Elements of the US special operations community have argued that the need for developing new "grey zone" or hybrid warfare indicators creates an intelligence collection requirement – and one that special operators are uniquely capable of fulfilling for the intelligence community. Specifically, this involves the collection of ambiguous "Human Domain"[55] data (e.g. population-centric information about the inhabitants of a conflict zone) relevant for strategic warning that is not being exploited either because it falls below, and outside of, traditional collection thresholds for war warning intelligence or because the human intelligence resources were not available.[56] For the US Special Operations community in particular, they see themselves in a position to leverage their deployment in allied or friendly states (or other operating environments) to identify subtle indications of hybrid warfare operations in its early stages.

The US Army Special Operations Command most likely intends to leave the actual construction of warning indicators of hybrid warfare to the warning intelligence experts. However, they intend to assist warning analysts with this indicator-building process by describing key characteristics of the grey zone/hybrid domain requiring new warning indicators. These key characteristics are based on their observations of hybrid operations in Ukraine and Crimea[57] and have been distilled and translated into what US Army Special Operations Command refers to as "seven leading indications of state-based aggression falling under the threshold of UN [Charter] Article 2 use of force".[58] These seven "indications" – perhaps better understood as an abstract description of the US Army Special Operations Command's understanding of the core problem of grey zone/hybrid warfare – are used to break up this hybrid warfare puzzle into a series of smaller, more concrete security problems that require new warning indicators to be built.[59]

In short, the US Special Operations community has identified what it perceives as a gap in the warning intelligence collection efforts related to grey zone/hybrid warfare threats and is arguing that it is uniquely suited as an organisation to supply the type of "human domain" intelligence required to help warning analysts fill this gap. It is essentially attempting to carve out a role for itself as a human intelligence collection source in deployed "hybrid environments" – like a future Crimea – by leveraging its ability to conduct long-term, embedded observation of subtle and ambiguous information in the "human domain". Whether or not this is true remains to be seen.

Unknown unknown part I: the Finnish model

The two previous case studies have looked at recent attempts to update and adapt the use of indicator-based warning to hybrid warfare by expanding the scope of known unknowns being monitored with indicator watch lists. This case study shifts the focus to some experimental work being conducted by the Finnish government on alternative methods for "discovering" the harder to detect "unknown unknown" hybrid threats. In this search for unknown unknowns, "discovery is not about pattern recognition or detection of known patterns: it is about pattern *discovery* or the identification of new patterns".[60] In a shift from the use and reliance upon indicators developed in the hunt of known unknowns, this Finnish approach to discovering new hybrid threats focuses on the detection of anomalies or the detection of harmful and unexplained effects to identify clues of possible ambiguous hybrid threats.

As a method seeking to identify and connect the potential bits and pieces of hybrid activity in many parts of society, enabling the analyst to see patterns that would not stand out by traditional security sector–oriented indicator-based methods, the Finnish government's attempt to develop a comprehensive domestic method to discover and detect potential hybrid threats is a case in point.[61] In the Finnish method a handful of analysts are placed in the Prime Minister's Office, reaching out horizontally to ministries, other governmental entities, as well as private actors. Rather than looking for specific indicators of known threats, selected contact points in these units or entities are instead tasked with reporting back on "all" incidents of an unusual nature, regardless of its apparent insignificance.

With respect to the operationalisation of what type of information to report, seven vital functions in society have been identified. The functions are:

1   Leadership
2   The ability to conduct international cooperation, for example as a part of the EU community
3   Military defence
4   The ability to uphold domestic security
5   The economy and civil infrastructure
6   Ensuring the basic civil services in society
7   Ability to mentally handle crisis in the population.[62]

Based on an individual assessment of whether an event is likely to threaten any of these seven functions, requiring extra actions from the authorities, the individual responsible for reporting is expected to notify the Prime Minister's Office about any potential event of relevance.[63]

To date, the information collected horizontally in its whole-of-government approach stands out as a "small data" method, where an Excel sheet is used to store the data. Hence, the model is vulnerable in the sense that it is heavily dependent on the various individuals' personal assessments, not seeking to make complete, uniform, and methodological rigorous analytical products of what potentially could represent an unusual hybrid activity. By scanning headlines, governmental reports, and whatever might come across the civil servant's desk, the method certainly has a weakness with respect to making valid claims of statistical significance. Nevertheless, in representing a qualitative approach, the experimental method also has its merit as it utilises personal skills and native knowledge. Hence, in its current version the Finish model differs from more ambitious – but yet unfinished – US programs involving multiple big datasets and cybernetic man-machine learning, where larger amounts of data are collected, stored, and processed.[64] However, while not collecting large bulks of data, one must assume that the data collected in the Finish system are categorised with a higher degree of accuracy than what might be the case with computer-based collection, where systematisation and statistical processing of written texts, such as news reports, are automatically conducted by machines.

The Finnish method represents an attempt to map activities that normally never would be put together by any intelligence or domestic counterintelligence agency. Moreover, the method aims to break down informational stovepipes between government agencies (and to the extent possible, the private sector) genuinely representing a national effort to combine information of potential hybrid character. The Finnish approach also involves bureaucratically elevating the hybrid analysis unit into the Prime Minister's Office, allowing rapid warning of hybrid threats if the need arises. Although there are vulnerabilities in its human-based collection structure, especially where the individuals involved might not have the proper education, the Fins are nevertheless working on these challenges, seeking actively to educate persons involved, aiming for bigger datasets over time and more resources, which perhaps in the near future can enable anomaly recognition and pattern recognition that can lead to the discovery of hybrid threats, and/or the discovery of previously unrecognised damaging effects from hybrid warfare.

Unknown unknown part II: the UK hybrid activity monitoring tool

Another example of a creative experimental method to discover potential hybrid threats is the "Hybrid Activity Monitoring Tool" (HAMT), developed by the British Ministry of Defence. This tool is designed to help identify hybrid activity that could stem from a malign actor and enable decision-makers to better understand the events as they take place – hence "support effective policy making in a hybrid threat environment".[65] Through seeking to understand what hybrid activity is happening and what "levers" the potential hostile state actor is using, the method is designed to support decision-making in an unclear hybrid terrain. The method is designed to be applied abroad through legal collection of openly available information from a UK embassy in a friendly country where hostile hybrid influence might occur. The individuals doing the collection would then look for relevant information, in accordance with specific criteria, pertaining to potential hybrid activity in the country of deployment. This information could additionally be combined with the general embassy reports being produced through standard diplomatic reporting procedures.

In this original set up of HAMT, the "levers" were selected to be:

1   Infrastructure
2   Political
3   Economic
4   Social
5   Military
6   Media/Information

In other words, it is quite overlapping with the earlier mentioned MPECI spectrum. Each lever is assessed on two dimensions: "Level of influence" and "Impact of influence", where potential findings on the first dimension is reported on a scale ranging from 1 to 10, where 1 is defined as "negligible" and 10 as "direct and traceable". The latter dimension is reported on a score between 1 and 5, where 1 is defined as "negligible" and 5 as "severe".

By following the aforementioned way of reporting an incident, a total score can be calculated by multiplying the level of influence with the impact of the influence.[66] By defining specific criteria to look for, and comparing collected information with an established "normal" baseline, a graphic visualisation of the potential hybrid activity level can also be produced. By experimenting with selecting information from areas of interest, such as "posting of fake news", "financial support of movements discrediting democratic institutions", "unusual purchases of properties", "or economic transactions with unusual motivations" – the examples are limitless, the method at least provides a basis for experimentation in seeking to identify and develop a method of warning of potential hybrid threats.

Moreover, if the foreign collection is combined with a domestic collection arrangement, then a coordinated state-run, centralised intelligence and counterintelligence apparatus might potentially provide a large enough set of data to over time improve our ability to identify hybrid threats at an earlier stage. Hence, the foreign deployed early warning arm should ideally be paralleled with a complementary homeland security early warning capacity.

Another interesting feature with the British undertaking is that the aforementioned collection unit, collecting information from abroad, potentially could be co-located with the "77th information brigade". The 77th Brigade was, when set up in 2015, characterised as a unit that "will use psychological operations and social media to help fight wars 'in the information age'".[67] Today, the Brigade states the following mission: "Our aim is to challenge the difficulties of modern warfare using non-lethal engagement and legitimate non-military levers as a means to adapt behaviors of the opposing forces and adversaries."[68] The Brigade furthermore describe themselves the following way: "77th Brigade is an agent of change; through targeted Information Activity and Outreach we contribute to the success of military objectives in support of Commanders, whilst reducing the cost in casualties and resources", describing what they do in short as: "Audience, actor and adversary analysis, information activity and outreach, counter-adversarial information activity, support to partners across government, collecting media content, disseminating media, monitoring the information environment [and] evaluating the information environment".[69]

The 77th Brigade represents an innovative capacity in many ways, not least in being a highly visible, uniformed, overt instrument of influence, enabling a dual mission of dissemination of strategic communication, psychological operations, as well as collection. Additionally, it can potentially legally be connected to military intelligence agencies, Special Operation Forces, as well as participate in the execution of kinetic action against enemy targets, as the Brigade is a part of the British Armed Forces.

To strengthen their capacity, the 77th Brigade is also set up with a research unit. The Brigade thus has the capacity, mandate, and skills to support collection through the HAMT, openly acting with personnel in uniform on the ground in deployed areas. Tasked with quite specific works such as "counter-adversarial information activity" or "collecting media content", the 77th Brigade could be an empowering element for the UK in its ability to not only detect but also respond to hybrid warfare.

Conclusion

Providing warning intelligence and making sure decision-makers are made aware of potential threats at the earliest stage possible is a critically important task for any intelligence service. Whereas during the Cold War intelligence services largely relied on the use of indicator-based methods that were heavily focused on monitoring military targets to provide warning intelligence, in light of today's more complex threat scenarios and because of the threats posed by hybrid warfare, this is changing. Our case studies demonstrate that intelligence analysts are experimenting with adapting old Cold War tools, such as the Centre of Gravity model, to address the need to create new indicators for non-military and non-kinetic hybrid threats to society at large. This kind of creative re-imagining of the types of indicators which are needed in order to provide early warning of an attack from weaponised economic, informational, and other non-military tools of statecraft is crucial for responding to hybrid warfare's challenge to warning intelligence. Hybrid warfare is also moving the threshold at which hybrid threats need to be understood as such and targeted with appropriate indicators to monitor their development. Since hybrid warfare is tailored to operate in a grey zone that falls short of, or outside of, our traditional understanding of warfare, new warning indicators will be needed to respond to this threat. While these first two case studies provide examples of how and why indicator-based methodologies are being expanded to cover a larger set of potential threats, the latter two case studies – focused on Finnish and British approaches to hybrid warfare early warning – point to alternative warning methodologies that move beyond indicators. Specifically, they demonstrate how intelligence agencies are responding to the fact that the nature of hybrid warfare increases the potential for threats emanating from "unknown unknowns" by developing creative approaches to "discovering" ambiguous or hidden hybrid threats by finding unanticipated anomalies from a given norm, rather than from watching for changes to a preconceived list of indicators. Future efforts to provide early warning against hybrid warfare would be well served by self-consciously experimenting with both approaches.

Notes

1 Andras Racz: "Russia's Hybrid War in Ukraine", Report No. 43, The Finnish Institute of International Affairs, 2015.
2 Van Jackson: "Tactics of Strategic Competition", *Naval War College Review*, Vol. 70, No. 3, 2017 pp. 39–61.
3 James K. Witheres: "Making Sense of Hybrid Warfare", *Connections: The Quarterly Journal*, Vol. 15, No. 2, 2016, pp. 73–87; Van Jackson, *op. cit.*
4 Dameien Van Puyvelde: "Hybrid War – Does It Even Exist?", *NATO Review*, 2015, www.nato.int/docu/review/2015/also-in-2015/hybrid-modern-future-warfare-russia-ukraine/EN/index.htm.
5 William Nemeth: "Future War and Chechnya: A Case for Hybrid Warfare", Thesis, Monterey, CA: Naval Postgraduate School, 2002; Patrick Cullen & Erik Reichborn-Kjennerud: "Countering Hybrid Warfare: Baseline Assessment", Report, Multinational Capability Development Campaign, 2016, pp. 5–6.
6 Frank G. Hoffman: *Conflict in the 21st Century: The Rise of Hybrid Wars*. Institute for Policy Studies. Arlington: Potomac, 2007, p. 7.
7 Frank G. Hoffman: "'Hybrid Threats': Neither Omnipotent Nor Unbeatable", *Orbis*, Vol. 54, No. 3, 2010, p. 443.
8 Cullen and Reichborn-Kjennerud: "Countering Hybrid Warfare: Baseline Assessment", *op. cit.*, pp. 8–13.
9 *Ibid.*
10 Personal communication with participants from the CHW campaign. Shrivenham, UK, October 2017.
11 Patrick Cullen & Erik Reichborn-Kjennerud: "Countering Hybrid Warfare Project: Understanding Hybrid Warfare", Report, 2017, p. 3.
12 *Ibid.*, p. 3.
13 For an account of the cyberattack on Estonia and a brief discussion of hybrid warfare as it relates to the cyber and digital realms, see Sascha-Dominik Bachmann: "Hybrid Threats, Cyber Warfare and NATO's Comprehensive Approach for Countering 21st Century Threats", *Amicus Curiae*, Vol. 88, Winter 2011.
14 "Russian 'Invasion' of Crimea Fuels Fear of Ukraine Conflict", *The Guardian*, February 28, 2014, www.theguardian.com/world/2014/feb/28/russia-crimea-white-house; Witheres, *op. cit.*; and Martin Murphy, Frank G. Hoffman, & Gary Schaub: "Hybrid Maritime Warfare and the Baltic Sea Region", Report. Centre for Military Studies, University of Copenhagen, 2016.
15 John Biersack & Shannon O'Lear: "The Geopolitics of Russia's Annexation of Crimea: Narratives, Identity, Silences, and Energy", *Eurasian Geography and Economics*, Vol. 55, No. 3, 2014, pp. 247–269.
16 Thomas, Ambrosio: "The Rhetoric of Irredentism: The Russian Federation's Perception Management Campaign and the Annexation of Crimea", *Small Wars & Insurgencies*, Vol. 27, No. 3, 2016, pp. 467–490.
17 Biersack & O'Lear, *op. cit.*; "Crimea Votes to Secede From Ukraine as Russian Troops Keep Watch", *The New York Times*, March 16, 2014, www.nytimes.com/2014/03/17/world/europe/crimea-ukraine-secession-vote-referendum.html; and Yuri Teper: "Official

Russian Identity Discourse in Light of the Annexation of Crimea: National or Imperial?", *Post-Soviet Affairs*, Vol. 32, No. 4, 2016, pp. 378–396.

18 Racz, *op. cit.*
19 Bettina Renz & Hanna Smith: "Russia and Hybrid Warfare – Going beyond the Label", *Papers Aleksanteri*, University of Helsinki, 2015.
20 Racz, *op. cit.*, p. 40.
21 "Why Didn't the U.S. Know Sooner?", *Politico*, May 3, 2014, www.politico.com/story/2014/03/united-states-barack-obama-ukraine-crimea-russia-vladimir-putin-104264.
22 *DOD Dictionary of Military and Associated Terms*, U.S. Department of Defence (DoD), 2017, www.dtic.mil/doctrine/new_pubs/dictionary.pdf.
23 Cynthia Grabo: *Handbook of Warning Intelligence*. Lanham, MD: Rowman & Littlefield, 2015, pp. 59–65; John A. Gentry: "Warning Analysis: Focusing on Perceptions of Vulnerability", *International Journal of Intelligence and CounterIntelligence*, Vol. 28, No. 1, 2015, pp. 64–88.
24 James J. Wirtz: "Indications and Warning in an Age of Uncertainty", *International Journal of Intelligence and CounterIntelligence*, Vol. 26, No. 3, 2013, pp. 550–562.
25 *Ibid.*, p. 552.
26 Grabo, *op. cit.*, p. 60.
27 Wirtz, *op. cit.*, p. 553.
28 *Ibid.*
29 Grabo, *op. cit.*, p. 346.
30 *Ibid.*, pp. 59–65, 115–117.
31 *Ibid.*, pp. 59–65.
32 Wirtz, *op. cit.*, p. 555; Joint Chiefs of Staff: Joint Publication 2–0. Joint Intelligence, 2013, p. II, www.dtic.mil/doctrine/new_pubs/jp2_0.pdf; and Myriam Dunn Cavelty & Victor Mauer: "Postmodern Intelligence: Strategic Warning in an Age of Reflexive Intelligence", *Security Dialogue*, Vol. 40, No. 2, 2009, pp. 123–144.
33 Grabo, *ibid.*, p. 113.
34 Roberta Wohlstetter: *Pearl Harbor: Warning and Decision*. Stanford University Press, 1962; Mark M. Lowenthal: *From Secrets to Policy*. Los Angeles: Sage, 2015, p. 92.
35 Wirtz, *op. cit.*; Gentry, *op. cit.*
36 Cullen & Reichborn-Kjennerud: "Countering Hybrid Warfare Project: Understanding Hybrid Warfare", *op. cit.*
37 Patrick Cullen & Erik Reichborn-Kjennerud: "Countering Hybrid Warfare Analytical Framework", *MCDC*, October 31, 2016, pp. 19–20.
38 Cullen & Reichborn-Kjennerud: "Countering Hybrid Warfare Project: Understanding Hybrid Warfare", *op. cit.*, p. 20; Interviews in the MCDC project with subject matter experts from the civil and military sector, from Finland and Norway fall 2017.
39 Ole Wæver: "The Rise and Fall of the Inter-paradigm Debate", in Steven Smith et al. (eds.): *International Theory: Positivism & Beyond*. Cambridge: Cambridge University Press, 2000; and Steve Smith: "Positivism and Beyond", in Steve Smith et al. (eds.): *op. cit.*
40 Carl L. Pritchard: *Risk Management: Concepts and Guidance*, 5th edition. Boca Raton: CRC Press, Taylor & Francis Group, 2015.
41 Christer Pursiainen: *The Crisis Management Cycle*. Abingdon and New York: Routledge, 2018, pp. 16–19.
42 *Ibid.*, p. 18.
43 For an application of these ideas in a non-hybrid warfare context, see Cavelty & Mauer, *op. cit.*, pp. 129–134.
44 Richards J. Heuer Jr. & Randolph H. Pherson: *Structured Analytic Techniques for Intelligence Analysis*. Los Angeles: Sage, 2015, pp. 5–6.

45 Presentation delivered by Austrian Army delegate at the Early Warning and Detection Syndicate Group of the Counter-Hybrid Warfare 2 Workshop, Multinational Capability Development Campaign, Granada, Spain, March 15, 2018.

46 Ian Kippen: "Centre of Gravity: Joining the Dots from Strategic to Tactical Level Plans", *Small Wars Journal*, October 2016.

47 Email correspondence with Austrian delegate to MCDC Counter Hybrid Warfare #2 power point presentation on March 18, 2018.

48 Presentation delivered by Austrian Army delegate at the Early Warning and Detection Syndicate Group of the Counter-Hybrid Warfare 2 Workshop, Multinational Capability Development Campaign, Granada, Spain, March 15, 2018.

49 Email correspondence with Austrian delegate to MCDC Counter Hybrid Warfare #2 power point presentation on, March 18, 2018.

50 The US defence community's discussion of Gray Zone warfare is similar to and overlaps conceptually with our (and EU, and NATO) understanding of hybrid warfare. For a discussion of Gray Zone warfare in this context, see Michael Mazaar: *Mastering the Gray Zone: Understa nding a Changing Era of Conflict.* Strategic Studies Institute, December 2015.

51 Hal Brands: "Paradoxes of the Gray Zone", *Foreign Policy Research Institute*, February 5, 2016, www.fpri.org/article/2016/02/paradoxes-gray-zone/.

52 Frank Hoffman places grey zone/ambiguous war – what we refer to as hybrid warfare – at the farthest left hand of his conflict spectrum. See, Frank Hoffman: *The Contemporary Spectrum of Conflict: Protracted, Gray Zone, Ambiguous, and Hybrid Modes of War.* Heritage Foundation, 2016, p. 25.

53 United States Army Special Operations Command: "Perceiving Gray Zone Indications", White Paper, March 15, 2016, p. i.

54 *Ibid.*

55 The "Human domain" concept is used to emphasize the role of Clausewitz's insight that strategy is played out with living opponents with interests, passions, decision options, and above all else, a will and goal of their own, and must be included in more traditional discussions of air, sea, land, space, cyber, etc., domains. For more on the Human Domain, see "Operating in the Human Domain", *US Special Operations Command*, August 3, 2015.

56 "Perceiving Gray Zone Indications", *op. cit.*, p. 1.

57 *Ibid.*, p. iii.

58 The indications identified are written in prose format and are too long to list here. However, they are organized into these seven categories: unconventional measures, nonmilitary measures, leverage population-based power, information measures, lawfare measures, technology measures; conventional measures. See "Perceiving Gray Zone Indications", *op. cit.*, p. iii.

59 *Ibid.*, p. ii.

60 Cavelty & Mauer, *op. cit.*, p. 132.

61 Edward Deverell: *Nordiska länders arbete för att identifiera och motstå informationspåverkan. En kartläggning av hur Danmark, Finland, Norge och Sverige arbetar avseende informationspåverkan [The Nordic Countries' Work to Identify Information Activities. A Mapping of Denmark, Finland, Norway and Sweden's Work on Information Operations].* Stockholm: Betenkning, Försvarshögskolan, 2018, p. 17.

62 Government of Finland: "Säkerhetsstrategi för samhället. Statsrådets principbeslut [Security Strategy for the Society, The Governments Decisions on Principles]", November 2, 2017.

63 Personal communication, Interviews, Prime Minister's office, September 5, 2017.

64 Presentation, Hybrid Threats Workshop NATO STRATCOM Center, Riga May 12, 2017.

65 *Monitoring and Visualising Hybrid Activity – A UK Food-for-Thought Paper for the MCDC Countering Hybrid Warfare Project*, UK Ministry of Defence, 2018.
66 *Ibid.*, p. 3.
67 "Army Sets Up New Brigade 'For Information Age'", *BBC*, January 31, 2015, www.bbc.com/news/uk-31070114.
68 "77th Brigade. Influence and Outreach", *The British Army*, 2018, www.army.mod.uk/who-we-are/corps-regiments-and-units/77th-brigade/.
69 *Ibid.*

Further reading

Agrell, Wilhelm: *The Black Swan and its Opponents: Early Warning Aspects of the Norway Attacks on 22 July 2011*. Stockholm: Försvarshögskolan, Senter for asymmetriske trusler, 2013.

Betts, Richard K.: "Fixing Intelligence", *Foreign Affairs*, Vol. 81, No. 1, 2002, pp. 43–59.

Gentry, John A., & Joseph S. Gordon: *Strategic Warning Intelligence: History, Challenges, and Prospects*. Washington, DC: Georgetown University Press, 2019.

Grabo, Cynthia: *Handbook of Warning Intelligence*. Lanham: Rowman and Littlefield, 2015.

Jervis, Robert: *Why Intelligence Fails: Lessons from the Iranian Revolution and the Iraq War*. Ithaca: Cornell University Press, 2010.

Wirtz, James J.: "Indications and Warning in an Age of Uncertainty", *International Journal of Intelligence and CounterIntelligence*, Vol. 26, No. 3, 2013, pp. 550–562.

Zelikow, Philip: "The 9/11 Commission Report", New York, 2004, www.9-11commission.gov/report/911Report.pdf.

8 Futures and forecasting

Kristian C. Gustafson

> I'm not sure what 2010 will look like, but I'm sure that it will be very little like we expect, so we should plan accordingly.
>
> – Linton Wells, US DoD[1]

Two strong and opposed currents help define the current state of international politics. The first is the rapid development of digital technology; the second is the difficulties that modern national governments have in keeping up with this development.

The pace of technological change is blistering.[2] This technological change has impacts which are surprising and which also cause clear changes in social and cultural behaviours. For instance, technology affects how we consume news, which in turn increases the impact of "fake news" in social media on politics.[3] At the same time, government projects are often slow and inept. For example, it can take decades for governments to deploy major capital military systems.[4] As the Australian Defence Science and Technology Office (DSTO) puts it, states must be able to "examine the wider socio-economic and strategic global factors that shape the long-term future and its impact on emerging trends in science and technology".[5]

Futures methodology is a potentially important tool to help modern governments prepare for challenges emerging from rapid technological innovation and change. Getting this methodology right is therefore also a key requirement of intelligence analysis in the digital age. These methods are not, by themselves, likely to eliminate intelligence surprise – which is likely an inevitable fact of life in the intelligence world[6] – but may increase the efficiency of intelligence organisations in making long-term predictions.

To demonstrate the potential significance of futures work for intelligence, this chapter will explain futures methodology, with a focus on so-called horizon scanning. Firstly, the problem these techniques are meant to counter will be examined and then the methodologies themselves. From there the chapter will examine where and how states have chosen to embed futures methodology in their national machinery, with a focus on how the UK Ministry of Defence (MoD) has embedded futures methodology into its doctrinal and acquisitions processes, via conceptual products and experimental exercises meant to prepare the UK Armed Forces for the perceived "future character of conflict".[7] Finally, some of the limitations associated with the methodology will be discussed.

Methodology for horizon scanning

Scenario generation is an analytical activity designed to provide creative analysis of future-focused questions. It is "most appropriate for early-stage analytical investigation, on future-focused questions that are primarily open and diagnostic (who, what, why, how), and relating to threats, opportunities or new developments".[8] The scenario is "the archetypical product of futures studies".[9] In general, scenarios deal with open, future-focused questions framed like "What will X be like at time T?",[10] with X being anything ranging from a technological field to a defined place or region, and the time frame generally being beyond the time frame one could normally directly predict. While there are a number of different methods to develop future-focused scenarios, all start with a few common steps. In almost all cases, the process starts with some version of (a) review of expert opinion, new literature, and abstracts in the field under inquiry; (b) identification of the key "drivers" that are conditioning the field of inquiry; and (c) some judgement or assumption about the direction those drivers are moving. Processes like the "Delphi Method" developed by Herman Kahn at the Rand Corporation in the 1950s to elicit and capture expert opinion systematically can stand in for the steps described here.[11] Varying methods exist for generating future scenarios. These methods help us examine how changes to certain drivers or forces might affect what we perceive as stable situations and help us produce plausible scenarios in a systematic way.[12] The Royal Dutch Shell/Global Business Network (GBN) matrix, the "Cone of Plausibility", and "Quadrant Crunching" are variants of such methods. Often, the next step begins with the development of a baseline scenario: If all trends continue in the way that we currently assume they are moving, what will the future look like? From this baseline the analyst can manipulate various factors and drivers identified in the first step to generate alternative future scenarios. The scenarios are generally expressed in the form of stories, by a narrative describing the situation at some future point, as if it were real. As we tend to view history as a collection of stories, futures work expresses its outcomes via specific creative stories which exemplify and describe the specific outcomes of the trends. The premium is placed on vividness and detail. "A good scenario grabs us by the collar", writes Peter Bishop.[13] A scenario is, then, effectively a "future history" to make a hazy potential future more concrete and relatable to decision-makers. The key idea is that the scenarios are not meant to be predictive but to provide "a specific manifestation of the general" and to cover the range of plausible future outcomes comprehensively.

It is clear that the outcome of this scenario-generating analytical process differs from the analytical process conducted more conventionally by the intelligence analyst. The intelligence analyst cannot predict the future, but what the analyst must do is assign probabilities to certain outcomes and events, as tasked. Judging by the most recent and well-sourced information, the intelligence analyst can determine, for example, that it is probable or certain (each word having a more-or-less well-defined percentage value) that country "R" will attack its neighbouring country "G" within time frame "T". By contrast, futures methods offer no probability, only noting that each scenario is plausible given the current knowledge. Futures methods can look at the assumptions on which any given analysis is based and then, through the various techniques common in scenario generation, investigate the relevant fields to see how far forward analysts can carry their linear predictions. Furthermore, the methods can look at which future shocks might change that system and thereby lead events from the probable outcome to an alternative or plausible outcome. The resulting products of scenario generating have clear positive implications for the field of intelligence. Intelligence analysts can use the scenario as a starting point to list indicators and warnings of undesirable events such as future shocks.[14]

Scenarios can serve as a more general way to cue more immediate intelligence collection on new political events and emerging technologies, or to monitor government response to the same. As former Joint Intelligence Committee (JIC) chairman Alex Alan commented, organisations like the UK Strategic Horizons Unit were "there to show gaps in the policy response" to the government "before this is actually apparent".[15] Last, scenarios can serve as the basis for planning policy responses to emerging issues. The use of futures work can thus be a critical component to policy planning and government response to emerging crises and act as an important bridge between policy direction and intelligence support for it.

The intelligence blind spot

In the digital age the intelligence community of Britain, like that of her major allies, has been dominated by what has been called the "tyranny of current intelligence".[16] The affairs of government have increased in tempo, and long-term global issues often received less attention than short-term and local issues.[17] As Espen Barth Eide shows in Chapter 3, pressure on leaders for informed decisions is increased by a global instantaneous media complex, and so intelligence customers want targeted and succinct reporting on matters of current concern, *now*. Accordingly, most staff time and effort go to producing short customer-driven products with an outlook of six months or less.[18] This demand for on-time reporting of current matters of interest has left a lacuna in intelligence reporting: long intelligence products, driven only partially by direct customer tasking, which forecast potential problems or tipping points. The lack of research and strategic view intelligence is a current problem for the British intelligence community. Indeed, the *Butler Review* warned that "assessments should not give undue weight to intelligence reports over wider analysis of historical, psychological or geopolitical factors".[19] Analysts caught up in current reporting will miss the deeper and long-term factors affecting their assessments.

There are many often-conflicting definitions of what constitutes horizon scanning. The UK Department for the Environment, Food, and Rural Affairs (DEFRA) defines it as "the systematic examination of potential threats, opportunities and likely developments including but not restricted to those at the margins of current thinking and planning. Horizon scanning may explore novel and unexpected issues as well as persistent problems or trends".[20] Sir David Omand, former Security and Intelligence Coordinator at the Cabinet Office, has defined horizon scanning as the "systematic search for potential developments to optimise action to manage future threats and hazards (and hazards that might spawn threats) and to exploit opportunities".[21] Common to both of these definitions is that horizon scanning is about probable future scenarios. It is not in itself predictive – it does not tell one what will happen – but it attempts to forewarn what could happen. As DEFRA says, horizon scanning

> does not predict the future, but on the basis of a thorough understanding and analysis of the subject in its broadest perspective and an awareness of different ways the future may develop, we can identify a range of possible outcomes.[22]

It involves analysts conferring with experts in widely scattered fields of physical and human sciences, engineering, sociology, and demography and examining whether new patents, technologies, or processes might lead the world to a future or plausible potential futures perhaps radically different from the probable one based on an inductive, linear extension from the world of today.

It might be asked if horizon scanning is an intelligence methodology – whether horizon scanning should be a task which specifically sits in an intelligence organisation. As Sir David Omand has noted, intelligence and horizon scanning are different in as much as the former's information culture is closed because of immediate threat and the latter's is open to detect potential hazard. Yet they have a "similarity of analytic role in enabling [the] reduction of risk".[23] As American intelligence practitioner and scholar Stephen Marrin has observed, the main reason we maintain an intelligence apparatus in government is that it "enables power to be applied with greater precision and with less collateral damage".[24] Or, as intelligence historian David Kahn said: "The function of intelligence is to optimize resources."[25] We have with these statements the most compelling reason to classify horizon scanning as a relevant intelligence methodology. Horizon scanning, when done properly as part of a greater intelligence analysis effort, can serve a strong 'cuing" function for the more secret and immediate components of the intelligence community.

The UK defence horizon scanning programme

So far, horizon scanning has been most extensively applied in other areas than intelligence. The UK government has a vigorous and long-standing appreciation of the value of horizon scanning.[26] This holds especially true for the Ministry of Defence, which arguably is a pacesetter in the UK for its use of robust scenario methodology. The use of scenario methodology is a clear acknowledgement of a threefold problem: the current quick pace of technological change; the often very long timelines of defence acquisitions even (or especially) in these new fields; and the squeezed defence budgets which put pressure on defence to get things right (as there is no more money if they get it wrong). The MoD is the most security-focused ministry with the greatest need for very long-term scanning. They are also, arguably, most immediately and acutely affected by any technological surprise.

The pressure on the military's long-standing way of warfighting is keenly sensed. In order to meet future challenges, horizon scanning and scenario-based products are produced through all levels of planning, with the aim of preparing the British Armed Forces for the future shocks that are presumed to be inevitable. It stands as a remarkably coherent effort to prepare the military for the future warfighting environment in a digital age which presents a "new geometry"[27] of the battlefield, conditioned by the prevalence of remote and autonomous systems (RAS), stand-off fires, and high-intensity information warfare.

The basis of the UK's defence horizon scanning is a connected system of products which stretch from the present to 30 years and more: Global Strategic Trends (GST), Future Operating Environment (FOE), and Future Force Concept (FFC). These key products are generated to provide a coherent, MoD-wide agreed view on realistic future scenarios.

The whole programme is on a rolling five-year renewal timeline and is inherently tied to funding. All UK defence spending begins by being joint, that is, across all three of the services. Money trickles down to the services when they can convince the Joint Force Development Command that their plans suit those concepts, which have been developed jointly. Hence, there needs to be a conceptually sound, agreed view of how conflict is evolving and how the UK fits into that future environment. The outcomes of this process are critical, as some capital equipment will remain in service for 35 years or more – such as the UK's Elizabeth-class aircraft carriers – after decades of development. The capabilities that new equipment must possess need to be considered in light of what they will bring not just into the "current force" but indeed into some "future force".[28]

Since 2001, the Defence Concepts and Doctrine Centre (DCDC) has been producing its landmark publication *Global Strategic Trends* (GST). GST

> describes a strategic context for those in the Ministry of Defence (MoD) and wider Government who are involved in developing long-term plans, policies and capabilities. . . . [I]t describes those phenomena that could have a significant impact on the future and combines these differing perspectives to produce a multifaceted picture of possible outcomes.[29]

It is produced without classification, so it can receive the maximum utility across various branches and levels of government. GST now serves as the longest-term and broadest-based horizon scan produced in the British Government.

The production of GST follows the standard methodologies of futures and scenario development. The entire process receives considerable engagement with those outside MoD, from academia, business, and government both domestically and internationally in order to avoid a single, subjective perspective.[30]

The document makes liberal use of scenario narratives and other classic horizon scanning tools. It presents its data both thematically and regionally. The themes include items as diverse as gender, urbanisation, corruption, and the environment, and the themes cover the entire globe. Throughout, the process is "red-teamed" to cross-check judgements via alternative analysis.[31] A small snippet of its key judgements provides an indicative sense of the whole:

> Technology is highly likely to change our working environment. By 2045, robots or 'unmanned systems' (able to carry out complex tasks without a human operator's direct involvement) are likely to be as ubiquitous as computers are today. Machines are likely to become more sophisticated and lifelike. We could also see robots used in many more areas of work and society, including caring roles, customer-service, surgery and in combat.[32]

The paper further describes the "significant challenges resulting from population growth, migration, greater demand for energy, climate change, continuing globalisation, rapid urbanisation and the exponential rate of change in readily available technologies".[33] In this way, GST provides broad-based judgements not purely primed for defence needs but instead covering the whole of the human experience. Accordingly, the next DCDC horizon scanning product, the Future Operating Environment (FOE), is needed to focus on the analysis to make it more relevant to the development of future force structures.

The FOE makes up the other half of the "Conceptual Force", the British Army's experimental land force concept for 2035 ("The Conceptual Land Force", CF(L) 35). The product's time horizon therefore extends far into the future. The previous edition of the document was titled "The Future Character of Conflict", and it may be the case that this title captures more clearly the function of the document.[34] The FOE restricts itself to 20 years outlook and makes a point of noting that, realistically, "some characteristics of the future operating environment in 2035 are likely to be similar to those apparent today".[35]

The FOE focuses uniquely on how the developments noted in GST will affect the ability of UK armed forces in future warfare. Working from the FOE documents, it is then the turn of the various services to convert the very long-term conceptual horizon into a product that can help force and capability planning in a 10- to 20-year horizon. For the Army, the key process is that of the Agile Warrior exercises. Agile Warrior is the army's "intellectual programme to test an alternative force structure based upon the future operating environment derived from DCDC".[36] Agile Warrior takes the DCDC publications as its starting point in order to set the social and political contexts of potential future environments, as well as the potentially disruptive or highly innovative technologies identified by other partners, and integrates them into how the army fights in order to see how the army will need to adapt. The futures scenario currently envisioned by Agile Warrior states:

> We should expect to fight in a contested Electro-Magnetic Spectrum (EMS) environment, often in complex terrain, amongst the people, and with pervasive

and usually less than accurate media. . . . The proliferation of cheap, accurate missiles will mean that massed formations, large immobile HQs, and supply areas are targeted. Our adversaries will have different, often shocking ethical frameworks and may employ both Remote or Robotic and Autonomous Systems (RAS) lethally before NATO. We will be able to augment the human, physically and cognitively.[37]

We can follow from here the judgements on robotics moving to a very specific point about their use in warfare; the scenario is more concrete and focused on land warfare, allowing the Army HQ to design a "Conceptual Force" for testing and experimentation. The Conceptual Force (Land) 2035 is thus the result of the army's view of how it should adapt to fight in a likely future, the outcome of a year-long series of futures and scenario-generating workshops and events, which began with the Global Strategic Trends. The Army's Conceptual Force meets the work of the two other services and is joined into a Joint Concept Note called the "Futures Force Concept". This product is then fed back up to the Joint Force level as the joint vision of the armed forces out to 20 years. Within the Army, CF(L) and its subsequent experimentation leading to actual change in how the army does its business. The requirement is that the customer – in this case, the General Staff – agrees to make the radical changes suggested by this horizon scanning and futures process, satisfies joint command, and gets funding.

Potential weaknesses to futures work

As one business scholar has noted, despite much research on strategic foresight and its methodologies, we still have little concrete data on its impact and value overall.[38] One review of UK government horizon scanning and futures has pointed out that Britain has a long tradition of horizon scanning in government, "but there were still gaps because of the way that we structured ourselves. Some of the main difficulties in trying to predict risk were looking robustly enough at where we would be in the future".[39] In short, the problem is that horizon scanning effectively is very hard no matter what. Policy customers, short on time and big on advice which adds value, seem to be aware of this. Comments by Chairman of the JIC Sir John Day in his review of cross-government horizon scanning in 2012 suggest why it is the DCDC that has taken the central position in government horizon scanning instead of the central government:

> Barriers to [use of horizon scanning] lie at multiple levels. Horizon scanning activity is often self-tasked or commissioned with a limited understanding of what it might be used to inform. . . . Ministers and senior officials are often accused of being too focused on tactical issues and it can be a challenge to find time to engage them on issues which might not impact for anything up to 50 years, if at all. Horizon scanning products are often lengthy, and poorly presented, making them harder to digest and easier to ignore. It is also rare

for them to include policy implications or an analysis of how the information presented could be used to inform decision making.[40]

Agreeing with this, studies of UK and Australian horizon scanning efforts have found that it is not well-tasked – that is, it does not align well with the priorities of the decision-makers or the rest of the institutional processes. Products of horizon scanning have encountered officials who cannot engage with uncertainty, suspend disbelief, and maintain an open mind. This has led to a lack of meaningful evaluation of horizon scanning outputs, which have not demonstrated how they could be used to inform decision-making.[41] All of this suggests that horizon scanning still struggles to demonstrate its utility to its core audience, and in a budget-driven world this failure to connect spells failure.

Questionable impact

It is most likely the case that horizon scans will fall foul of the same problem encountered by intelligence analysts producing warning intelligence, as outlined by Erik J Dahl: If policymakers are not psychologically receptive towards a particular threat, then warnings, no matter how specific, will not cause them to take preventative action. Success comes only in the instance of high policymaker receptivity; thus, only highly specific warnings will cause them to shift their mindset and act. Dahl calls this the paradox of strategic warning and suggests that the critical factor is not "the presence or absence of brilliant analysts, or the organisation of intelligence agencies, but rather the availability of precise intelligence and receptive policymakers".[42] Director of Central Intelligence Richard Helms said "it is not enough to ring the bell . . . you've got to make sure the other guy hears it".[43] Dahl effectively argues that this can never happen. Since futures scenarios are by definition indefinite and imprecise – indeed, they consciously use fictional narratives to illustrate their scenarios – they may be very easily dismissed.

One might counter that futures work is what prepares policymakers for the possibility of some of those future threats – it helps make them more receptive by priming them to what might otherwise be dismissed as outlandish possibilities. But made aware of the rise of a new technology, but with only some indications of how it could be used, it may be too much to expect policymakers to adjust resources to a distant threat as yet unrealised. Some scholars on horizon scanning agree with this critique in general, noting that the information gathered about them frequently comes from fringe sources in the first instance, and "tends to lack conventional measures of credibility and authority to sufficiently influence policy making".[44] Consequently, horizon scans on new technologies are viewed with lower levels of confidence as a source of evidence for policy development.[45]

Technological determinism

A problem cited frequently in discussions of futurology is the tight focus on the impact of technology at the expense of other factors, or technological determinism.[46] British historian and strategist Sir Lawrence Freedman in his recent book, *The Future of War: A History*, notes how studies of future war over the last century have focused on new weapons and how they can be deployed in war-winning knock-out-blow strategies, but

> far less thought was given to the consequences of a first blow . . . or how a war's course might be increasingly determined by non-military factors, including the formation and breaking of alliances, underlying economic or demographic strength or the public's readiness to make sacrifices and tolerate casualties.

Militaries, Freedman has noted, have tended to focus on large capital systems, rather than fully exploring the impact or use of the smaller or more mundane technological systems.[47] They focus on building the Death Star, one commentator has noted, rather than the much less vulnerable and far more useful droid.[48]

A reasonable counterargument is that modern horizon scanning makes use of a wide range of tools and, like the GST, starts by considering social and demographic trends. Unfortunately, historically we have seen that prediction and forecasting in these domains have been highly inaccurate and prone to hyperbole both positive and negative.[49] In large part this is because most experts are remarkably bad at prediction – and we turn to experts to help build our futures scenarios. As we know from the work of Philp Tetlock and the IARPA "Good Judgement Project", the aptitude to be an accurate forecaster is relatively rare.[50] Our 30-year predictions are – we might judge simply by looking at the very poor base rates of analytical accuracy – unlikely to be particularly accurate.

It is easy to note that while social and demographic trends feature heavily in GST, below that level the place of technology in the scans becomes more central. The predominant focus on technology, perhaps a comfortable space for soldiers, may not be particularly comfortable in the long run. As science fiction author (and inventor of the term "cyberspace") William Gibson suggested, "the street finds its own uses for things".[51] Technologies rarely end up doing what their creators think they will do. The creation of the iPhone is a case in point. It is one of the most disruptive pieces of technology of the last 20 years, but its underlying technology (capacitive touchscreens, GPS modules, accelerometers, lithium-ion batteries, and microprocessors) had all existed for many years before they were combined into the juggernaut – that is, the iPhone.[52] Understanding each of those technologies by means of horizon-scanning would have been unlikely to foresee the iPhone or its effects, because these were cumulation of the non-linear behaviour of millions of people in a cultural and behavioural sphere, not a technological one. People and societies co-adapt to new technologies, and rarely do new technologies fundamentally change social functions. We use iPhones to enhance or change social behaviours, communicate, and socialise, rather than it causing entirely new behaviours.[53] It is not unreasonable to project that the same goes for military technologies. Indeed, one Canadian Forces officer noted that Agile Warrior's focus on technology risked dazzling the analysts involved and that warfare "is still (as it always has been) about massing combat power at the decisive time and space, and all adversary efforts will be about stopping that mass".[54] New technologies will not change war; war will co-adapt with it.

Resilience as key

Despite our best efforts, it is likely that forecasts of potential futures will remain largely unrepresentative of the future that actually comes to pass. Tetlock determined that prediction beyond five years dropped to an accuracy no better than chance – simply the result of the butterfly effect in non-linear systems.[55] Taleb notes, as has Tetlock, Gardner, and others, that the prediction record on political and economic events by most forecasters is so poor as to be pointless.[56] This raises questions about what states achieve out of their efforts at horizon scanning and scenario development. Unsure and worried about the future, we have a propensity to seek prediction beyond the actual ability to predict.[57] We are naturally drawn to forecasting as the solution rather than looking backwards, perhaps because we overestimate how different the future will be from now. This may be part of what Christopher Andrew has called "Historical Attention Span Deficit Disorder",[58] where policymakers not only do not know much history but fail to perceive its significance to policy. With such a mindset, futures scenarios may seem more realistic than they might to someone with a deeper historical knowledge or a good understanding of the weakness of forecasts. Basing future force decisions on horizon scanning inherits into that force all the errors of the futures work that precedes it.[59]

This does not argue against horizon scanning efforts but suggests the product be used for different purposes. It may be that horizon scanning fits into the older maxim frequently attributed to Dwight D. Eisenhower: "peace-time plans are of no particular value, but peace-time planning is indispensable".[60] What should most beneficially result from futures work is a raised awareness of where risk may lie, rather than the nature of the risk itself. This should lead planning staffs to weigh resilience and flexibility over the hope that the right piece of equipment is purchased or the right policy is pursued. Richard Danzig argues against seeking single answers to forecasted areas of challenge, and for the preparation of a wider range of unforecast events more common to the digital age.[61] The Future Force Concept seems to acknowledge that a key hurdle is simply quicker adaptation to change, noting that "to exploit the increasing pace of technological change, we must become more institutionally agile in our acquisitions system".[62] It was noted in the Agile Warrior conference that armies excel at buying and maintaining capital systems, and that this was not the way to handle the fielding of new AI and robotics systems, which will need quick purchases and quick turnover, to be effectively disposable systems.[63] The Australian army seems to acknowledge the need for competition of ideas in its experimentation on unmanned aerial vehicles (UAVs), having issued fixed-wing UAVs to all regular, reserve, and even cadet units to see who could come up with the most interesting concepts for their use. "It is only once we put these systems in soldiers' hands that we will truly discover the breadth of missions we could use them for", said Australian Maj Gen Kathryn Toohey, though this understates the genius of issuing them to teenaged cadets to see what the youngest population with the fewest preconceptions might come up with.[64] One British officer made a telling observation which further supports Danzig's rules, noting that

> we spend too much time trying to figure out if it's better to paint our vehicles tan or green – where will we fight most in the future, deserts or forests? – but this is irrelevant. What matters is how quick you can paint them red when you're told you'll be fighting on Mars.[65]

This officer's choice of Mars as the future destination may partly be in jest, but it makes a significant point: Horizon scanning techniques do not predict the future; they only offer a very few selections from among the infinite number of possibilities. This is some endorsement to the ideas behind the British Army's experimental land-force concept CF(L) 35, which above all is meant to be a more responsive, agile, and adaptable force, better able to cope with new forms of warfare. The ability to quickly adapt to change is the most frequent lesson in the history of forecasting the future. Military conservatism, and its close partner bureaucratic inertia, may be the nemesis of this need for resiliency. The challenge is therefore to balance the ability and agility to change with the caution and wisdom to adapt wisely. This is no small challenge.

Conclusion

Horizon scanning and futures methods offer us potentially very powerful tools to help cope with the inherent uncertainty of the future. These methods are closely allied to intelligence analysis methods, even if they are not always deployed directly to intelligence tasks, so it is important that intelligence practitioners remain aware of, and engaged with, their employment. A look at how the British Government and the military have embraced horizon scanning shows the variety of approaches that can be taken and the significant outcomes the process can have. We must however always remain sceptical of what horizon scanning scenarios can teach us. It is highly unlikely that the future war envisioned by the Agile Warrior programme, as one example only, will come to pass. At the same time, these futures methods can help tune current intelligence collection to the most significant or worrying trends in technology and warfare that may threaten our states. Furthermore, the act of futures inquiry itself, when done with valid data and careful methods, can help the staffs and decision-makers focus on the most critical uncertainties. Should the futures process cause governments to better prepare for the changes brought by the digital age, then it has accomplished its central goal.

Notes

1 Linton Wells: "Thoughts for the 2001 Quadrennial Defence Review", *The Rumsfeld Archive*, W000454-1, April 12, 2001.

2 UK MoD: "Strategic Trends Programme Future Operating Environment 2035 First Edition", 2015, https://library.rumsfeld.com/doclib/sp/2382/2001-04-12%20To%20 George%20W%20Bush%20et%20al%20re%20Predicting%20the%20Future.pdf.

3 Tom Simonite: "Moore's Law Is Dead. Now What?", *MIT Technology Review*, 2016, pp. 1–5.

4 David Thornton: "DoD Acquisition 'Slow by Design,' Can't Handle Cybersecurity Defense", *Federal News Radio*, October 24, 2017, https://federalnewsradio. com/cybersecurity-2017/2017/10/dod-acquisition-slow-by-design-cant-handle-cybersecurity-defense/.

5 Mark Sexton: "UK Cybersecurity Strategy and Active Cyber Defence – Issues and Risks", *Journal of Cyber Policy*, Vol. 1, No. 2, 2016, p. 223.

6 Richard K. Betts: "Analysis, War, and Decision: Why Intelligence Failures Are Inevitable", *World Politics*, Vol. 31, No. 1, 1978, pp. 61–89.

7 UK MoD: "The Future Character of Conflict", Shrivenham, UK, 2010.

8 Nick Hare & Peter Coghill: "Driver-Based Scenario Generation". London: Aleph Insights, 2016, www.alephinsights.com.

9 Peter Bishop, Andy Hines, & Terry Collins: "The Current State of Scenario Development: An Overview of Techniques", *Foresight: The Journal of Futures Studies, Strategic Thinking and Policy*, Vol. 9, No. 1, 2007, p. 5.

10 Hare & Coghill, *op. cit.*

11 Bishop, Hines, & Collins, *op. cit.*, pp. 5–25.

12 Norman Dalkey & Olaf Helmer: "An Experimental Application of the DELPHI Method to the Use of Experts", *Management Science*, Vol. 9, No. 3, 1963, pp. 458–67.

13 Bishop, Hines, & Collins, *ibid.*, p. 5.

14 *Ibid.*

15 Intervju med UK JIC Chairman Alex Allan, May 28, 2009.

16 UK MoD, "Quick Wins", *op. cit.*; Bishop, Hines, & Collins, *op. cit.*

17 House of Lords: "The Lord Speaker's River Room Series Seminar: The Global Risk Register", London, 2011.

18 Interview with UK JIC Chairman Alex Allan, *op. cit.*

19 Richards J. Heuer & Randolph H. Pherson: "Structured Analytic Techniques", in *Structured Analytic Techniques for Intelligence Analysis*, Los Angeles: CQ Press, 2011, p. 25.

20 DEFRA: Horizon Scanning and Futures Home, http://horizonscanning.defra.gov.uk/.

21 David Omand: "From Whence Owe We This Strange Intelligence: Organising Horizon Scanning", framført ved Gregynog, University of Wales Conference Centre, May 2, 2009.

22 DEFRA, Horizon Scanning and Futures Home, *op. cit.*

23 Omand: "From Whence Owe We This Strange Intelligence . . .", *op. cit.*

24 Stephen Marrin: "Intelligence Analysis Theory: Explaining and Predicting Analytic Responsibilities", *Intelligence and National Security*, Vol. 22, No. 6, 2007, p. 827.

25 David Kahn: "An Historical Theory of Intelligence", *Intelligence and National Security*, Vol. 16, No. 3, 2001, pp. 79–92.

26 UK Cabinet Office: "Review of Cross-Government Horizon Scanning", London, 2013, p. 1.

27 Anthony King: "Future Small Units and the Urban", Agile Warrior Conference, Worthington Gunner, February 22, 2018.

28 Interview with B1, UK OF-4, London, January 13, 2018.

29 UK MoD: "Strategic Trends Programme: Global Strategic Trends – Out to 2045", Shrivenham, UK, 2014, p. vii.

30 *Ibid.*, p. vii.

31 Intervju med Paul Norman, DCDC, Shrivenham, UK, February 12, 2018.

32 UK MoD: "Global Strategic Trends", *op. cit.*, p. xiv; UK MoD: "A Guide To Red Teaming: DCDC Guidance Note", Shrivenham, DCDC, 2010.

33 UK MoD: "Strategic Trends Programme Future Operating Environment 2035 First Edition", *op. cit.*, p. 1.

34 UK MoD: "The Future Character of Conflict", Shrivenham, DCDC, 2010.

35 UK MoD: "Strategic Trends Programme Future Operating Environment 2035 First Edition", *op. cit.*

36 UK Army HQ: "Agile Warrior Quarterly", Vol. 1, 2018, p. 1.

37 Army HQ: CF(L)35, 1* Draft.

38 Riccardo Vecchiato: "Strategic Planning and Organizational Flexibility in Turbulent Environments", *Foresight*, Vol. 17, No. 3, 2015, p. 258.

39 Bishop, Hines, & Collins, *op. cit.*

40 UK Cabinet Office, *op. cit.*, p. 2.

41 K. Garnett et al.: "Integrating Horizon Scanning and Strategic Risk Prioritisation Using a Weight of Evidence Framework to Inform Policy Decisions", *Science of the Total Environment*, Vol. 560, 2016, p. 83.

42 Erik J Dahl: *Intelligence and Surprise Attack.* Washington, DC: Georgetown University Press, 2013, p. 25.

43 Tim Wiener: *Legacy of Ashes.* London: Allen Lane, 2007, p. 479.

44 Garnett et al., *op. cit.*

45 Wendy L. Schultz: "The Cultural Contradictions of Managing Change: Using Horizon Scanning in an Evidence-based Policy Context", *Foresight*, Vol. 8, No. 4, 2006, pp. 3–12, https://doi.org/10.1108/14636680610681996.

46 Ben Anderson & Paul Stoneman: "Predicting the Socio-Technical Future (and Other Myths)", in Paul Warren, John Davies, & David Brown (eds.): *ICT Futures: Delivering Pervasive, Real-Time and Secure Services.* Chichester: John Wiley & Sons, 2008, s. 3.

47 Lawrence Freedman: *The Future of War: A History.* London: Allen Lane, 2017, p. 240; Paul Shawcross: "This Isn't the Petition Response You're Looking For", *Wired*, 2013, www.wired.com/2013/01/white-house-death-star/.

48 Freedman, *op. cit.*, p. 240.

49 Dan Gardner: *Future Babble.* New York: Random House, 2010, pp. 22–25.

50 Philip Tetlock & Dan Gardner: *Superforecasting: The Art and Science of Prediction.* London: Random House, 2015, pp. 16–19.

51 William Gibson: *Burning Chrome.* New York: Ace Books, 1987.

52 Jason Griffith: "The Problem with Experts – Why Uber, Tesla and the iPhone Are Disruptive Innovations", *Medium*, 2015, https://medium.com/snappea-design/the-problem-with-experts-why-uber-tesla-and-the-iphone-are-disruptive-innovations-54a03ea7c1fd.

53 Anderson & Stoneman, *op. cit.*, pp. 4–5.

54 Interview with Lt. Col. Shane Gifford, Canadian Land Warfare Centre, in Winterbourne Gunner, Salisbury UK, February 21, 2018.

55 Tetlock & Gardner, *op. cit.*, p. 244.

56 Nassim Nicholas Taleb: *The Black Swan: The Impact of the Highly Improbable*, Revised edition. London, 2010, p. xxiv.

57 Richard Danzig: "Driving in the Dark: Ten Propositions About Prediction and National Security", Washington, DC: Centre for a New American Security, 2011, pp. 9–10.

58 Christopher Andrew: "Reflections on Intelligence Historiography Since 1939", in Wilhelm Agrell & Gregory F. Treverton (eds.): *National Intelligence Systems: Current Research and Future Prospects.* Cambridge: Cambridge University Press, 2009, p. 55.

59 Danzig, *op. cit.*, p. 17.

60 "Letter from Dwight Eisenhower to Hamilton Fish Armstrong, December 31, 1950", in Louis Galambos et al. (eds.): *The Papers of Dwight David Eisenhower*, Vol. XI. Baltimore, MD: Johns Hopkins University Press, 1984, p. 1516.

61 Danzig, *op. cit.*, pp. 18–28.

62 UK MoD: "JCN 1/17 Future Force Concept", https://assets.publishing.service.gov.
   uk/government/uploads/system/uploads/attachment_data/file/643061/concepts_uk_
   future_force_concept_jcn_1_17.pdf.
63 Agile Warrior Conference, February 20–22, 2018, Winterbourne Gunner, Salisbury,
   UK.
64 Major General Kathryn Toohey: "Head Land Capability Speech to Defence and Security
   Equipment International", London, September 11, 2017, www.army.gov.au/our-work/
   speeches-and-transcripts/robotics-and-autonomous-systems-smart-machines-address-to-the.
65 Interview with B1, UK OF-4, London, January 4, 2018.

Further reading

Danzig, Richard: "Driving in the Dark: Ten Propositions about Prediction and National
   Security", Washington, DC: Centre for a New American Security, 2011.
Freedman, Lawrence: *The Future of War: A History*. London: Allen Lane, 2017.
Gardner, Dan: *Future Babble*. New York: Random House, 2010, pp. 22–25.
Garnett, Kenisha et al.: "Integrating Horizon Scanning and Strategic Risk Prioritisation
   Using a Weight of Evidence Framework to Inform Policy Decisions", *Science of the
   Total Environment*, Vols. 560–561, 2016, pp. 82–91.
Global Strategic Trends: The Future Starts Today, 6th edition. Shrivenham, UK: DCDC, 2018,
   https://assets.publishing.service.gov.uk/government/uploads/system/uploads/attachment_
   data/file/771309/Global_Strategic_Trends_-_The_Future_Starts_Today.pdf.
Tetlock, Philip, & Dan Gardner: *Superforecasting: The Art and Science of Prediction*. London:
   Random House, 2015.
Vecchiato, Riccardo: "Strategic Planning and Organizational Flexibility in Turbulent Envi-
   ronments", *Foresight*, Vol. 17, No. 3, 2015, pp. 257–273.

9 Capturing the customer's attention

Lars Haugom

Communicating intelligence to decision-makers is a final and decisive step in the intelligence process. Without efficient communication with intelligence customers, collection and analysis are both quite futile activities. If intelligence is to function as decision support, the analyst must not only have a good product but also be able to capture and hold on to the decision-makers' attention so the message can be received and perceived correctly. Capturing the customer's attention has never been an easy exercise, regardless of whether these customers are government ministers, government officials, military chiefs, or business leaders. Such professionals have busy agendas with only limited time to focus on each and every item on it. An intelligence analyst must therefore perform the art of presenting complicated issues in a simple and concise manner without compromising his or her professional integrity.[1]

This challenge has become greater in the digital age. Increasing amounts of information, faster information flows, more sources of information, and ever-more advanced communication technology are all intensifying the competition for people's attention – both in people's daily lives and in the workplace. New digital devices that can be carried everywhere and the opportunity to stay online continuously affect both our own ability to concentrate and the ability to get and keep the attention of others. In the book *Captivology*, journalist and IT entrepreneur Ben Parr discusses this development. Attention has become a scarcity, he writes. What this means is that if we want our product to be a success, be it a business idea, a work of art, a book, or a research report, we are increasingly forced to fight for the attention of others.[2]

Here, there is also an asymmetry between the intelligence analyst and the decision-maker that shapes their relationship with each other. The analyst must constantly consider the decision-maker's need for relevant and timely intelligence, while the decision-maker may choose to disregard the intelligence in favour of other sources of information. This asymmetry has become even more evident in the digital age because the access to alternative sources of information has grown to such a great extent. Consequently, in order to succeed in their work, intelligence analysts must be able to communicate well with their customers. As Espen Barth Eide writes in his chapter in this volume, this is a two-way process. The analyst must understand the customer's needs, while the customer in turn must develop so-called user competence – that is, an understanding of what kind of information intelligence analysis is able to produce. Put differently, in order to communicate correctly, the analyst and the customer must develop a good working relationship with each other.

In the literature on intelligence, intelligence communication has received far less attention than collection and analysis. Communication of intelligence is often regarded as a matter of structuring products and presenting briefs in the correct way.[3] Challenges regarding communication that intelligence services face in the digital age are even less discussed in the academic literature.[4] The aim of this chapter is to remedy such a shortage by highlighting some challenges related to intelligence communication in the digital age and then discuss some options intelligence agencies have to meet these challenges. The chapter can therefore also serve as the starting point for a future research agenda.

How to communicate intelligence

As stated in Chapter 1, this book equates intelligence with decision support. In order to work as decision support, intelligence must be reliable, timely, and relevant. Customers must be able to rely on what the services tell them, information and assessments must come prior to important decision points, and the intelligence must be of importance for decisions to be made. These requirements place demands on how intelligence is *communicated* to policymakers – whether it is in the form of a written report or a briefing. It is not sufficient just to deliver a product to the customer. As far as possible, intelligence analysts must also make sure that the product is perceived, understood, and *remembered* correctly by the decision-maker. In other words, the message must *stick* in the minds of those who make decisions so that it will have a lasting effect on them. Only then can we say that intelligence works as decision support in a real sense of the word.

One of the most effective tools the intelligence analyst has for communicating a message is undoubtedly the structure of his or her product. An intelligence report is not a crime novel where the mystery is solved towards the end of the book or a scientific article in which painstakingly constructed arguments culminate in a conclusion on the last page. In intelligence assessments, the main conclusions are presented first, usually in the form of bullet points or a brief summary. This is followed by a main section that elaborates on the conclusions with more details, with discussion and argumentation. Often, this main body will be structured by organising information and arguments in a prioritised order, with the most important information put first. This structure allows busy decision-makers to get to the key points quickly without having to read a whole report or listen through a full briefing. At the same time, supplementary information is available to the decision-maker's circle of advisors and professional expertise, who have more time and opportunity to focus on the details of the case.

Intelligence products are also characterised by a particular style of writing. Compared to other genres, intelligence texts can appear simple and sober with little room for literary effects and pompous formulations. James S. Major, a former intelligence analyst with the Defense Intelligence Agency (DIA) and later a lecturer at the Joint Military Intelligence College in the United States, sets out six principles on how to write a good intelligence product. The text must be clear, concise, and correct. In addition, it should be *tailored* to the reader's needs, *complete* as to the case analysed, and *coherent* so that it appears as a whole with focus on a central theme. In other words, the analyst should strive to write so that he or she is properly understood, use as few words as possible to formulate the message, and avoid ambiguous concepts that may confuse the reader. Above all, the analyst must write with regard to the customer and his needs.[5]

In addition, intelligence products should indicate the uncertainty associated with their content. Such uncertainty is associated with the content of the product itself – that is, the validity of the assessments – and with the information the product is based upon – that is, how solid and unambiguous the information is. For a decision-maker, knowledge of both of these types of uncertainty is essential in order to assess if and how intelligence information can be used as a basis for decision-making.

Uncertainty attached to intelligence assessments are most often indicated by probabilities. Probability concepts in use vary between national intelligence services but can, for example, take the form of a scale ranging from "very unlikely" via "unlikely" and "likely" to "very likely", possibly with more finely graded levels in between. Since people will always understand probability concepts differently; numerical scales have been developed that link the concepts to percentual probabilities. The NIS is using the following standard for probability concepts (Table 9.1).[6]

However, as Karl Halvor Teigen and Eirik Loehre, among others, have pointed out, even such scales can create differing perceptions of probability with the sender

Table 9.1 Standard for probability concepts in the Norwegian Intelligence Service

National standard	Definition	NATO standard
Highly likely ("meget sannsynlig")	The assessment is based on an unambiguous information base	Highly likely (<90%)
Likely ("sannsynlig")	The assessment is based on a relatively unambiguous information base	Likely (60–90%)
Possible ("mulig")	The assessment is based on an ambiguous information base	Even chance (40–60%)
Unlikely ("lite sannsynlig")	The assessment is based on a relatively unambiguous information base	Unlikely (10–40%)
Highly unlikely ("meget lite sannsynlig")	The assessment is based on an unambiguous information base	Highly unlikely (>10%)

and the receiver.[7] For example, a 70 per cent probability can give rise to differing interpretations depending on how the message is formulated linguistically by the sender and the degree to which the recipient perceives a given outcome as probable or unlikely. The statement "it is 70 percent certain that the Syrian regime was behind the chemical weapons attack last week" may give the receiver a different perception of likelihood than if the analyst writes: "*the service* is 70 per cent sure the Syrian regime was behind the attack with chemical weapons last week". Both statements actually say the same thing but can establish different perceptions of probability for decision-makers. The first statement refers to an "external" probability that initially seems more objective and reliable but which says little about the analyst's own judgement. The second statement refers to an "internal" probability, making the assessment seem more dependent on the analyst and therefore less reliable. On the other hand, the second statement may emphasise the analyst's own beliefs as a professional and therefore may strengthen the impression of probability.

Personal characteristics of the receiver can also affect how statements of probability are perceived. Preconceptions can, for example, stem from both attitudes and existing knowledge of the matter at hand.[8] For instance, a decision-maker may choose to place greater emphasis on some issues over others in an intelligence report based on his own attitudes to the subject or reject the likelihood of a given development outlined in the report based on his own knowledge and beliefs. An alternative to communicating probabilities in the text is to use graphical figures and charts. Charles S. Weiss has discussed various ways of communicating uncertainty and probability in this way, including box, line, and pie charts. By means of such tools, the uncertainty and probability of a particular outcome can be made clearer and less ambiguous for the receiver.[9]

However, a good structure, precise language, and the indication of uncertainty are not in themselves sufficient to support intelligence customers in a decision-making process. Intelligence communication is not just about having a good product but also about attracting the attention of decision-makers so that a message will be correctly perceived, understood, and remembered. Psychological studies of organisation and management since the 1960s have shown that decision-makers have limited rationality and ability to concentrate on information. Moreover, they tend to have a preconceived attitude to what information they focus on and which decisions they make based on this information. There is much to suggest that humans are only able to access and store a certain amount of information in their short-term memory, and only information that is perceived as sufficiently relevant. The presumed irrelevant is filtered out, while that which is perceived as relevant enough is stored in the long-term memory, which has virtually unlimited capacity.[10]

On the other hand, studies of social influence have shown that it is quite possible to awaken people's attention and get a message through. Knowledge of people's preferences, strategies for shaping the context of communication, and linguistic techniques to arouse interest and engagement are some options highlighted in these studies.[11] The more we know about the person we want to communicate with, and the more it is possible to shape the actual communication situation, the more the message can be structured to appear relevant and important, and made to "stick" with the receiver.

Intelligence services can have some advantages over other institutions in this context. Firstly, these services are usually given specific tasks by decision-makers and are expected to resolve the tasks before specified deadlines. In other words, there is already an established relationship between intelligence services and decision-makers, and the services enjoy a certain status and priority as contributors to the decision-making process. Usually, intelligence services will also have a privileged access to national decision-makers. For example, until the Trump administration, the US Director of National Intelligence held a daily briefing for the US president.[12]

In addition, intelligence services presumably have access to sources that other professional advisors do not and should therefore be able to contribute vital information, analyses, and assessments to decision-makers. This means that they are listened to in a special way compared to other sources – especially in national crises where there will often be a lack of reliable information and the time factor is critical. Traditionally, intelligence services have also had access to technology and resources that did not exist outside the intelligence community – for example, data collection from satellite and radar. This gave intelligence analysts the opportunity to document movements and developments in other states and from non-state actors in a unique way. Intelligence services can also take advantage of the aura of secrecy that still surrounds their work. Few things are better suited to attract attention than being initiated into secrets that not everyone else has access to.

However, intelligence services are not the only source on which national decision-makers base their decisions. As Espen Barth Eide writes in Chapter 3, most decision-makers will have their own apparatus of advisors and professional experts to lean on in the decision-making process. In addition, they have access to other sources such as diplomatic cables, research reports, the media, and their colleagues at home and abroad. In this context, one can say that intelligence services complement other sources of information and help decision-makers by broadening their decision-making basis.

Although intelligence agencies will often have a privileged position and access to national decision-makers, they will not necessarily have a decisive influence on the decisions being made. Stephen Marrin, associate professor of intelligence studies at James Madison University, has, for example, asked why strategic intelligence in the United States has had so little influence on US foreign policy. One possible explanation is the decision-makers' bias, based on their own attitudes to and knowledge of foreign policy issues. Another explanation is that policymakers must take a number of considerations into account that are not directly related to the issue at hand, such as internal bureaucratic struggles, the domestic political situation, and budget costs associated with different policy options.[13]

However, Marrin believes that preconceptions and such "external" considerations are insufficient to explain why strategic intelligence generally has had little influence on US foreign policy decisions. Instead, he points out that decision-makers are often very well informed about their fields of expertise. In many ways, they are their own analysts and do not readily accept assessments presented by intelligence services. As already discussed, decision-makers have access to information and expertise outside intelligence service channels. Much of this information comes through their own network with colleagues at home and abroad, and by way of contacts in the state apparatus, academia, and business. This enables decision-makers to make their own analyses and possibly arrive at other conclusions than the intelligence services. In addition, intelligence assessments – to the extent that they deviate from the decision-maker's own conclusions – can increase uncertainty and complicate the decisions to be made. Intelligence assessments can therefore be perceived as "bothersome" if they go against established beliefs and policy. According to Marrin, it is more likely that intelligence assessments that go against established policy will be discarded than the policy itself.[14]

What is new in the digital age is that competition for attention has become much sharper. The amount of information, the speed of the information flow, and the rapid development of new information and communication technology all contribute to an increased competition for the ear of decision-makers. In addition, there is a cultural change regarding how decision-makers wish to receive and process information. This change challenges the established forms of intelligence communication.

New forms of intelligence communication

In a world with more and more impressions and a growing number of channels for information, the competition for people's attention also becomes greater. For example, a study made by the Norwegian School of Economics showed that the average Norwegian checks his cell phone 150 times a day.[15] Further, it can take up to 20 minutes from being distracted until we regain full concentration, and thus the time intervals when we are really focused become short.[16] There is little reason to believe that decision-makers represent an exception from the general population in this context. From checking the first email in the morning until writing the last message late at night, a decision-makers' day is filled with information. In this sea of information, it has become more challenging to perceive everything, separate the essential from the non-essential, and filter out true from false.

Another feature of the digital age is that technology offers new opportunities to shape and communicate a message. "Single media products" in fixed formats – such as written reports, newspaper articles, oral presentations, and traditional radio and television programmes – are being replaced by online multimedia products – for example, the online editions of newspapers. In multimedia products, text, graphics, maps, photographs, and video clips can be combined in one and the same page to give a more comprehensive presentation of an issue. Online services have also made users increasingly accustomed to digital communication formats. Such services provide continuous access to news and entertainment, creating expectations among users of getting information quickly, often at the same time as a situation arises and develops, whether it is a terrorist attack somewhere in the world, a sporting event, or an interactive game. One can therefore say that this technological development has resulted in a cultural change regarding where and when we receive and process information. In addition, many users of web-based services are no longer just consumers of information but actively participate in its production by publishing photos on Instagram, video clips on YouTube, blog posts on WordPress, and updates on Facebook and Twitter.

Randolph H. Pherson, former CIA analyst and founder of the analysis company Pherson Associates, and Rubén Arcos, professor of communication science at King Juan Carlos University of Spain, expect a generational shift among national policymakers regarding how they want intelligence communicated. The new generation will want control over when, where, and how they are informed. They will want the freedom to search for information and analysis at times that suit them best and decide for themselves how much information about a topic they receive. They will want updates that they can choose to read or ignore depending on their daily schedule.[17] In short, in the digital age, decision-makers are no longer passive receivers of information; they also want to take a more active part in the communication process. One example is former President Donald Trump, who frequently communicated with the world through Twitter. Trump was not alone among world leaders to use social media, of course, but he distinguished himself by posting highly personalised messages at odd times of the day.

A final and significant feature of the digital age is that state intelligence services are experiencing increasing competition from private, commercial actors that provide information and analysis covering many of the same geographical areas and subjects as the intelligence services do. Many of these private actors also have access to resources that were previously the exclusive domain of intelligence and security organisations. Analysis firms such as Stratfor, Jane's, and Oxford Analytica offer assessments and situation updates that are quite similar to intelligence products. By means of an international network of analysts and informants, and with the help of civil satellite imagery and advanced computer technology, several of these agencies are able to maintain a continuous coverage of several of the world's conflict areas. In some cases, private organisations provide assessments that rival those of state intelligence services. These organisations therefore challenge the position of intelligence services as providers of unique information and analysis. The point here is not that commercial actors can or will replace intelligence services in supporting national decision-makers but only that intelligence products do not appear as exclusive as they did before. One can therefore further argue that intelligence products now face stiffer competition from commercial sources when it comes to attracting the attention of customers.

In order to remain timely and relevant in the digital age, intelligence services must adopt new technologies and adapt to new forms of communication and collaboration. For analysts, this may entail changes in writing style, production formats, and ways of collaboration. Three concrete measures in this regard may be to acquire more of the news journalists' language and writing style, use online multimedia formats to communicate with decision-makers, and enter into new forms of collaboration on production.

Look to the news journalists

One means of tackling the competition for attention is to apply a style of writing that arouses interest and engagement, and that makes the message stick with decision-makers.[18] Journalists already write in this way. Parallels have previously been drawn between intelligence analysts and traditional news journalists as professional groups.[19] Both aim to explain the facts, driving factors, and potential outcomes of constantly evolving situations. In order to be relevant, both also rely on timely deliveries to their audiences and work against strict deadlines. The analysis environment in an intelligence service can also be reminiscent of a newsroom, with analysts working on time-limited tasks. Journalists and analysts will also in many cases focus on the same questions, although their target groups are somewhat different.

Furthermore, both journalists and analysts must catch the receiver's attention in order to get their message across. The difference is that journalists rely on this to a much greater extent than analysts. Intelligence analysts find themselves in an institutional context where policymakers actively seek information from them. Journalists have a far looser relationship with their readers and viewers, and must work continuously to capture and hold on to the interest of their audience.

There are also some striking similarities between how intelligence analysts and journalists write. If we compare a textbook in intelligence analysis with guidelines for a journalist at the *Reuters* news agency, there is a great deal of correspondence between how a news article and an intelligence report is produced. Both the news journalist and the intelligence analyst have decision-makers among their target audience – although the journalist, of course, also writes for the general public. Both have integrity, independence, and impartiality as guiding ideals, and their texts should be clear, concise, and correct in terms of how the information is presented and in the linguistic precision of the text. The main points of a text should always come first in the form of a preamble or summary; the case itself should be established early in the text by specifying "Who ?", "What?", "Where?", and (optionally) "Why?"; the text must be brief, with well-founded arguments; and the different points should come in order of priority so that it is possible to "cut from below" without losing the core messages. Source references and source criticism are central in both professions, although the intelligence analyst will not normally refer directly to their sources in the text. Titles and headlines should be sharp and clear and tell the reader as clearly as possible what the text and individual sections of it are about. Both for the news journalist and the intelligence analyst, it is more important to be forward-looking than backward-looking in their perspectives. Finally, in both professions, quality control is mainly done by means of "peer review" where colleagues in the newsroom or analysis department read and comment on the content before the text is submitted for final approval.[20]

However, at one point journalists and other professional writers differ in their style of writing. As pointed out by Peter Cole, former news journalist and now professor of journalism at the University of Sheffield, it is crucial that a news story is interesting or entertaining so people will read or hear it. Journalism is basically about recognising a story and telling it to others. Ultimately, there is only one purpose of a newspaper journalist's work: getting a general public to read the story. Journalism differs from both fiction writing and scientific research. The regular newsreader does not spend much time reading a newspaper article – unlike the reader of a novel or a scholarly article. The newsreader will often skim an article first to find out if it is worth reading through or not. The journalist must therefore capture the reader's attention immediately – and then hold on to it until the story is read. If not, the reader will quickly browse or click on to something else that appears more interesting.[21]

As Cole points out, it is difficult to write in an easy and engaging way so the reader wants to continue reading and to explain so clearly that all readers understand and want to understand. However, this is the journalist's job.[22] It is not difficult to see a parallel here to the intelligence analyst who not only has to convey her message to busy decision-makers but also must make sure that it is perceived, understood, and remembered correctly.

So what can intelligence analysts learn more from the writing style of news journalists?

Firstly, journalists strive to write in a simple way on complex issues so that the reader can easily understand what the issue is about and wants to understand more. Professional experts, on the other hand, tend to write too complicated for an audience of non-experts. In the book *Made to Stick* by Dan and Chip Heath, this phenomenon is called "the curse of knowledge". The curse of knowledge is that "once we know something, we find it hard to imagine what it was like not to know it. Our knowledge has 'cursed' us. And it becomes difficult for us to share our knowledge with others, because we can't readily re-create our listeners' state of mind". According to Heath and Heath, it is therefore necessary to reshape the message we have so that it is actually understood and remembered by those we want to reach.[23]

Secondly, journalists try to write engagingly to keep the reader's attention through a text. This can be done by comparing facts in the text with something that is easy for the reader to relate to, including quotes and statements from people mentioned, or by using unexpected titles and subheadings that will "awaken" the reader. For example, it would be more effective to compare the devastation of war in a part of Syria with the size of the reader's hometown than to specify the area in square miles. Quotes from heads of state or warlords can express their intentions better than just describing those intentions in the text. And a catchy title or sub-heading is better suited to attract readers' attention and engagement than descriptive phrases.

Last but not least, journalists will often structure their texts as storytelling, giving rise to the designation of a news article or television report as a "story". Mary O'Sullivan, a former CIA officer who is now working as a developer with the private analytics agency Pherson Associates, has advocated using just storytelling to structure intelligence products. Storytelling is the oldest form of communication we know, and a good story is something we remember to a much greater extent than an analysis report or the briefing of a professional question.[24] Intelligence analysis and storytelling also have many corresponding key elements. Intelligence analysis should explain what or how something happened, who was behind it, when and where it happened, why it happened, and what it means (which implications it has). Storytelling, for its parts, includes a plot, characters, a setting, a theme, and a goal for the action. The structure of storytelling may therefore also be suitable for intelligence communication.

Info box 9.1 Key elements of storytelling and intelligence analysis

Storytelling	Intelligence analysis
• Plot	• What/how?
• Characters	• Who?
• Setting	• When/where?
• Theme	• Why?
• Goals for action	• What does it mean?

Stories stick with us to a greater extent than other forms of communication. Why some ideas and stories live on through generations, while others crumble and die, is also the main question in Chip and Dan Heath's book *Made to Stick*. Why is it that some ideas are understood and remembered and have a lasting effect on those who hear about them? The authors found that surviving ideas are characterised by six principles:

1 They are *simple* in that they contain a single thought that is easy to reproduce.
2 They contain an *unexpected* element that makes them arouse curiosity and interest.
3 They are *concrete* in that they refer to common human experiences that are easy to recognize.
4 They are *credible*, either because the person presenting the idea is an expert, or because the idea itself can easily be tested.
5 They awaken the *emotions* of the recipient.
6 They are presented as a *story*.

By means of these principles, we can also reshape our own message so that it sticks better with the receivers.[25]

It is neither possible nor desirable for intelligence products to contain *all* the features of storytelling. Too many of these features may appear artificial in a report or a briefing, and therefore they are more likely to arouse irritation than interest. However, intelligence analysts may find it helpful to use one or more of the six principles in their writing to give a message greater impact on decision-makers.

Intelligence analysts are trained to think in a critical, systematic, and logical manner. The idea of structuring their products as a story may therefore seem strange. However, as O'Sullivan points out, there is no contradiction between logical thinking and storytelling. Both are legitimate ways of organising information. The former relies on the power of argument, while the latter relies on analogies and vividness in order to convince. In either case, the analyst must be aware of his or her assumptions and bias, and avoid logical flaws and abuse of emotionally charged twists and turns.[26]

All analytical work is also basically about persuasion. Every analyst has a basic idea that he or she wants to convince others of. The question is how this can be done in the most efficient way. For intelligence analysts, it is not about using tools to manipulate or control an audience but to inform, alert, update, or impress a new perspective on a decision-maker.[27]

For this reason, the intelligence analyst must also be alert to the fine line between stories as a writing technique and storytelling. By structuring his or her products as a story, the analyst may inadvertently put a spin on assessments that in the worst case could mislead decision-makers rather than inform them. Applying a more journalistic style would therefore require that analysts are well aware of the risk of advocacy when writing their products.

Writing in a simple and engaging way, and making the message stick with the receiver, is an acquired art that requires lots of training. For intelligence analysts it may be challenging to change their writing style in such a manner. This is not to say that intelligence analysts write in a complicated and boring way to begin with, only that they generally have not faced the same requirements as journalists when it comes to catching the attention of an audience.

One way to introduce more of the journalists' writing style and language in intelligence analysis may be to employ former journalists in the analysis branches of intelligence services. This can stimulate learning and transfer of knowledge to the intelligence community and create acceptance for a more journalistic form in intelligence communication. Another way would be to develop basic internal guidelines for good language and structure in intelligence products.

Using multimedia products

Another way intelligence analysts can meet the increasing competition for decision-makers' attention is to rely more on online multimedia products in intelligence communication. Multimedia can be defined as any combination of text, graphics, video, audio, and animation in a shareable format that users can communicate with using a digital device.[28] Decision-makers are already familiar with this format from open online services, and potentially the format can give them the same flexibility when receiving and processing intelligence. For intelligence services, multimedia products also provide better opportunities for communicating intelligence to decision-makers – in terms of both quantity and content.

Decision-makers are already accustomed to receiving multimedia information on digital media, giving them the freedom to read information they find relevant at times that suit them best. "Single-media products", such as an intelligence report or a briefing, do not give decision-makers the same flexibility. With a traditional intelligence report, it is in many ways the analyst who decides what the decision-maker needs to know (within the scope of a given request), and an intelligence briefing requires the decision-maker to be present at a specific time to receive information.

Evidently, intelligence analysts are already using multimedia products to some extent. For example, presentation tools such as Microsoft PowerPoint make it possible to combine text with images and links to video and audio files. However, this software is relatively limited compared to the opportunities offered by online solutions. Web-based multimedia formats are powerful tools that allow for the integration of images, video, audio, maps, and other information graphics, providing completely different opportunities to shape and convey a message than the traditional intelligence report and briefing. Information graphics are also better suited than plain text to arouse emotions and engagement in the receiver, for example when outlining future scenarios and their implications.

Furthermore, with online multimedia solutions, it is possible to update decision-makers faster and more continuously by adding new information as it becomes available, without having to publish a new report or schedule another briefing. In this way, decision-makers can potentially achieve much of the same flexibility when receiving and processing intelligence information as when reading a newspaper article or a research paper report online. The intelligence report can still be written according to a fixed format but with links in the text to previous reports and supplementary information regarding the same issue. Video clips or podcasts with a briefing on the issue can also be integrated into the report format. In sum, multimedia products contribute to the transition from a system where customers "pull" information from the intelligence services by issuing information requirements to a system where the services actively "push" information to customers, making relevant intelligence accessible to decision-makers as new information becomes available.

From time to time, customers will request to see the unprocessed intelligence that assessments are based upon.[29] Intelligence services usually find it difficult to comply with such requests because single-source reports only give a small snippet of a larger image and do not contextualise the information. In addition, unprocessed intelligence may contain sensitive data on sources and how the information was obtained. However, multimedia products provide opportunities to include "washed" versions of single-source reports and to place them into a larger context, for example by using explanatory text to indicate how the report should be understood, the accuracy of the data, the credibility of the source, and how much the analyst relies on the content for his or her own assessments.[30] For example, parts of the source material can be added as attachments to the intelligence report, appearing as hyperlinks on a web page.

Generally, multimedia products give intelligence services increased opportunities for making different types and amounts of information available to customers. Links in a report can, for example, give access to biographies of people who have been featured in the text, background information on past events and developments, and basic data on geographical locations and organisations. It is also possible to link to information about the analytical framework used to produce the report, such as the main assumptions behind assessments, critical information gaps, and indicators used in scenario-building.

In the intelligence community, it is debated whether this type of information should be shared with customers. It can be argued that the analytical framework used by an intelligence service is an internal work tool that should not be made known outside the organisation, mainly because it says something about the service's line of thinking and its capabilities. The counterargument is that knowledge of work methods, way of thinking, and information basis increases the customers' understanding of the intelligence products they receive and enables them to use the products better as support for decisions.

The quantum of extensive changes intelligence analysts must be prepared for with the introduction of online multimedia formats is not so easy to predict. We do not know to which extent the new formats will be introduced. However, changes in news journalism can give some clues as to the type of restructuring that potentially awaits intelligence analysts in the digital age. In their book *Newspaper Journalism*, Peter Cole and Tony Harcup write that it is no longer sufficient to tell a good story. New technology has contributed to the transformation of newspapers into media houses. A media house disseminates news and entertainment in various channels, more or less erasing the distinction between newspaper, the Internet, and television. The need for good layout and structure is now secondary to the need for a good and functional website architecture, because readers must be able to find relevant information on the website with as few clicks as possible. Today's journalists are expected to deliver content as much as writing a story, and what they write should be applicable to both newspaper and web and television media.[31]

Moreover, for online journalists, daily deadlines are history. News is published continuously and updated as a situation or event develops. The only requirements are that the information is ready for publication, that it can be updated regularly, and that a decision is made as to where, how, and when the information will be published.[32]

Rubén Arcos has argued that analysts should have the same expertise as online journalists when it comes to using multimedia in intelligence analysis.[33] Transferred to intelligence analysis, one can envision a future production setting where analysts primarily communicate with customers using websites containing text, image, sound, graphics, and animations that are tightly integrated, and where such websites largely have replaced both the traditional intelligence report and briefing. For example, reporting on an event or situation can be disseminated simultaneously in the form of a written text and as an oral briefing on a video clip or audio file. Instead of reporting at regular intervals, web pages can be updated when new assessments or information from the intelligence service become available. These updates can be received by customers on digital devices and processed at times that are convenient for them.

Multimedia products communicated by digital devices have already begun to enter the intelligence world. For example, according to the *Washington Post*, former US President Barack Obama received several of his intelligence briefings on a tablet, which allowed analysts to add video clips, audio files, and interactive graphics to the daily report.[34]

New forms of collaboration

New information technology also opens up for novel forms of collaboration, internally in intelligence services, between different services, and between intelligence analysts and decision-makers. This offers entirely new opportunities to engage and involve decision-makers in the production and communication of intelligence, which in turn can help ensure that intelligence services remain timely and relevant. The new technology can also help to break up the traditional organisation model for intelligence services where collectors and analysts work in separate "silos" with little contact across the professional environments.

Using web-based wikis, several intelligence analysts can contribute directly to the same report or briefing, without having to give individual inputs to a joint draft that requires continuous revisions. A wiki is a website that allows users to collaborate on content, editing, and structure. Because access rights for these users can be defined at different levels, the use of wikis opens up for multiple participants in the production process – from both inside and outside individual intelligence services. For example, the technology enables collection branches to participate directly in the production process by adding information and data into a product draft rather than sending reports to the analysts. If several national secret services are expected to contribute to the same product, analysts from these services can also use wikis to work together rather than spend time on coordinating individual drafts. Customers can also be invited into the actual intelligence process, both to provide relevant information from channels other than those intelligence services have access to and to adjust and address information needs as new intelligence becomes available or a situation develops. The technology also allows for the use of virtual conference rooms on the web where analysts and decision-makers can meet for briefings, updates, and discussions without leaving their workplaces.[35]

The possibilities and limitations of intelligence communication

The new technology can contribute to the continued timeliness and relevance of intelligence services in several ways.

Firstly, it can make the production and communication of intelligence faster and more efficient. Information can be obtained and turned into intelligence products more quickly than today. Instead of having agreed deadlines for reports and fixed dates for briefings, the new technology can enable intelligence services to keep decision-makers continuously updated on top prioritised issues and developing situations. At the same time, analysts can have an ongoing dialogue with policymakers about information needs and how these needs should be adjusted. Intelligence services could thus approach the same 24-hour continuous cycle found in many international news media.

Secondly, the technology can make national intelligence and security services more coordinated and, to a greater extent, speak with one voice on issues where their areas of responsibility overlap. In a Norwegian context, this may, for example, apply to transnational issues where both the NIS and the Police Security Service are responsible for supporting decision-makers. If analysts from different national services can collaborate directly on the same product draft, this can result in a qualitatively better product, a simpler production process, and a more consistent basis for decision-makers when they are making decisions. In addition, where there is real professional disagreement between services, such disagreement can be better expressed in a joint product than in several individual products from the different services.

Thirdly, the new technology could build down organisational divides in the intelligence community, both within and between intelligence services, and between the services and decision-makers. By allowing analysts, collectors, and customers access to the same web-based production environment, albeit at different levels and with different user rights, they can all become contributors to the overall process and no longer be just producers or users of intelligence. When it comes to decision-makers, this type of access to and participation in the production process may give them a stronger sense of ownership and commitment to the intelligence products they receive. The introduction of new information and communication technology could thus help maintain much of the privileged position and access that intelligence services have had to national policymakers.

Nevertheless, there is reason to believe that the nature of the intelligence business will restrict how quickly and far this technological development can and should go. Four factors are of particular importance here: capacity, reliability, trust, and security.

Switching to online websites that can be updated continuously can easily create expectations among decision-makers that the intelligence services will provide new information about situations and events 24–7. This would challenge the capacity of both intelligence analysts producing the information and the decision-makers consuming it.

Switching from a "pull system" to a "push system" for communication with decision-makers would in itself be resource-intensive as deliveries can be continuous and not tied to agreed deadlines or fixed times. In addition, such a change can make the services prioritise current production and publishing over more long-term analytical work. If analysts become more occupied with filling web pages with content than producing solid analyses, it may lead to a decline in the quality of intelligence products over time. Such a development has already become evident in many media houses where journalists spend more and more time adapting content to different formats (paper, website, web-TV, etc.), and less and less time researching and writing their own articles.[36]

This is also relevant to the discussion on how intelligence services should deal with so-called "non-change". These are cases where there have been no significant changes in a situation that analysts follow. One point of view in this discussion is that intelligence services need to be timely; therefore, they should continuously be reporting on developments in prioritised areas. There will always be *some* development in a country or conflict area that is worthy of reporting. The counterposition is that intelligence services need to be relevant and thus should report to decision-makers only when significant changes occur. Over-reporting can give decision-makers the impression that a development is more significant than it is and burden them with information that they strictly do not need. The debate among intelligence professionals on what to report and when is likely to intensify with the introduction of web-based reporting, as websites provide such great opportunities to communicate and continuously update their customers.

For intelligence services, one possible solution to these challenges would be to use a "push system" fully during a national crisis and other situations that require continuous attention over a period of time, but only to a limited extent under normal circumstances. In other words, intelligence products will be communicated using online multimedia formats, but the updating frequency will vary between different focus areas and according to the customers' priorities.

With increasing use of multimedia formats, intelligence services also need to get around the so-called firehose-syndrome[37] – that is, that decision-makers become so overwhelmed by updates and additional information that they are not able to effectively use the intelligence as decision support. In order to avoid such overloading of customers, intelligence products must be structured so that the most important assessments appear first, with the possibility to move on to more specific information. The appearance of an online intelligence report may therefore be similar to existing document formats, even if the report will also contain new options for including information. For example, decision-makers will be able to choose among reading the report in its entirety or just the main assessments, reading background material, finding the intelligence service's basic assumptions about the subject, or watching the report being briefed in a video clip. There could also be options to access source material and give feedback to the analyst who has written the report.

It will also be imperative for intelligence services to make sure that the ambition to remain timely and relevant in the digital age does not detract from the need to be reliable. Decision-makers must be able to trust that the information provided by intelligence services is as accurate as before. As already mentioned, there are limits to how entertaining and engaging an intelligence report can be without compromising its reliability.

Another reason why intelligence analysts should be cautious with using literary effects is the need to be taken seriously by customers. Intelligence assessments can easily be regarded as unserious if the style of writing is too similar to tabloid newspapers or fiction. Ultimately, the raison d'etre of intelligence services is based upon the decision-makers' trust in them, and this confidence can easily be undermined if the products appear as sensational news or sheer storytelling. There are some expectations attached to all literary genres, including intelligence products.

Furthermore, trust between intelligence services and policymakers is built through face-to-face contact, often over a long period. In this context, intelligence analysts act as trusted interlocutors for customers, both by delivering analytical products and by maintaining the dialogue between the intelligence service and their customers.[38] Neither multimedia products nor other forms of communication technology can replace this contact without at the same time risk undermining the trusting relationship that has been built up. Most likely, therefore, new formats and forms of communication will come in addition to the established forms of interaction and face-to-face dialogue with policymakers.

Finally, the use of new technology, formats, and forms of collaboration must be weighed against security concerns. If policymakers are to read and process intelligence in the same way that they manage open-source information and emails, this will require a completely new security regime for intelligence communication. This is partly about security for transferring data and for digital media units such as tablets and smartphones, but also about developing security awareness in decision-makers as to when, where, and how they can receive and read intelligence information. It seems unlikely that intelligence reports and briefings can be received "on the fly" and be read by decision-makers on their way to a meeting or waiting in an airport. More likely, decision-makers will be trusted with special digital units accompanied by strict user guidelines. Classified information on digital media must be secured as satisfactorily as a hard copy of an intelligence report, or a meeting room used for intelligence briefings. Security concerns will therefore inevitably put restrictions on how extensive the technological revolution in intelligence communication can be. For decision-makers, there will still be a difference between receiving an intelligence report and a news report from *Reuters*.

Conclusion

The digital age has brought forth new demands and expectations regarding how information is communicated. This is a reality that intelligence services must also take into account. Established forms of intelligence communication such as reports and briefings are no longer sufficient if intelligence analysts are to succeed in capturing the customers' attention and getting their message across. This chapter has argued that analysts should look to the media business when facing the challenges of the digital age, both by acquiring the writing techniques of journalists and by adopting new multimedia formats and modes of communication. Such an adaptation will help intelligence services remain relevant and timely to their customers in the new information reality that we live in. At the same time, the uniqueness of the services will limit how fast and far this adaptation can go. For example, the requirements for timeliness and relevance may not compromise the equally important requirements for reliability and security. Decision-makers must still have trust in the assessments that intelligence analysts provide, and that classified information is handled responsibly. New formats and technology will therefore not be able to fully replace the traditional forms of intelligence communication. Not least, a good relationship between the services and their clients will depend on intelligence analysts still meeting decision-makers face to face, and not just through new formats such as web-based presentations and video meetings.

Notes

1 See for example Robert D. Blackwill & Jack Davis: "A Policymaker's Perspective on Intelligence Analysis", in Loch K. Johnson and James J. Wirtz (eds.): *Strategic Intelligence: Windows into a Secret World*. Los Angeles, CA: Roxbury Publishing Company, 2004, pp. 120–126.
2 Ben Parr: *Captivology: The Science of Capturing People's Attention*. New York: Harper Collins, 2015, pp. 2–5.

3 See for example James S. Major: *Communicating with Intelligence: Writing and Briefing in the Intelligence and National Security Communities*. Lanham, MD: The Scarecrow Press, 2008.
4 An important exception is Rubén Arcos and Randolph H. Pherson (eds.): *Intelligence Communication in the Digital Era: Transforming Security, Defence and Business*. Lanham, MD: The Scarecrow Press, 2015.
5 Major, *op. cit.*, Chapter 2.
6 Norwegian Intelligence Service (NIS): *Fokus*. Oslo: Etterretningstjenesten, 2019, p. 102.
7 Erik Løhre & Halvor Teigen: "There Is a 60% Probability, But I'm 70% Certain; Communicative Consequences of External and Internal Expressions of Uncertainty", *Thinking and Reasoning*, Vol. 22, No. 4, 2015, pp. 369–396. See also Karl Halvor Teigen: "On the Nature of Probability Judgements", *Psykologisk rapportserie*, University of Bergen, Vol. 5, No. 1, 1984.
8 Charles Weiss: "Communicating Uncertainty in Intelligence and Other Professions", *International Journal of Intelligence and Counterintelligence*, Vol. 25, No. 1, 2008, pp. 69–70.
9 *Ibid.* pp. 71–76.
10 See for example Richard Heuer: *The Psychology of Intelligence Analysis*. Washington, DC: Government Printing Office, 1999; and Daniel Kahneman, Paul Slovic, & Amos Tversky (eds.): *Judgement under Uncertainty: Heuristics and Biases*. Cambridge: Cambridge University Press, 1982.
11 See for example Kevin Hogan: *Invisible Influence: The Power to Persuade Anyone, Anytime, Anywhere*. Hoboken, NJ: Wiley, 2013; and Robert Cialdini: *Influence: The Psychology of Persuasion*. New York: Collins, 2009.
12 Adrian Wolfberg: "The President's Daily Brief: Managing the Relationship between Intelligence and the Policymaker", *Political Science Quarterly*, Vol. 132, No. 2, 2017.
13 Stephen Marrin: "Why Strategic Intelligence Has Limited Influence on American Foreign Policy", *Intelligence and National Security*, Vol. 32, No. 6, 2017, pp. 725–726.
14 *Ibid.*, pp. 727–730.
15 Ida Kvittingen: "Why Some Become Addicted to the Mobile Phone" (in Norwegian), *Forskning.no*, August, 2017, https://forskning.no/samfunn-mobiltelefon-psykologi-teknologi/2017/08/derfor-blir-du-avhengig-av-mobiltelefonen.
16 Parr, *op. cit.*, p. 2.
17 Randolph H. Pherson & Rubén Arcos: "Introduction", in Rubén Arcos & Randolph H. Pherson (eds.): *Intelligence Communication in the Digital Era: Transforming Security, Defence and Business*. Houndmills, Basingstoke: Palgrave Macmillan, 2015, p. 3.
18 Mary O'Sullivan: "Presentational Tradecraft: A New Skill", in Randolph H. Pherson & Rubén Arcos (eds.), *op. cit.*, p. 25.
19 One of the first to point out this parallel was Sherman Kent in *Strategic Intelligence for American World Policy*. Princeton, NJ: Princeton University Press, 1949. See also Wilhelm Agrell & Gregory F. Treverton: *National Intelligence and Science: Beyond the Great Divide in Analysis and Policy*. Oxford: Oxford University Press, 2015, pp. 80–109.
20 See for example, Major, *op. cit.*; and *Reuters Handbook of Journalism*, http://handbook.reuters.com/index.php?title=Main_Page.
21 Peter Cole: "How Journalists Write", *The Guardian*, September 25, 2008, www.theguardian.com/books/2008/sep/25/writing.journalism.
22 *Ibid.*
23 Chip Heath & Dan Heath: *Made to Stick: Why Some Ideas Take Hold and Others become Unstuck*, Kindle edition. London: Random House, 2007, p. 20.
24 Mary O'Sullivan: "Presentational Tradecraft: A New Skill", in Randolph H. Pherson & Rubén Arcos (eds.), *op. cit.*, pp. 32–36.
25 *Ibid.*, pp. 14–18.

26 *Ibid.*, p. 34.
27 *Ibid.*, pp. 32–36.
28 Vic Costello, Susan Youngblood, & Norman E. Youngblood: *Multimedia Foundations: Core Concepts for Digital Design.* Waltham, MA: Elsevier, 2012, p. 12.
29 Randolph H. Pherson & Rubén Arcos: "Introduction", in Rubén Arcos & Randolph H. Pherson (eds.), *op. cit.*, p. 7.
30 *Ibid.*
31 Peter Cole & Tony Harcup: *Newspaper Journalism.* London: SAGE Publications, 2010, pp. 102–107.
32 *Ibid.*, p. 105.
33 Rubén Arcos: "Communication Analysis in a Digital Age", in Rubén Arcos & Randolph H. Pherson (eds.), *op. cit.*, p. 16.
34 Greg Miller: "Oval Office iPad: President's Daily Intelligence Brief Goes High-Tech", *The Washington Post*, April 12, 2012, www.washingtonpost.com/blogs/checkpoint-washington/post/oval-office-ipad-presidents-daily-intelligence-brief-goes-high-tech/2012/04/12/gIQAVaLEDT_blog.html?utm_term=.dbd389f34f52.
35 Randolph H. Pherson: "Establishing a New Paradigm of Collaboration", in Rubén Arcos & Randolph H. Pherson (eds.), *op. cit.*, pp. 57–58.
36 Cole & Harcup, *op. cit.*, pp. 116–120.
37 The concept "firehose-syndrome" is borrowed from computer science, and describes what happens when a large number of packets of data are received by a server that is unable to handle the load. It is derived from the saying that drinking from a fire-hose is a good way to rip your lips off. *Oxford Reference*, www.oxfordreference.com/view/10.1093/oi/authority.20110803095819706.
38 Pherson, *op. cit.*, pp. 68–69.

Further reading

Arcos, Rubén, & Randolph H. Pherson (eds.): *Intelligence Communication in the Digital Era: Transforming Security, Defence and Business.* Houndmills, Basingstoke: Palgrave Macmillan, 2015.

Heath, Chip, & Dan Heath: *Made to Stick: Why Some Ideas Take Hold and Others Become Unstuck.* London: Random House, 2007.

Major, James S.: *Communicating with Intelligence: Writing and Briefing in the Intelligence and National Security Communities.* Lanham, ML: The Scarecrow Press, 2008.

Marrin, Stephen: "Why Strategic Intelligence has Limited Influence on American Foreign Policy", *Intelligence and National Security*, Vol. 32, No. 6, 2017.

Parr, Ben: *Captivology: The Science of Capturing People's Attention.* New York: Harper Collins, 2015.

Weiss, Charles: "Communicating Uncertainty in Intelligence and Other Professions", *International Journal of Intelligence and CounterIntelligence*, Vol. 25, No. 1, 2008.

10 Avoiding politicisation*

Wilhelm Agrell

Speaking truth to power

Shortly before noon on October 16, 1962, possibly the most crucial intelligence briefing of the Cold War started in the Cabinet Room at the White House in Washington DC. Attending the briefing were, apart from President Kennedy himself, key members of the government, the Chairman of the Joint Chiefs of Staff and three intelligence officials, the Deputy Director of the Central Intelligence Agency (CIA) Marshall Carter, the Director of the National Photo Interpretation Center Arthur Lundahl, and the technical expert Sidney Graybeal.

Kennedy and the other key players were not completely unprepared when the briefing started but were not far from it. The president's national security adviser McGeorge Bundy had received a telephone message the previous evening from Ray Cline at the CIA that "those things we've been worrying about – it looks as though we've really got something". This cryptic wording referred to a growing political controversy over the possibility of Soviet nuclear missiles on Cuba. Over the last weeks, Republicans on Capitol Hill campaigning for the upcoming midterm election had challenged what they saw as the administration's weak foreign policy and inability to react to a mounting threat from the Soviet build-up on Cuba. There was no hard intelligence backing up this claim, and the eventuality of such a provocative step had been discarded by the senior analysts at the CIA in mid-September.[1] As recently as 14 October 1962, Bundy had himself denied the presence of Soviet nuclear missiles on Cuba in a TV interview on the ABC news programme. Receiving the piece of bad news from the CIA, Bundy took the decision not to inform the president of the imminent crisis, letting him have a good night's sleep after a day of campaigning and then delivering the bad news after breakfast.

The minutes from the meeting in the Cabinet Office constitutes a rare documentation of an interaction between intelligence officials and policymakers. The president did not just listen but opened up a barrage of detailed queries on just what the intelligence specialists knew, how certain their conclusions were, and what assessments they made on the time frame of the ongoing Soviet preparations. Kennedy virtually cross-examined Graybeal – referred to as the "missile man" in the minutes – on how he could tell that the objects on the high-altitude

U-2 photographs really were Soviet missiles of the types described. He was obviously satisfied, and what unfolded as the Cuban missile crisis thus rested on the confidence of the President in the technical knowledge and reliability of the intelligence specialist. Graybeal and his superiors were "speaking truth to power" in two ways. Firstly, they were delivering unwelcome news for the President, both affecting the relations with the Soviets and supplying the Republicans with arguments against the administration. Secondly, "speaking truth" during this briefing also meant that the intelligence officials admitted what they didn't know and how approximate their assessments of the time frame for the finalising of the Soviet preparations were. Intelligence experts and decision-makers had a tacit mutual understanding of roles and knowledge claims, all based on trust. The intelligence people were not trying to manipulate the picture or give a false impression of the underlying material. And the president and his advisers listened and accepted the facts and the assessments, even though they were highly undesirable.[2]

Politicisation from below and from above

The October 1962 intelligence briefing appears as more or less a handbook case of intelligence-executive interaction, where the distortion of politicisation appears to be absent. In this ideal concept of intelligence, its role is to provide facts and unbiased assessments, whatever the implications or wider consequences. In this ideal world, intelligence should not only be a provider but also be the servant whispering the truth in the emperor's ear.

This role is firmly based on the dominating intelligence culture. Michael Herman defines this culture as a set of perceptions, separating various kinds of intelligence personnel from "normal" civil servants. Within the intelligence community, the fundamental perception is a sense of being different, of belonging to a closed and separate entity, an entity with a different and more pronounced sense of mission. The sense of being different and of having a unique mission is amplified by the secrecy that transcends organisations, information flow, and routines.[3] A not uncommon consequence is that "the others" by definition are regarded as less able to grasp the significance and implications of the intelligence picture and instead are preoccupied with different – from the perspective of intelligence – less relevant and pressing matters. This notion of being in possession of vital and exclusive knowledge is shared by many other professionals, as lawyers, doctors, and not least scientists. The latter in some cases assume that it is pointless and a waste of time even to try to explain scientific problems to a lay person, since she or he will get it all wrong anyway.[4] But while the scientist at least under some circumstances can enjoy the privilege of not interacting with the external environment, the intelligence official cannot do the same. Interaction, that is giving political decision support, is their raison d'être.

The notion of exclusive knowledge, and the sense of a unique mission, can be an incentive for politicisation from below – that is, attempts by experts to influence policy beyond "speaking truth to power", in some cases including the manipulation of dissemination or assessments. Sometimes, this could be done unintentionally when the intelligence officers or scientists think that they are providing "clean" expert advice, while they in fact are giving policy advice. A nuclear scientist does not necessarily know about public perceptions of risk or a reasonable trade-off between conflicting policy goals. Major General Shlomo Gazit, the former head of Israeli military intelligence, makes a similar observation regarding intelligence advice to policymakers. Intelligence experts tend, according to Gazit, to disregard the complexity of the policy arena and hence the limitations of their own expertise.[5] Politics is neither science nor dispassionate intelligence analysis, and decisions sometimes are taken, and must be taken, contrary to such advice, however well founded. The handling – or mishandling – of the Covid-19 pandemic offers a wide range of cases of such interaction.

Politicisation is focused on a bilateral relation between intelligence and policymakers, and their respective roles. On one end of this scale, intelligence could limit or even control policy, a phenomenon associated with the notion of the "deep state". On the opposite end, intelligence becomes either irrelevant or simply a provider of disinformation or distorted assessments. In the first case, intelligence has become the power; in the latter, truth has been replaced by convenience.

Politicisation from above appears when policymakers disregard such advice on the grounds that it runs contrary to their desires or intentions. Warnings are unwanted, or justifications for a certain course of action are not provided. Politicisation from above can employ a variety of techniques, such as focusing on certain aspects of an assessment while ignoring others. One step further is to ask for or create a demand for certain intelligence, or assessments pointing in a prescribed direction, or simply remove the bearer of bad news. Direct pressure to alter the intelligence output in a given direction is an exception in countries with independent intelligence organisations. In authoritarian regimes things are different, although the underlying friction between roles tends to prevail. In Nazi Germany, the SS internal security service *Sicherheitsdienst* produced a biweekly summary of the reports from the extensive network of informers, including circulating anti-government statements, rumours, or jokes. At the end of 1943, however, this flow became too much for the SS chief Heinrich Himmler, and the circulation to the top Nazi officials was discontinued, even though the production of the biweekly summary continued.[6] Not even in a totalitarian state the wish for more optimistic reports could in the long run be satisfied.

In a democratic country politicisation from above is management and guidance that deviates from, or goes beyond, the accepted division of roles in the intelligence dialogue. Such guidance challenges the autonomy of intelligence organisations and the integrity of the intelligence process, and as a consequence of this the professional fundamentals of the intelligence culture as well. In its blunter forms, politicisation from above results in a breakdown of professional codes, similar to the effects of scientific fraud. The historical development of the concept of intelligence also plays a vital role for the rise of this kind of politicisation. As long as intelligence was conducted in a pre-modern fashion, focused on the collection of certain (secret) pieces of information, there was hardly an arena where politicisation could take place. Politicisation presupposed the emergence of a strategic planning and decision-making process, and the parallel institutions for intelligence assessments. The histories of the development of intelligence analysis and of intelligence politicisation are, if not identical so, at least closely related.

Politicisation by default

Politicisation, thus, could refer to either policy pressure on the intelligence process or the use of intelligence to influence policymaking. However, this phenomenon could also appear in a more indirect form, as a systemic malfunction, rather than an element in a tug of war between actors and professional roles, much in the same way as Roberta Wohlstetter's analysis of the warning of failure prior to the Pearl Harbor attack. Her main conclusion is that no agency had a clear responsibility for the total intelligence picture and for converting warning to contingency measures.[7] This constitutes a third form of often unintended and undetected politicisation that ironically can stem from attempts to limit the risk of politicisation. If politicisation is perceived as a consequence of intermingling roles between analysts and decision-makers, then a preventive measure is to establish borders and no-go areas. In one sense this is uncontroversial. Analysts should refrain from speculating about the preferability of alternative policies, and policymakers should, unless there is a very good reason, refrain from side-tracking by collecting their own intelligence and making their own often biased assessments. But efforts to stay clear of politicisation, and avoid acting outside the assigned role, might create a tendency towards overcautiousness, where important aspects of a complex issue are either bypassed or simply overlooked, a kind of politicisation by default.

In his study of how the British intelligence estimated the growth of German military power after the Nazi rise to power in 1933, Wesley Wark offers insights into how threat assessments that were written during the decade were characterised not only by varying uncertainty but also by elements of politicisation. Wark's main finding is that the British intelligence estimates can be separated into four distinct successive phases.[8] This meant that the British estimates went from basically ignoring the rise of the German threat, to relaxation based on the assumption of political reconciliation, to a sudden shift towards perceptions of overwhelming German superiority, to finally a more balanced view, too late to avoid war, but enough to finish appeasement and the hope that this could save the peace in the long run. While the main story is one about insufficient intelligence assets and the inability to grasp the magnitude of shift from the peaceful détente-oriented Weimar Republic to the Nazi Third Reich, there were elements of politicisation in one of its standard forms: the ignoring and suppression of "unwanted" intelligence data and assessments. For the proponent of the policy of laissez-faire and later that of appeasement, indications of a growing threat would serve no other purpose than to undermine policy. This dilemma is perhaps most vividly illustrated in Sir Winston Churchill's fierce criticism in the House of Commons of the government's appeasement policy. Certainly, Churchill made ample use of intelligence in his campaign against appeasement, and to the extent he could draw from backchannels to classified intelligence, this did constitute politicisation from below, though in this case in typical Churchill manner it was justified by the fact that he was right and the others were not.

The politicisation that appears in Wark's analysis is however of a more indirect and subtle character. One example of this was the prevailing efforts to look for some ground for optimism when all lights flashed red. Analysts tended to supply the government with assessments that seemed to confirm the present line of policy, and thus to reassure rather than to challenge the fundamentals of the dogmatic appeasement policy. In drafting the 1939 strategic assessment, an air staff member of the Joint Planning Sub-Committee (JPC) wrote a note to his colleagues arguing that the picture in the draft was a too gloomy one. He went on underscoring that there was considerable evidence available that "Germany's belt is already as tight as she can bear" and that Germany, through achieving the current advantage in initial military strength, had used up all hidden resources.[9] As we know today, the remark of the group captain was both right and wrong: right in the sense that Germany did indeed not have the sufficient resources for a prolonged war – and especially not before conquering the bulk of the European continent – but fatally wrong because Germany had no intention in waging such a war, instead bypassing the Maginot Line and the resource threshold with the Blitzkrieg concept.

The relations between intelligence and foreign policy were close at this time, and there were no other equivalents to Churchill's assaults in the House of Commons. In fact, as Wark notes, at no stage during the 1930s were there any fundamental contradictions between intelligence reporting and the foreign policy of the government. While this could be regarded as a final proof for the lack of politicisation of intelligence, the obvious failure of the British foreign policy in the face of the Nazi expansionism nevertheless indicates something different. Either there was simply a massive, or rather several successive, intelligence failure or intelligence was influenced, if not outright dictated, by the virtue of political necessity. Churchill turned out to be right, and in retrospect, the docile intelligence assessments could be criticised because appeasement ultimately failed. Wark concludes that the main negative impact of intelligence was the tendency to supply assessments that seemed to confirm the present line of policy and thus to reassure rather than to challenge the fundamentals of the dogmatic appeasement policy.[10]

The Germans were in this respect no better off. Between 1942 and 1945, Fremde Heere Ost (Foreign Armies East), the German Army General Staff's military intelligence section focusing on the Eastern Front, produced a series of forecasts underestimating the capacity of the Soviet military. The reason behind this poor performance was partly due to the lack of intelligence coverage of the Soviet heartland, but the tendency to underestimate also reflected the Nazi leadership's preconceptions about the Soviet society and industrial capacity.[11]

Intelligence among the cogwheels of government machinery

In his study of US intelligence assessments prior to the fall of the Shah regime in 1979, Robert Jervis describes another, and subtler, type of politicisation by default, characterised by its invisibility even to those most closely involved.[12] The CIA had, prior to the crisis, only a tiny unit monitoring and assessing develop-ments in Iran and the growing internal opposition towards the regime. There was a lack of intelligence from relevant segments of the Iranian society and an over-dependence on reports supplied by the regime's own security apparatus, but these were not the main reasons for the failure to discover the gravity of the situation. A string of intelligence assessments was based on the assumption that the regime, if the situation deteriorated, would crack down on the opposition. American dip-lomats had the aim of averting such a development by compelling the Shah to make concessions to the opposition, thereby further weakening the regime, until its final collapse.

In the post-mortem done by Jervis shortly after the fall of the Shah, he discov-ered the fatal discrepancy between the assumptions that the intelligence assess-ments were based on and the consequences of US pressure on the regime. The problem was that the intelligence analysts, in order to stay clear of interfering in the domains of US diplomacy, did not take this into account as one of the key fac-tors determining the outcome. But the analysts not only stayed clear of this "blue dimension", they were unaware of this serious limitation in their analysis.[13]

Western assessments of the Iraqi weapons of mass destruction (WMD) pro-gramme prior to the 2003 war are perhaps the most well-known intelligence-policy interactions in recent history. This is a case illustrating not only the complexity of politicisation but also the impact of a more profound change in the role of intel-ligence in an increasingly medialised political landscape, from that of supplying facts and assessments to a provider of munitions in a domestic and international political struggle over the presumed threat from Iraqi WMDs.

After 2003, the Iraqi WMD estimates and politicisation have generally been regarded as inseparable. The erroneous estimates, finally confirmed by the find-ings or rather non-finding of the vast intelligence excavation effected by the Iraqi Survey Group (ISG),[14] were generally perceived as a clear-cut case of top-down politicisation, where the US and British intelligence communities simply pro-duced and disseminated the assessments and supporting evidence that the poli-cymakers needed to make their case for war, domestically and internationally. However, both the investigation conducted by the US Senate and the British Hutton and Butler inquiries failed to find any proof that the intelligence process and assessments had been distorted due to direct pressure from the policymak-ers.[15] These investigations approached politicisation from a legalistic perspective, where the policymakers were acquitted mainly due to the lack of sufficient evi-dence of direct involvement in the intelligence process. Especially, the US Senate put the blame entirely on the intelligence community, framing the Iraqi estimates as a case of devastating intelligence failure due to flawed analysis and inadequate or ignored quality control, thus as a case of "politicization from below".[16]

Few other cases of intelligence failures, and possibly no other instance of intelligence-policymaker interaction, have been so thoroughly investigated, studied, and debated as the Iraqi WMD case.[17] This in itself constitutes a problem of validity, similar to the focus on intelligence failures. Specific estimates under intense scrutiny can stand out as odder and more controversial if the background "noise" of similar but less known cases is ignored.[18] But how wrong were actually the assessments prior to the 2003 war?

In his "corrected" version of the October 2002 Special National Intelligence Estimate (SNIE) on the Iraqi WMD programmes, Richard K. Betts made remarkably small changes, mainly by inserting more explicit descriptions of the uncertainty, in the assessments. But the overall conclusion, that Iraq probably was hiding stocks of chemical and biological weapons and was pursuing active development and production programmes for these as well as nuclear weapons, remained more or less the same.[19] Betts puts the finger on a paradox overlooked in many of the post-war comments on an apparent intelligence failure, that the assessments from a methodological standpoint were not entirely wrong. Intelligence was stuck between the irresponsible standpoint of not offering any judgement at all and the need to take a reasonable stand based on previous knowledge and available intelligence.

Robert Jervis, in his efforts to map the causes of the failure, argues along similar lines that the analysis was trapped by the fact that the "truth", as it eventually turned out, was so implausible. The eventual findings of the Iraqi Study Group would have sounded not only improbable but also directly ridiculous if presented before the war – for instance, that the lack of confirmation of the destruction of large quantities of anthrax after the 1991 war was due to fear for Saddam's anger if he found out that it had been dumped near one of his palaces.[20] A fully correct estimate could simply not have been substantiated with the available intelligence, context, and sound reasoning. A wild guess could have got it right but would have been useless to policymakers faced with handling the Iraqi quagmire. The dilemma was that "facts" would have appeared as unfounded, while "alternative facts" made sense.

If the Iraqi estimate was not "dead wrong", why did it nevertheless slide off the mark and overstate certainty, boost intelligence from shaky sources,[21] and not least miss the very possibility of alternative interpretations? The answer is in one sense very simple: The long history of the Iraqi WMD issue, the underestimates prior to the 1991 war, and the continued evasion in dealing with the United Nations Special Commission (UNSCOM) all produced a context, albeit biased, in terms of an overwhelming list of crimes.[22] Jervis points at the pitfall of believing that scientific methods would make the difference. On the contrary,

> intelligence strives to follow scientific methods, and every day scientists see results that contradict basic scientific laws, which they react to not by rushing to publish but by throwing out of the data because they know it cannot be right.[23]

The somewhat surprising outcome of the analysis by both Betts and Jervis is that the unprecedented intelligence failure in this case had less to do with equally unprecedented flaws in the analytic process and more to do with specific problems associated with the Iraqi case, and the broader political context. Betts argues that it was not only the perception of the Iraqi WMD programme that was flawed, it was the whole belief that sound intelligence analysis *must* be able to deliver the correct conclusion. And he concludes: "Hindsight inevitably makes most people assume that the only acceptable analysis is one that gives the right answer."[24] This strikes at the very heart of the positivist intelligence culture and the claim of possessing and conveying the truth. If there is no such thing as the truth, who is then best suited to speak to power, and with what knowledge claims?

Politicisation and the medialisation of intelligence

But then what about politicisation? Was the US post-mortem of the intelligence work that was done prior to the Iraq war wrong in putting the entire blame on the intelligence community's poor performance but right in concluding that the failure was not caused by political pressure down the chain of command, which is politicisation from above? Few who have studied the case and the post-mortems seem to agree on this point, viewing the framing of the post-mortems as a part of a "blame game".[25] Jervis on this ground dismisses the post-mortems as "almost as flawed as the original estimates and partly for the same reason: the post-mortems neglected social science methods, settled for more intuitive but less adequate ways of thinking, and jumped to plausible, but misleading conclusions".[26] In the case of politicisation, this meant that the investigators were simply searching for evidence of the wrong kind of influence. It was not so much orders down the chain of command but the whole collective perception of the coming war and what was expected by – and appreciated from – the intelligence services in the countries trying to assemble an international coalition.

Politicisation in this respect had more to do with the transforming producer-customer relation after the end of the Cold War, where intelligence in many instances had to make their services and input relevant, by identifying new issues and new categories of customers. From this perspective, the surge from spring 2002 in the demand for intelligence underpinning the gravity of the Iraqi WMD threat was simply an all-time high in customer pull and producer euphoria. This sudden peak in overlapping interests is perhaps best caught in the memo from Tony Blair's press secretary Alastair Campbell to the Chairman of the Joint Intelligence Committee (JIC), where Campbell expressed his gratitude for the services rendered by "your team" in producing the text for the public dossier to be known as the September Report: "I was pleased to hear from you and your SIS (Secret Intelligence Service) colleagues that, contrary to media reporting today, the intelligence community are taking such a helpful approach to this in going through all the material they have." In the preceding line, Campbell sums up the changing role of intelligence: "The media/political judgement will inevitably focus on 'what's new?'".[27]

Since the 1950s, the political domain has been increasingly medialised, first with the breakthrough of television, followed by the Internet and the rapid growth and impact of social media. The Iraq crisis highlighted not only this transformation but also the new and possibly unexpected role intelligence came to play in such a medialised context. Especially for the British government, the crucial issue was how to persuade the parliament and the public of the necessity of a massively unpopular war.[28] This created a demand for another kind of intelligence product than the traditional estimates and threat assessments and more in line with the annual Soviet Military Power, produced by the US Department of Defense between 1981 and 1990.[29]

As the critical debate in the British Parliament on an Iraq war drew close, the Prime Minister's Office and the staff of the Joint Intelligence Committee worked with increasing speed to produce an open intelligence summary, supported by all the credentials of the key intelligence. The result was the later much-debated "September-dossier", in itself not very rich in substance but implying the existence of a more extensive but classified bulk of intelligence.[30]

The post-mortem of the process behind the September-dossier illustrates the consequences when intelligence is rerouted from the intelligence/policy interface to the policy/media interface. This was not a case of JIC informing the Government, their main task for over 60 years, as Tony Blair underlined in the first paragraph of his foreword to the dossier.[31] For the first time this trusted intelligence provider and adviser was reaching out with an unclassified version of the classified intelligence assessments. But, as the Butler Inquiry observed, the JIC put their reputation at stake when taking responsibility for the intelligence content of something that in effect was a skilfully drafted policy product with the result that "more weight was placed on intelligence than it could bear".[32]

But the effects of politicisation in this case went one step further. As Philip H.J. Davies found, there are reasons to believe that the drafting of the public dossier "contaminated backwards" on the parallel drafting of a classified intelligence assessment. Time-pressure and staff overload simply choked the process and prevented the employment of normal review procedures.[33]

The rise of competitors

The September-dossier appeared in an information environment where intelligence still possessed a knowledge monopoly in most respects. There were no reliable alternative sources available inside or outside Iraq for journalists or sceptic politicians to turn to.

Furthermore, intelligence still had the upper hand in terms of credibility and enjoyed the considerable advantage of being able to refer to, or hint at, the existence of secret intelligence material. Much of these advantages were lost in the post-Iraq *melée*. But something else, and potentially more damaging, was about to happen to the role played by intelligence.

The search for new areas of interest and new customers was hampered in many Western countries with the increased focus on terrorism after 2001. Instead, the process was continued by other actors, as private risk and intelligence firms, NGOs, and other non-intelligence agencies, capitalising from the rapidly growing availability of open sources. Reports and assessments made by well-staffed think tanks could compete with, and in some cases outmatch, products from traditional intelligence agencies. This output had the considerable advantage of being available either in the public domain or on a commercial market, and without the severe limitations of reliance on classified sources and methods. Furthermore, an open market for assessments meant that second opinions could be available or were possible to commission. To the extent intelligence agencies still enjoyed an advantage, this was increasingly based on their access to special sources, first of all from technical collection systems.

But also in this respect the monopoly was increasingly challenged by non-state actors. With the growth of digital flows over the Internet, non-state actors or single individuals could conduct intrusive intelligence collection against persons, companies, or government agencies.

And finally, the citizens themselves started to supply surveillance data and sensitive personal information on an unprecedented scale in real time, creating collection opportunities not only for the traditional intelligence agencies but also for a wide span of new actors. After the downing of the Malaysian airliner MH-17 over Eastern Ukraine in 2014, the movement of the missile battery involved could be reconstructed by the volunteer group *Bellingcat* using social media forensics. Back in 1962 the overall picture of a weapons deployment could only be pieced together by an intelligence system with vast and exclusive resources. Now it could be pieced together through volunteer cooperation, using data available everywhere and to everyone.

Both the conflict in Eastern Ukraine and the use of chemical weapons in the Syrian war have underlined the shift in the availability of raw intelligence from war zones, where footage and social media postings not only supplement traditional intelligence sources but, in some respects, outmatch them by being accessible, timely, and easy to use for political purposes. The suppliers, whether journalists, NGOs, or ordinary citizens, can unintentionally be transformed into actors in a fragmented intelligence process.[34]

But the most spectacular and for the traditional intelligence agencies damaging development was the string of leaks of classified material out in the open domain, heralded by WikiLeaks and followed by the Snowden revelations. The damage was not so much the information revealed as the fact that the most protected governmental bodies and most sensitive international intelligence corporations were unable to prevent leaks on this unprecedented scale and that those affected seemed unable to cope with the situation. As Michael Warner concludes, technology has blurred the line between states and non-state actors in the intelligence field, thereby putting an end to a century-long intelligence monopoly.[35]

Is ignorance a strength?

"Alternative facts" might be a new term, emanating from a famous White House press briefing in 2017. However, as a phenomenon, and a challenge to intelligence, it is far from new. The dominating totalitarian ideologies of the twentieth century rested on quasi-scientific concepts, disinformation, and systematic propaganda, a negation of the established scientific methods and principles for knowledge production. The regimes set up in the name of these ideologies constructed powerful "bubbles", enforced by propaganda, surveillance, and the isolation of the population from information outside the bubble. Under these regimes, intelligence either became a part of the bubble or had, as most journalists, writers, and scientists, to renounce the ambition of intellectual autonomy and objectivity.

From the 1970s onwards, several of the traditional producers of knowledge in what Karl Popper called the "open society" have been increasingly called into question. Not only intelligence has been challenged by media but also science, where attention has shifted from a predominantly uncritical reporting of exciting discoveries to a critical scrutinising of scientific results, controversies, and performance failures.[36] Science – and later intelligence – has been subject to a transformed media logic. This media logic has tended to exaggerate the criticism of experts and their institutions beyond the point that would be reasonable from the idealistic perception of a more confined watchdog role. Media is, according to this interpretation, simply exploiting inaccurate criticism on the pretext of making a social contribution, while in fact making a commercial one.[37] With the advent of the digital age and the rise of social media, scepticism has turned towards traditional media and their crumbling information monopoly.

In this brave new world, all authorities have eroded, and all knowledge claims can – and will – be called into question. Navigating in these new and uncharted waters, struggling to remain relevant and informed, and being both transparent and able to protect sensitive information will be major challenges to traditional intelligence agencies. With policymakers likewise struggling to keep afloat, the power and ability to define trust and reliability will inevitably be the key issues. Politicisation, in this broad respect, is thus likely to transform from a distortion in an ideal system to the core element in the future intelligence-policymaker interface.

Conclusion

In the past, politicisation was something that concerned mid- and top-level managers, while the analyst could remain on safe ground, relying on speaking the truth, the whole truth, and nothing but the truth. At a time when alternative fact and alternative definitions of truth and reliability exist, the individual analyst is no longer in the background but at the frontline. No one else can or will face up to the challenge of defending the intellectual high ground that constitutes the very essence of intelligence analysis.

Is it then possible to avoid a development towards increasing politicisation in different forms? Presumably, such a goal is both unrealistic and in the worst case misleading. If the struggle between narratives is the new normal, it is pointless to try to reverse the development back to an ideal state that seldom or never existed. To try to avoid politicisation using various general measures is probably just as counterproductive as trying to avoid intelligence assessments that in retrospect turn out to be wrong. In both cases, the result might be a profession that is overcautious and unwilling to confront alternative narratives and its proponents, thus running the risk of marginalising itself.

Notes

* This chapter is partially based on my previous writing on the subject in Wilhelm Agrell and Gregory F. Treverton: *National Intelligence and Science: Beyond the Great Divide in Analysis and Policy*. Oxford: Oxford University Press, 2015; and Wilhelm Agrell: *Essence of Assessment: Methods and Problems in Intelligence Analysis*, 2nd edition. Malmö: Gleerups, 2016.

1 "The Military Buildup in Cuba", SNIE 85–3–62, September 19, 1962, in Mary S. McAuliffe: *The CIA Documents on the Cuban Missile Crisis 1962*. Washington, DC: Central Intelligence Agency, 1992.

2 For the transcripts of the briefing, see Timothy Naftali & Philip Zelnikow (eds.): *The Presidential Recordings: John F. Kennedy. The Great Crises*, Vol. 2. New York: W.W. Norton & Company, 2001.

3 Michael Herman: *Intelligence Power in Peace and War*. Cambridge: Cambridge University Press, 1996, pp. 327–331.

4 Dorothy Nelkin: *Selling Science: How the Press Covers Science and Technology*. New York: Freeman, cop. 1995, pp. 7–8.

5 Shlomo Gazit: "Intelligence Estimates and the Decision-Maker", in Michael I. Handel (ed.): *Leaders and Intelligence*. London: Frank Cass, 1989.

6 Hienz Boberach: *Meldungen aus dem Reich*. Berlin: Hermann Luchterland, 1965. The complete series of reports has later been published in the 18 volumes *Meldungen aus dem Reich, 1938–1945: die geheime Lageberichte des Sicherheitsdienste der SS*. Editor: Hans Boberach. Herrsching: Pawlak Cop. 1984–1985.

7 Roberta Wohlstetter: *Pearl Harbor: Warning and Decision*. Stanford: Stanford University Press, 1962.

8 Wesley Wark: *The Ultimate Enemy: British Intelligence and Nazi Germany, 1933–1939*. London: I.B. Tauris & Co Ltd, 1985.

9 Wark, *op. cit.*, p. 226.

10 *Ibid.*, pp. 235–236.

11 Magnus Pahl: *Fremde Heere Ost: Hitlers militärische Feindaufklärung*. Berlin: Ch.Links. 2012.

12 Robert Jervis: *Why Intelligence Fails: Lessons from the Iranian Revolution and the Iraq War*. Itacha: Cornell University Press, 2010.

13 *Ibid.*, pp. 19–20.

14 The Iraqi Survey Group (ISG) was a 1,400-strong team searching for traces of WMD-programs in post-war Iraq. ISG published its findings in September 2004 in the so-called 'Duelfer Report'. ISG should not be confused with the Iraq Study Group, also known as the Baker-Hamilton Commission, a bi-partisan commission on future U.S. policy on Iraq appointed by the U.S. Congress in 2006.

15 "Report on the U.S. Intelligence Community's Prewar Intelligence Assessments on Iraq", Senate Select Committee on Intelligence (SSCI), United States Senate, July 7, 2004; "Report of the Inquiry into the Circumstances Surrounding the Death of Dr. David Kelly C.M.G.", *The House of Commons*, January 28, 2004, https://fas.org/irp/world/uk/huttonreport.pdf (Hutton-inquiry); "Review of Intelligence on Weapons of Mass Destruction, Report of a Committee of Privy Counsellors", *The House of Commons*, July 14, 2004, http://news.bbc.co.uk/nol/shared/bsp/hi/pdfs/14_07_04_butler.pdf (Butler-inquiry).

16 SSCI, *op. cit.*

17 See Jervis, *op. cit.*; Richard K. Betts: *Enemies of Intelligence: Knowledge and Power in American National Security*. New York: Columbia University Press, 2007; Richard K. Betts: "Two Faces of Intelligence Failure: September 11 and Iraq's Missing WMD", *Political Science Quarterly*, Vol. 122, No. 4, 2007–2008; Charles A. Duelfer & Stephen Benedict Dyson: "Chronic Misperception and International Conflict: The

U.S.-Iraq Experience", *International Security*, Vol. 36, No. 1, 2011, pp. 73–100; Liesbeth van der Heide: "Cherry-Picked Intelligence: The Weapons of Mass Destruction Dispositive as a Legitimation for National Security in the post 9/11 Age", *Historical Social Research*, Vol. 238, No. 1, 2013, pp. 286–307; John N.L. Morrison: "British Intelligence Failure in Iraq", *Intelligence and National Security*, Vol. 26, No. 4, 2011; Olav Riste: "The Intelligence-Policy Maker Relationship and the Politicization of Intelligence", in Wilhelm Agrell and Gregory F. Treverton (eds.), *op. cit.*

18 Examples of attempts to contextualize the Iraqi estimates can be found in the Butler Report, comparing Iraq with other cases of proliferation concerning Iran, Libya, North-Korea and Pakistan. Also the second US inquiry on the Iraqi assessments, the Ross-Silberman Commission discussed this wider intelligence setting.

19 Betts: *Enemies of Intelligence*, *op. cit.*, pp. 121–123; and Betts: "Two Faces of Intelligence Failure", *op. cit.*, pp. 603–606.

20 Jervis, *op. cit.*, p. 147.

21 The most prominent case being the Iraqi Humint source with the ill-fated Covername Curveball. See Bob Drogin: *Curveball. Spies, Lies and the Man behind Them: The Real Reason America Went to War in Iraq*. London: Ebury Press, 2007. *Curveball* was however far from the only shaky or unverified source the U.S. and British assessments were based on. See Philip H.J. Davies: *Intelligence and Government in Britain and the United States*, Vol. 2. Santa Barbara: Praeger, 2012, pp. 273–291.

22 Jervis, *op. cit.*, pp. 150–153.

23 *Ibid.*, pp. 149–150. Though, as he remarks: "There is no such thing as 'letting the facts speak for themselves' or drawing inferences without using beliefs about the world, and it is inevitable that the perception and interpretation of new information will be influenced by established ideas."

24 Betts: *Enemies of Intelligence*, *op. cit.*, pp. 122–123.

25 Davies, *op. cit.*, pp. 373–403.

26 Jervis, *op. cit.*, p. 123.

27 Hutton Inquiry: "Report of the Inquiry into the Circumstances Surrounding the Death of Dr. David Kelly C.M.G.", *The House of Commons*, 28 January 2004, https://fas.org/irp/world/uk/huttonreport.pdf.

28 Davies, *op. cit.*, p. 274.

29 U.S. Department of Defense: *Soviet Military Power*. Washington, DC: Department of Defense, 1981–1990.

30 Joint Intelligence Committee: *Iraq's Weapons of Mass Destruction: The Assessment of the British Government*. London: Stationery Office, 2002.

31 *Ibid.*

32 Butler Inquiry: "Review of Intelligence on Weapons of Mass Destruction, Report of a Committee of Privy Counsellors", *The House of Commons*, 14 July 2004, http://news.bbc.co.uk/nol/shared/bsp/hi/pdfs/14_07_04_butler.pdf.

33 Davies, *op. cit.*, p. 284.

34 Rune Saugmann: "The Civilian's Visual Security Paradox: How Open Source Intelligence Practices Create Insecurity for Civilians in Warzones", *Intelligence and National Security*, Vol. 34, No. 3, 2019, pp. 334–361.

35 Michael Warner: *The Rise and Fall of Intelligence: An International Security History*. Washington, DC: Georgetown University Press, 2014, p. 318.

36 Winfred Göpfert: "The Strength of PR and Weakness of Science Journalism", in Martin W. Bauer & Massimiano Bucci (eds.): *Journalism, Science, and Society: Science Communication between News and Public Relations*. New York: Routledge, 2007, p. 215.

37 Björn Fjaestad: "Why Journalists Report Science as They Do", in Martin W. Bauer & Massimiano Bucci (eds.), *op. cit.*

Further reading

Agrell, Wilhelm, & Treverton, Gregory F.: *National Intelligence and Science: Beyond the Great Divide in Analysis and Policy*. Oxford: Oxford University Press, 2015.

Bar-Joseph, Uri: "The Politicization of Intelligence: A Comparative Study", *International Journal of Intelligence and CounterIntelligence*, Vol. 26, No. 2, 2013, pp. 347–369.

Betts, Richard K.: *Enemies of Intelligence: Knowledge and Power in American National Security*. New York: Columbia University Press, 2007.

Eisenfeld, Beth: "The Intelligence Dilemma: Proximity and Politicization – Analysis of External Influences", *Journal of Strategic Security*, vol. 10, no. 2, 2017, pp. 77–96.

Jervis, Robert: *Why Intelligence Fails: Lessons from the Iranian Revolution and the Iraq War*. Ithaca: Cornell University Press, 2010.

11 A professional code of ethics

Kira Vrist Rønn

A hallmark of professions is that they have ethical guidelines. Such guidelines for professional conduct are, for example, well developed within medicine, with detailed specifications of responsibilities related to a doctor's behaviour towards the patient, society, the medical profession, and herself or himself. Adam Diderichsen understands professional ethics as an opportunity to stop and take a personal stand towards an issue and its purpose. This is different from legal requirements for a professional:

> Where law is about clear and objective demands made by society on certain professions and citizens in general, ethics is about . . . how the individual manages her social role with regard to overarching values.[1]

Discussions about the evolution of professional guidelines in intelligence analysis are little developed so far. At the same time, such guidelines are becoming more relevant in light of the increasing professionalisation of the field. This chapter is meant to be a contribution towards developing a professional ethics for intelligence analysts by discussing some ethical challenges that analysts are confronted with in their work and by suggesting some practical ethical guidelines for analysts.

New tasks and roles for the intelligence analyst in the digital age confront us with several ethical dilemmas. Analysts work less with what previous chapters have referred to as "secrets" and more with "mysteries". The latter concept refers to questions that do not have clear answers, and where the task of the analyst is to give decision-makers situational understanding of a certain case rather than present them with an unambiguous and true answer. Such tasks demand total honesty from the analyst regarding her or his own assessments, and a demand not to reach beyond what the intelligence provides a basis for. Another feature of the digital age is that analysts use open-source information to a much greater extent than before and are themselves able to collect much of the information they need from news services, web pages, and social media. Collection methods from open sources (OSINT) represent a grey zone between intelligence collection and intelligence analysis because analysts can collect from open sources themselves. Such collection raises ethical problems too – for example, the fact that even if people publish information about themselves on the net, this does not mean that they know about or consent to the exploitation of this information for intelligence usage.

Intelligence and ethics

As a consequence of the ongoing professionalisation of intelligence, ethics is increasingly thought of as a relevant and inevitable component of modern intelligence conduct. Discussions of morals never refer to one single correct course of action, and ethical considerations entail much more than referring to obviously questionable conduct (lies, deceit, etc.) as generally impermissible in a moral sense. Most moral philosophers will actually consider actions that include lying, manipulation, and secrecy as morally permissible under certain circumstances, when there are good reasons to act in such a way.[2] This type of discussion reflects the fundamental tensions in moral philosophy between *deontology*, saying that the morality of an action should be based on whether that action itself is right or wrong, and *consequentialism*, saying that a morally right act is one that will produce good outcomes.

Intelligence methods are commonly perceived as inherently "unethical". This notion also reflects a common approach to the role of ethics in the context of intelligence. In fact, the phrase *intelligence ethics* is often described as *an oxymoron* – a contradictory term. Ethics are said to be irrelevant, unnecessary, or impossible, since intelligence activities are always immoral in some way, due to their often deceiving, manipulating, and covert nature.[3]

Whether this notion is correct depends on which perspective on ethics one has. Communication intelligence (COMINT), which per definition implies a violation of privacy, can, for example, be unacceptable from a deontological perspective but not from a consequentialist perspective.

Additionally, some scholars have argued that the legal frameworks governing intelligence services are often vague and broadly formulated, in order to ensure the efficiency and to safeguard the sources and methods of the services.[4] The same intelligence scholars argue that, precisely because of the vague nature of the rule of law in this context, ethics play an even more important role. Ethics can regulate in another way than the law, and this makes ethical considerations very relevant in the context of intelligence, since they can provide guidance that is otherwise absent or very broadly formulated.[5]

Collection and analysis: two sides of the same coin?

The intelligence cycle, as presented in Chapter 1, is virtually always placed centre stage in attempts to articulate and define what intelligence is. Many scholars and practitioners would claim that the cycle has gained too much attention and that it presents a flawed vision of how intelligence is in fact conducted. This critique has been particularly applicable when it comes to the strict division between the collection and analysis of intelligence. Opponents would claim that the collection and analysis of intelligence occur as dialectic processes, rather than as a linear, chronological process, as expressed in the image of the cycle (shown in Chapter 1). Even if the strict division between the two disciplines has previously resulted in the practice of keeping the two types of intelligence professionals more or less separated from each other, many intelligence organisations have now softened the divide. Recently, more and more intelligence services have started to combine roles and collocate units in order to achieve synergy between the two types of intelligence activities, reflecting how these intelligence activities are dependent on each other.

A central question to pose is whether it would be equally relevant to merge the ethical considerations concerning intelligence collection with those concerning intelligence analysis. Naturally, some ethical considerations would be relevant for both types of activities, especially since intelligence analysts sometimes become collectors, and vice versa. Additionally, intelligence collection is never an "objective" process, and the act of identifying the relevant information when collecting intelligence will, in most instances, be a way of commencing the analytical and interpretive endeavour of intelligence analysis.[6] Similarly, the intelligence analyst cannot be absolved of responsibility associated with collection since her or his analyses are based on collected data.

However, it makes good sense to differentiate between discussions of the ethics of intelligence collection, or "gaining access" when it comes to digital information, and the ethics of intelligence analysis – at least on a theoretical level.[7] The core activity of collecting information differs in terms of scope and, most importantly, in terms of the individuals affected by intelligence analysis. In addition, intelligence collection is apparently surrounded by many more and very different types of ethical dilemmas than analysis of the intelligence. A common understanding within the scholarly literature on intelligence ethics is that the collection of intelligence often turns out to either wrong or harm the person who is a target of a specific intelligence collection activity, for example, phrased as violation of the individual right to privacy.[8] This is not necessarily true of intelligence analysis to the same extent. On the other hand, ethical considerations pertaining to the analysis of intelligence will most often concern the way in which the analyst treats the collected intelligence. This includes the way she or he concludes and infers on the basis of the collected intelligence and other types of information, and subsequently interacts with decision-makers when providing them with intelligence in order to help construct an informed decision-making framework.[9]

Honesty in making assessments

The scholarly literature on the ethics of intelligence analysis is much less developed than the literature on the ethics of intelligence collection. This is primarily due to the fact that the collection process affects the targeted individuals in a far more obvious way than intelligence analysis.

Some scholars, however, specifically address the ethics of intelligence analysis, and they often focus on the personal ethics of the professionals conducting intelligence analysis. One of the fundamental questions when addressing the ethics of intelligence analysis is: When is an intelligence analysis considered morally problematic? Underpinning this is the question: What are the norms that govern intelligence analysis? A common reply to the latter question is that the aim of intelligence analysis is to discover the truth about a specific topic. This is reflected, for example, in the mantra of "speaking truth to power".[10] As regards so-called manufactured intelligence, the case concerning the non-existing weapons of mass destruction in Iraq leading to the invasion of Iraq in 2003 is one of the most prominent recent examples of the intelligence analysts and the intelligence community not living up to this standard of truth.[11]

Uri Bar-Joseph has provided two simple guiding principles which, in his opinion, should guide the intelligence analyst in a moral direction when it comes to speaking truth to power. These principles should help the analyst become aware of what Bar-Joseph calls motivated and unmotivated biases.[12] The unmotivated biases refer to shortcomings in the analyst's recognition, such as group think, confirmation bias (the tendency to only include information that supports a specific hypothesis), and other judgemental heuristics in which a flawed or untested conclusion is reached due to dynamics that are external to the topic of the intelligence analysis. Such biases often result in an excessive confidence in one's own opinions.[13] The biases are described in greater detail in Richards Heuer's book *The Psychology of Intelligence*, a classic within intelligence studies. Though unmotivated cognitive biases are in fact very difficult to avoid, Bar-Joseph suggests introducing a guiding principle for intelligence analysts as a way of potentially avoiding or at least minimising their influence on the conclusions of the intelligence analysis. His suggestion is to apply the Socratic sentence "I do not think that I know what I do not know" as a guiding norm for intelligence analysis, in order to become aware of the common pitfalls related to cognitive biases and to minimise their influence on the intelligence conclusions. Though this may appear rather simplistic, other scholars in the field of cognitive psychology have similarly suggested systematically posing the question "In what ways could I be wrong?" in order to minimise the influence of cognitive bias, resulting in overconfidence in one's own beliefs, which is considered to be a general cognitive bias in everyday decision-making.[14]

The motivated biases, on the other hand, are described as conscious choices made in order to mislead or manipulate the conclusions of an intelligence report, for example in the Iraq case. Here, Bar-Joseph introduces the second norm: "tell the truth, the whole truth, and nothing but the truth" in order to overcome this type of motivated bias. With motivated biases, false or misleading conclusions are intentionally presented to the decision-makers in order to intentionally mislead their decisions. Bar-Joseph's boldly phrased guideline would make it possible to avoid such misleading, if the analysts disclose what is known and not what, for example, is expected or wanted by the decision-makers ("intelligence to please").

Both these guiding principles are valuable for promoting a more specific code of conduct for intelligence analysts. Ideally, both types of bias or misleading should be avoided, according to Bar-Joseph. His guiding principles thus reflect the shared ideal of intelligence analysts and the underlying norm that intelligence analysis should speak the truth to decision-makers.

The division into motivated and unmotivated biases contributes to the highly relevant debate on misinformation and disinformation. This debate has attracted more and more interest in the wake of the US presidential election in 2016 and the focus on so-called fake news.

Misinformation can be understood in line with the unmotivated biases presented by Bar-Joseph, since misinformation equals information which unintentionally misleads its recipients.[15] Disinformation, on the other hand, can be seen as equivalent to motivated biases, since it constitutes the intentional misleading of the recipients. Both misinformation and disinformation are part of the discussion of fake news.

Nevertheless, it is an interesting question whether *the truth* is, in fact, a feasible norm in all types of intelligence analysis. In academic literature, several researchers distinguish between two different types of intelligence analysis: intelligence as *secrets* and intelligence as *mysteries*.[16]

Secrets are cases of intelligence analysis whereby a truthful and correct solution is feasible. These are cases where the question posed is factual – for example, the answer to the question: How many missiles does an adversary have? Or what is/was the specific location of Osama Bin Laden? These questions are not easy to answer, but a correct and true answer is possible. In the case of mysteries, simple answers are not feasible, since they often involve the future-oriented interpretation of complex questions. An important consequence of this division is that the governing norm of intelligence analysis should be flexible to the type of task at hand. One cannot expect one correct and true answer in cases that are characterised by mysteries. Such nuances are very relevant to the discussion of the ethics of intelligence analysis, since the truth-norm only pertains to a specific type of analysis – those resembling secrets. Naturally, this does not lead to the conclusion that intelligence analysis in cases of mysteries and complexities is random. The norms governing the latter type of intelligence analysis should still be to detect misinformation and disinformation. Yet the norms governing the resolving of mysteries might be better understood as speaking *comprehension* to power rather than the truth. The core aim of these types of analysis is thus to facilitate the best possible understanding of a specific question or task, thereby making sense of the question at hand. The norm of intelligence analysis is phrased as an attempt to be *neutral* and *apolitical*.[17] Yet even though this norm is vague, it seems to be fundamentally contested by the fact that intelligence services are inherently political, since they play a central role in the governmental machinery and primarily aim to serve policymakers, the political decision-making process, and the political system. Hence. a central question is whether intelligence can be apolitical when it is so closely connected to those in power.

This question leads us back to the discussion of how the relationship between decision-makers and intelligence analysts should ideally be. This question has been debated by the father of intelligence studies Sherman Kent and by other well-known researchers in this field such as Willmoore Kendell and Robert Gates. Kent viewed intelligence analysis as similar to scholarly research, whereby the fundamental aim is to be distanced from the research object and from potential stakeholders in striving for scientific objectivity. Following Kent's strict understanding of "political", even a decision-maker's presentation of an intelligence requirement could, in principle, be problematic and be considered a form of politicisation. According to Kent, even the initiative and identification of intelligence requirements should ideally be placed on the side of the analyst. Nowadays, this requirement of a complete absence of interaction between analysts and decision-makers seems to be quite a radical norm, and at least infeasible to uphold in practice. The relationship would thus in practice be more equivalent to a Gates-like understanding of a dynamic and close relationship between intelligence analysts and decision-makers. However, the fact that intelligence analysis is inherently political does not mean that we can conclude that intelligence is inherently politicised. Politicisation occurs when intelligence professionals – including decision-makers – intentionally manipulate the conclusions they have identified in order to promote a specific political agenda.

Awareness in using open sources

A common-sense notion of OSINT is that the term refers to information from the press, the media, or similar publicly available sources. A general saying within the intelligence services is that up to 80 per cent of all the relevant information about an adversary is available via OSINT – and this percentage is probably increasing in the digital age.[18]

Since the availability of online information is increasing, there is the question of whether, why, and when the use of intelligence from open sources (OSINT) in general and intelligence from social media intelligence (SOCMINT) in particular can be considered as unproblematic. How can we assess new and non-traditional collection methods in a period characterised by speed and an overwhelming access to information? Which ethical dilemmas arise in the wake of an increasing emphasis on OSINT in intelligence analysis, for example by utilising information from social media? This type of intelligence work blurs the boundary between collectors and analysts, because OSINT is accessible to both.

A starting point in the existing literature on intelligence ethics is that the process of collecting intelligence is never "neutral" because it often involves some form of intrusion or wronging of the person who is the target of the collection activity.[19] Naturally, the degree of intrusion entailed in a specific activity depends on the type of collection measure applied. Most HUMINT methods will, for example, entail some degree of deception, lying, or manipulation, since such means (the use of informants, undercover agents, spying etc.) are designed to make the targeted individual reveal information, which she or he would not have done, if she or he knew the intentions and motives of the specific intelligence collection operation. Technical intelligence measures can entail similar types of intrusion of the targeted individuals as HUMINT – for example, in cases of wiretapping or bugging of private rooms. Here, the affected individual is being deceived as she or he does not know that the collection activity is going on. In general, the wronging entailed in most intelligence measures would however often be phrased as a violation of the right to privacy of the targeted individual.[20]

The right to privacy is not an easy concept to define. For example, Gary Marx says:

> Persons often have trouble articulating what seems wrong with a surveillance practice beyond saying that privacy is invaded. Privacy is a vague catch-all phrase that includes a variety of concerns, such as respect for personhood, dignity, and autonomy of the individual.[21]

Despite the difficulties connected to specifying the concept of privacy violations, it seems intuitively right to claim that many intelligence measures entail some degree of morally problematic intrusion into the private life of the affected individuals. Thus, since intelligence activities and surveillance in general are most often characterised by information gathering without the *consent* of the affected parties,[22] and since intelligence is often characterised as being a "game between hiders and finders",[23] the claim that most intelligence activities harm, wrong, and/or violate the right to privacy of the affected individuals seems in general plausible.

The next question is, then, whether such wronging can ever be morally permissible. Naturally, the answer to this question is yes, since we have already concluded that intelligence ethics is not an oxymoron. The right to privacy is not an overriding right, which can never be overruled by other concerns. However, the same goes for national security and public safety. Roughly speaking and ideally, there should be a balance between considerations of intrusion and wronging on the one hand and attempts to safeguard the public from unwanted events such as terrorism on the other. There is a need to assess this balance in each individual case when initiating an intelligence activity. Nevertheless, even if scholars generally agree on the need for such a balance, there is no agreement on when the balance is adequate and when it is not.[24] Quite on the contrary, huge disagreements occur. Some scholars would even claim that the use of the balance metaphor is inadequate, since privacy can in some cases be seen as a way to ensure security, and that the two aspects (privacy versus security) will not necessarily constitute counterparts in a null-sum-game.[25]

The basic assumption in this chapter is that intelligence collection can be viewed as morally permissible even though it entails some degree of intrusion, harm to or wronging of the affected individuals. Hence, the next question is: How should we go about deciding whether a specific intelligence collection activity is morally permissible? Or in other words: How should we assess whether there is a morally right balance between the wrongs on the one side and security and safety benefits on the other?

Toni Erskine maintains that the answer to this question would depend on the moral theory used as a backdrop of the assessment. According to her, a moral assessment would look different depending on whether the underlying moral theory is *deontology*, which claims that some actions are inherently unethical (e.g. lies and deception), or consequentialism, which ascertains that the consequences of an act, not the means, should decide whether the action is morally permissible or not.[26]

Some scholars have addressed this question from the perspective of practitioners in an attempt to identify some guidelines that can apply to the actual decision-making process.[27] I will briefly present one of these contributions and afterwards discuss whether and how such guidelines are relevant for the challenges faced by intelligence services in the digital age.

John Kleinig suggests six specific questions to consider when deciding on the moral permissibility in the context of knowledge acquisition within police organisations. These questions can, for example, be posed when initiating acts of surveillance or intelligence collection with the aim of disrupting or preventing a specific crime. Internally in an intelligence service, this type of questions would also form the basis for a legal assessment before collection is initiated. Kleinig describes the kind of assessment taking place when deciding on the moral or legal permissibility in the context of surveillance as a "means-ends reasoning". The person in charge of the assessment would ask herself or himself whether the means applied in order to acquire a specific piece of information justifies the expected ends of the specific collection activity (referring to the balance metaphor described earlier). Kleinig lists six distinct questions which should be satisfactorily answered before any collection activity is initiated:

1   Are the ends good or good enough?
2   Are the means proportionate to the end?
3   Can the ends be secured in a less invasive manner?
4   Will the means secure the ends?
5   Is there something intrinsically problematic about the means?
6   Will the means have deleterious consequences that would make their use inappropriate?[28]

These questions are rather broad and must be applied to specific cases if we want to determine their utility for decision-making.[29] In "traditional" intelligence cases, for example when an intelligence service intends to initiate a specific HUMINT operation, the six questions could be useful as guiding principles in order to spark discussions on, for example, the core reason for initiating the activity, whether alternative and less invasive methods would apply, and whether the operation would be proportionate in relation to the results sought.

Naturally, these questions are not easy to answer and they call for further specification: How to interpret central elements, such as the concept of proportionality? However, in this chapter I will not go into more details on how to apply the guidelines. The presentation of the six questions serves mainly as an introduction to one way of including ethical considerations into the context of intelligence collection.

Even though it might be difficult to apply these guiding principles in a strict and literal sense, they would enable discussions on the moral permissibility of intelligence collection. Such practical guidelines should therefore be considered as a valuable and constructive element when pushing towards a professionalisation of intelligence, not least when it comes to collection from open sources.

One could argue that since intelligence collected from open sources is publicly available, for example online, no one is wronged by the intelligence collection activity. Thus, it would be a bold claim to say that the collection and use of open-source information pose the same kind of ethical dilemmas as the collection of intelligence via clandestine means, since the affected individuals' right to privacy and the methods will not be deceiving in the same way as traditional collection methods. After all, the information is already available without intruding into the personal lives of the affected parties. On the other hand, the affected parties have not consented to the use of their personal details, or may have consented on a general basis where it is often unclear what one agrees to, for example by accepting a privacy policy when entering a social media platform or a specific web page. Naturally, some information on these platforms is intentionally public, for example blogs that are used to communicate certain views to as many people as possible. However, OSINT units in police and intelligence services would, in fact, rarely equate reading news and similar publicly available sources with their notion of OSINT. On the contrary, in many cases the collection of OSINT and SOCMINT refers to the collection of information through the use of sophisticated software tools designed to penetrate otherwise closed social media platforms and/ or by exploiting the ignorance of internet users in terms of privacy configurations on Facebook and other similar platforms. Thus, software tools can easily and legally enable intelligence services and any other parties to gain access to Facebook accounts and similar social media profiles. Hence, "open-"source intelligence seems to be situated in a grey zone between private and public information, and the exploitation of such information raises new questions about the nature and privacy of online information.[30]

Access to social media profiles is possible because most users of social media platforms lack technical know-how on how to safeguard against intrusion. The user will in fact often believe that her or his information is only communicated to a closed circle of people, as their followers and friends, when this is not always the case. Additionally, the users have accepted broad consent policies of the providers, and there is therefore nothing illegal in gaining access to and exploiting the "openly" available information. Even if one disregards the legal aspects, the question of whether there is something morally problematic with the exploitation of online information by intelligence services still remains. Annabelle Lever, among others, emphasises people's interest in having privacy online, even if much online communication in its nature is public. She argues that even if a space is public, this does not mean that people should be comfortable about being monitored in this room. We usually assume a certain amount of privacy even in public space. Consequently, the collection and analysis of information are not morally permissible by the fact that the information is publicly available.

The use of fake profiles, as a way of gaining access to information on social media platforms or chat forums, is another and much more active way of engaging in intelligence gathering. This approach is also easier to identify as morally problematic because it involves deceiving the person who is the target of the collection activity.

Deciding on whether a specific online collection activity is morally problematic raises new and challenging ethical questions regarding what is private and what is personal online, and on how far intelligence services can go in order to gain access to such semi-private/public information. In general, ethical considerations concerning the collection and exploitation of online information need critical scrutiny from legal and moral scholars, especially since some cases of OSINT collection seem to be intruding and morally problematic even though they do not include elements like deception, lies, or manipulation.

Conclusion

The digital age is about to change the working day of the intelligence analyst. The changes involve among other things what questions analysts work on, which sources they use to find information, and what role they have in assessing this information for decision-makers. Such changes emphasise the need for a professional ethics for intelligence analysts, both by creating an ethical awareness around the analyst's role and by clarifying guidelines for how this role should be exercised. This chapter has suggested some general principles that can serve as a foundation for a professional ethics for intelligence analysts. Naturally, the preparation of ethical guidelines requires a broader discussion within intelligence communities on how a professional code for analysts will look like. Hopefully, this chapter will both motivate and contribute to such a discussion among analysts.

Notes

1 Adam Diderichsen: *Ethics for Police Officers* (in Danish). Frederiksberg: Samfundslitteratur, 2011, p. 23.
2 Ross Bellaby: *The Ethics of Intelligence: A New Framework*. London and New York: Routledge, 2014; Ross Bellaby: "What's the Harm? The Ethics of Intelligence Collection", *Intelligence and National Security*, Vol. 27, No. 1, 2012, pp. 93–117; and Toni Erskine: "'As Rays of Light to the Human Soul'? Moral Agents and Intelligence Gathering", *Intelligence and National Security*, Vol. 19, No. 2, 2004, pp. 359–381.
3 Hans Born & Aidan Wills: "Beyond the Oxymoron: Exploring Ethics through the Intelligence Cycle", in Jan Goldman (ed.): *Ethics of Spying: A Reader for the Intelligence Professional*, Vol. 2. Lanham, MD: Scarecrow Press, 2010; and Kira Vrist Rønn: "The Professional Ethics of Intelligence: On the Feasibility of Ethics as Internal Self-regulation of Intelligence activities", in N. Fyfe, H.O.I. Gundhus, & K.V. Rønn (eds.): *Moral Issues in Intelligence-led Policing*. London and New York: Routledge, 2017, pp. 121–139.
4 Born & Wills *op. cit.*; and Emil B. Greve: *The Police Intelligence Service: A Legal Elucidation of the Service's Activity and Overall Control System* (in Danish). Copenhagen: Jurist og Økonomiforbundets Forlag, 2014.
5 Greve, *op. cit.*; and Rønn: "The Professional Ethics of Intelligence", *op. cit.*
6 Nick Fyfe, Helene O.I. Gundhus, & Kira Vrist Rønn: "Introduction", in Nick Fyfe, Helene O.I. Gundhus, & Kira Vrist Rønn (eds.): *Moral Issues in Intelligence-led Policing*. London and New York: Routledge, 2017, pp. 1–23.

7 For a discussion of the distinction between gaining access to digital information, and collecting information using traditional intelligence gathering methods, see Sir David Omand, Jamie Bartlett, & Carl Miller: "Introducing Social Media Intelligence (SOC-MINT)", *Intelligence and National Security*, Vol. 27, No. 6, 2012, pp. 801–823.

8 Bellaby: "What's the Harm?", *op. cit.*; and Gary T. Marx: "Ethics for the New Surveillance", *The Information Society*, Vol. 14, No. 3, 1998, pp. 171–185.

9 Uri Bar-Joseph: "The Professional Ethics of Intelligence Analysis", *International Journal of Intelligence and CounterIntelligence*, Vol. 24, No. 1, 2011, pp. 22–43.

10 Len Scott & Peter Jackson: "The Study of Intelligence in Theory and Practice", *Intelligence and National Security*, Vol. 19, No. 2, 2004, pp. 139–169; and Kira Vrist Rønn: "Introduction", in Kira Vrist Rønn (eds.): *Intelligence Studies* (in Danish). Frederiksberg: Samfundslitteratur, 2016, pp. 11–39.

11 Robert Jervis: "Reports, Politics, and Intelligence Failures: The Case of Iraq", *The Journal of Strategic Studies*, Vol. 29, No. 1, 2006, pp. 3–52.

12 Bar-Joseph, *op. cit.*

13 Michael A. Bishop & J.D. Trout: *Epistemology and the Psychology of Human Judgement*. Oxford: Oxford University Press, 2005.

14 *Ibid.*

15 Sille Obelitz Søe: "Misleadingness in the Algorithm Society: Misinformation and Disinformation", *Medium*, March 6, 2017, https://medium.com/big-data-small-meaning-and-global-discourses/misleadingness-in-the-algorithm-society-misinformation-and-disinformation-28f78f14e78f.

16 Gregory F. Treverton: "The Future of Intelligence: Changing Threats, Evolving Methods", in Isabelle Duyvesteyn, Ben de Jogn, & Joop van Reijn (eds.): *The Future of Intelligence: Challenges in the 21st Century*. London and New York: Routledge, 2014, pp. 27–38.

17 Olav Riste: "The Intelligence-policy Maker Relationship and Politicisation of Intelligence", in Wilhelm Agrell & Gregory F. Treverton (eds.): *National Intelligence Systems: Current Research and Future Prospects*. Cambridge: Cambridge University Press, 2009, pp. 93–114.

18 See for example Arthur Hulnick: "The Dilemma of Open Sources intelligence: Is OSINT Really Intelligence?", in Loch K. Johnson (ed.): *The Oxford Handbook of National Security Intelligence*. Oxford: Oxford University Press, 2010, pp. 230–241.

19 John Kleinig: "The Ethical Perils of Knowledge Acquisition", *Criminal Justice Ethics*, Vol. 28, No. 2, 2009, pp. 201–222.

20 Bellaby: "What's the Harm?", *op. cit.*; and Marx, *op. cit.*, pp. 171–185.

21 Marx, *op. cit.*, p. 173.

22 Kevin Macnish: "An Eye for an Eye: Proportionality and Surveillance", *Ethical Theory and Moral Practice*, Vol. 18, No. 3, 2015, pp. 529–548.

23 Jervis, *op. cit.*, p. 11.

24 See for example Adam D. Moore (ed.): *Privacy, Security and Accountability: Ethics, Law and Policy*. London: Rowman & Littlefield, 2016.

25 Annabelle Lever: "Democracy, Privacy and Security", in Adam D. Moore (ed.) *Privacy, Security and Accountability: Ethics, Law and Policy*. London: Rowman & Littlefield, 2016, pp. 105–124.

26 Erskine, *op. cit.*; and Kira Vrist Rønn: "What Is Intelligence Ethics? A Critical Review and Future Perspectives", *International Journal of Intelligence and CounterIntelligence*, Vol. 29, No. 4, 2016, pp. 760–784.

27 For some exceptions, see Bellaby: "What's the Harm?", *op. cit.*; Kevin Macnish: "Just Surveillance? Towards a Normative Theory of Surveillance", *Surveillance & Society*, Vol. 12, No. 1, 2014, pp. 142–153; and Kleinig, *op. cit.*

28 Kleinig, *op. cit.*

29 See for example some fictitious cases in James M. Olson: *Fair Play: The Moral Dilem-mas of Spying*. Washington, DC: Potomac Books, Inc., 2006. For a more detailed dis-cussion of the principles, see Rønn: "The Professional Ethics of Intelligence", *op. cit.*
30 For a more extensive discussion of the concept "privacy", see for example Lever, *op. cit.*

Further reading

Bar-Joseph, Uri: "The Professional Ethics of Intelligence Analysis", *International Journal of Intelligence and CounterIntelligence*, Vol. 24, No. 1, 2011.
Bellaby, Ross: *The Ethics of Intelligence: A New Framework*. London and New York: Routledge, 2014.
Kleinig, John: "The Ethical Perils of Knowledge Acquisition", *Criminal Justice Ethics*, Vol. 28, No. 2, 2009.
Moore, Adam D. (ed.): *Privacy, Security and Accountability. Ethics, Law and Policy*. London: Rowman & Littlefield, 2016.
Omand, David, & Mark Phythian: *Principled Spying: The Ethics of Secret Intelligence*. Oxford: Oxford University Press, 2018.
Omand, David, Jamie Bartlett, & Carl Miller: "Introducing Social Media Intelligence (SOCMINT)", *Intelligence and National Security*, Vol. 27, No. 6, 2012.

12 Conclusion

Towards an analyst-centric intelligence process

Brigt Harr Vaage and Knut Magne Sundal

As pointed out in the Introduction, intelligence is an ancient activity in a new age. Several of the previous chapters have detailed the contents of this new age: Intelligence users perceive increased tempo, complexity, and volatility in international political developments. This experience alters the requirements directed at intelligence as decision support. In the digital age, the main effort of intelligence is no longer limited to exposing, contextualising, and disseminating secrets. Rather than "speaking truth to power", intelligence in the digital age is about making uncertainties less uncertain to the decision-makers. In this concluding chapter, we will review some of the changes happening to intelligence. We will claim that the intelligence process has become analysis-centric rather that collection-centric – which puts new charges to analysts. Analytic work becomes increasingly interdisciplinary and demands analysts with solid knowledge of intelligence as such as well as of the subject matter. In order to be an intelligence analyst in the digital age, *knowing the world is not enough.*

From "secrets" to "mysteries"

In the intelligence literature, one finds the dichotomy between "secrets" and "mysteries".[1] Traditionally, intelligence has been tasked with warning of impending threats, understood as the ability and intent of an adversary to inflict damage. Clandestine collection reveals truths about abilities and developments which the adversary tries to keep hidden. In the literature, these truths are referred to as *secrets*. Said otherwise, collection of facts can reveal the opponent's secrets (abilities and intentions) – for example, the reach of Iran's newest missiles or the coup plans of a small group of officers. Divulging secrets is the main task of an intelligence organisation's collection assets.

During the bipolar rivalry of the Cold War, uncovering the adversary's secrets was the central feature of intelligence work. Intelligence analysis contributed to contextualising the collected facts, assessing their features, and interplay.[2] Intelligence became *truth-seeking*, and collection assets were its core capacity. Intelligence was to present collected facts and provide neutral assessment to the decision-makers, regardless of political consequences. In this regard, intelligence adhered to the guidelines prescribed by Sherman Kent in the early years of the Cold War,[3] which since have dominated Western intelligence services: Intelligence shall divulge and disseminate secrets, like a servant whispering truth in the emperor's ear.

This tradition is clearly reflected in the motto of the NIS: "Knowledge of the world for the protection of Norway." The same goes for a statement attributed to Admiral Torolf Rein, former Norwegian Chief of Defence: "The Intelligence Service is tasked with viewing the world as it is, not like the rest of us desires it to be."[4] His observation coincides with Kent's view. Truth-seeking intelligence is objective and independent, remedying politics, media, and other sources of information. This approach dominated intelligence thinking during the Cold War and remains a keystone to understanding modern intelligence.

In the digital age, intelligence is still tasked with ascertaining useful knowledge and facts, banishing misconception and ignorance, as well as mitigating "alternative truth" and "fake news". In October 2017, for instance, the NIS publicly repudiated allegations that the Russian Zapad 2017 military exercise included a mock invasion of Svalbard. The Service could correct and shorten a debate on the threat from Russia by presenting collected facts.[5]

Still, in the digital age, the enterprise of intelligence is more than to unveil, contextualise, and disseminate secrets. Sir David Omand shows this development in Chapter 2, and in the subsequent chapter, Espen Barth Eide describes how Norwegian decision-makers have been experiencing change in international relations since the Cold War. The space for manoeuvre and the intentions and capacities of both state and organisational actors seem less constant. Certainty and truth have become increasingly fluctuant. What was correct yesterday may appear different tomorrow. As mentioned in Chapter 1, a white paper written by the Norwegian Ministry of Foreign Affairs in 2017 opens with the statement: "Unpredictability has become the new normal."[6] By necessity, these conditions affect intelligence's mission, area of responsibility, and work process. If users perceive the world as capricious and unpredictable, intelligence must focus on more than merely revealing secrets. The decision-maker must be emboldened to deal with insecurity and uncertainty. When giving decision-making support in the digital age, understanding intelligence as truth is required but not sufficient. Intelligence work has extended into forecasting and prediction.[7]

Intelligence literature refers to this as the assessment of *mysteries* and treats it as the counter-point to the unveiling of secrets. The term implies that it refers to a future idea not yet thought of, a course of action not fully planned, or, at the very least, a non-articulated concept which is not yet a manifested, thus collectable, fact. Furthermore, mysteries are the future outcomes of the actions of more than one actor: the course of an armed confrontation between Russia and NATO, the result of an assassination of a head of state, a revolution or an important multinational summit. In the current complex, composited, and rapidly alternating threat environment, intelligence analysts must increasingly work with mysteries, assessing and predicting the likelihood of different alternative trends and outcomes. Their work is founded on both collected secrets and their own expertise on the subject matter. But this is not sufficient. More than anything, the analysis requires creativity, imagination, and sound analytic techniques.

When intelligence analysts in the digital age develop predictions, they work with uncertainty, not with certain facts. Probability, rather than truth in itself, has become the ambition and yardstick of assessments. The analyst measures the likelihood of a number of hypotheses on future development. Collection assets and captured secrets remain pivotal to successful intelligence decision-making support, but in dealing with mysteries, *analysts* have become the agencies' core capacity.

These changes reflect on all concepts of intelligence: process, product, and organisation.

The analyst at the core

In the age of truth-seeking intelligence, collection assets were the core activity of the intelligence process. The intelligence mission was initially translated to collection requirements, which in turn unveiled facts about the topic, region, or actor in question. Thereafter, analysts elucidated collected data and turned them into intelligence reporting. Such a process surmises that truth has a certain shelf life – that its "best before" date does not run out. And it preserved, sort of: 40 years ago, it may have been meaningful to state that Soviet armed forces, a certain number of weeks into an armed conflict, would have moved into a certain geographical area with a doctrinally predetermined entity. As the Russian annexation of the Crimea in 2014 demonstrated, today such a prediction would be void of meaning and use. When intentions and abilities fluctuate and old rules rarely apply, the playing field for state and non-state actors alike becomes much larger. Saying anything meaningful about assets and timing just becomes more difficult.

In our age, therefore, the intelligence process is centred on assessing different, possible future developments, by way of the tools, scenarios, and creativity of the analytic craft. The intelligence mission is implemented by analysts, who sketch different future outcomes based on end-user requirements. Only at the next step are the hypotheses discussed with collection assets, which in turn can conduct targeted searches for information which confirm or refute any possibility or scenario. The intelligence process has become *analyst-centric*. This does not, mind you, demerit collection – quite the contrary. But its role in the process is changed. Intelligence has moved from "analyse this" to "collect that".[8]

This challenges the traditional cyclic model of the intelligence process. Although still valid as an illustration of four different sub-processes, the traditional model under-communicates that in the digital age the essence of the intelligence process is the link between the various components. In order to understand the process at large, and work as part of it, it is more rewarding to study the links between the components rather than the components themselves. It is here intelligence is made and promulgated.

The pulse of these relations is called *externalisation* in the intelligence literature.[9] Thoughts, ideas, reservations, or concerns are of slim value if retained by individuals or groups and not shared with those who can learn from, elaborate, or refute them. The errors most commonly discussed in intelligence literature stem from such lack of communication between employees and components of an intelligence organisation. Likewise, misunderstanding and befuddlement between the intelligence provider and the end users are classic sources of failure.[10] Intelligence dialogue must be done with openness and without reservation. This way requirements are more evident and precise, and the user harnesses a better understanding of what the intelligence organisations can – and cannot – supply. The intelligence product is not submitted, as such, before the procurer is certain the user has understood the contents correctly.

All in all, modern intelligence work requires greater openness. While external cover can be maintained, involved parties at all levels internally need to share knowledge, method, ideas, and reservations. When intelligence deals with and disseminates the uncertain, the intelligence process itself must manifest certainty throughout.

A continuous dialogue

In the age of truth-seeking intelligence, the context of the intelligence product was rather constant, and therefore it could have value over time. The idea of preparedly collected and analysed *basic intelligence* presupposes that intelligence is to reveal something permanent – "the world as it *is*". Reporting provides works of reference, to be consulted as per user requirements. The counterpart, *current intelligence*, involves short-term analyses, comprising comments on on-going developments. The basic/current dichotomy remains a point of reference in the intelligence literature and doctrine and is one of the most vibrant examples of modern intelligence striving and struggling to achieve an outdated ambition.

In our age, current and basic intelligence have become *reflexive*: By working on both short- and long-term projects and event horizons, intelligence professionals become more proficient at both. Of course, intelligence agencies still put forward products that may *look* current or basic – dealing with ongoing or long-term developments. However, all products are more than anything the outcome of a concerted effort – a correlation of all collection and analysis functions. Today, mental and physical thresholds between current and basic intelligence work are ground down, along with compartmentalisation of subject matter and discipline specialists. Different groups of experts work together, according to the requirements of the task, product, and real world, not according to organisational divisions.

This challenges the dissemination of intelligence products to the end user. Gone are the courier-borne reports delivered in sealed, classified folios. Dissemination has become an interactive service. The conversation between agency and user has become closer and continuous – *the conversation is the product*. It encompasses both assessments, the elucidation of current development and of the uncertain future, and clarifying ongoing and new assignments. Only when the conversation is fluent, trusting, and close can intelligence deliver relevant and timely decision-making support. This proximity deviates from Kent's ideal, albeit isolationist, view of the role of intelligence, accentuating the *applicability* of the intelligence support instead of the objectivity of the process. Robert Gates pointed out this position to the US intelligence community from the early 1990s.[11]

Still, intelligence should not speak to the decision-maker about the world "as they desire it", but when tempo increases, it is vital that the two parties understand each other's demands, abilities, and language. And when the user needs the best possible assessment of possible outcomes and future change, closer cooperation becomes a necessity. The daily interaction between them is a continuation of Gates' position on proximity, while both parties preserve their disparateness and integrity, like Sherman Kent called for.

While truth, of course, still exists, the new normal of the digital age is that intelligence is less absolute and less lasting than in previous times. Reporting is more about validating possible future development than about verifying truth about the world as it currently is. As decision-making support, in the digital age intelligence must reduce doubt and opaqueness about tomorrow, rather than solely seek to increase the user's knowledge about today. Prediction can never be knowledge, and thus neither truth nor science. It may be based on collected facts and experience, but it never reaches beyond the horizon of probability.

Knowing the world is not enough

In the age of truth-seeking intelligence, collection and analysis were both procurers of knowledge. As intelligence has come to deliver much more than secrets and knowledge, the requirements put to the individual intelligence professional and to the organisation as such change.

Previously, collectors were technicians or discipline specialists with thorough knowledge of the kind of data their sensor collected. Their knowledge was first and foremost based on hands-on experience. Today, sources, sensors, and collection techniques change at a higher pace, as illustrated by the current need for collection in digital communication. Similarly, analysts recruited were previously country or subject-matter experts. They were educated on the state or region in question, in language or religion, and were thus well-suited to extract significance from the large amounts of data delivered by the collection assets. Then, they could write thorough, basic intelligence reports, trusting full well the lasting value of the assessments. All in all, intelligence could describe a continuous, incremental reality. However, current assignments, incident management, and other small-spectrum assessments were troublesome spots of friction in the basic and pre-planned machinery.

Still, analysts must be specialists in their assigned subject matter. Neither analytic techniques, as Stig Stenslie argues in Chapter 4, nor artificial intelligence, as Lars Haugom, Cato Yaakov Hemmingby, and Tore Pedersen discuss in Chapter 5, can alone replace the subject-matter specialist. It is still more efficient to recruit a Chinese specialist and teach her or him intelligence work than to thoroughly familiarise a discipline specialist in Chinese language, society, and politics. "How long does it take to develop an intelligence analyst with 25 years of experience on Iran?" an intelligence instructor once asked rhetorically. This remains unchanged. Subject-matter knowledge is crucial, and any intelligence analyst needs to be among the top professionals nationally within his or her primary topic.

In our age, "knowing the world" is no longer a sufficient quality. Today, analysts are also the central resource in overseeing and running the intelligence process, interpreting assignments, and providing guidance to collection. To do this, they need to understand opportunities and limitations in all parts of the intelligence process, and they need to comprehend and be poised to discuss user requirements.[12] They must run the internal and external dialogue just as well. The age of the wise analyst, deliberating in the isolation of his office, has passed. Today, groups of analysts, collectors, and information coordinators work together. It may still be one single analyst with thorough topical expertise who eventually pens the assessment, but the preceding mental process has certainly not been hers or his alone.

This kind of work demands – and fosters – open conversation as well as traceable tools and methods. As Chapters 4 and 5 of this book demonstrate, intelligence professionals now more than ever need to understand, discuss, and use a plethora of tools and techniques for analysis: Ranging from tangible computer programs which can model and visualise volumes of information to mental and conceptual ways to exacerbate, discuss, and externalise ideas on evolution and change – they are all required and employed as need be. The tools are means and ways; thus, they do not regularly constitute part of the finished product, but they can assist groups of analysts to reciprocally understand and describe the basis of the assessments that are eventually put forth. To a modern intelligence organisation, the ability and will to exercise intelligence through traceable and structured methods are just as vital as subject-matter expertise.

To be an intelligence analyst, therefore, is something much more than being the cleverest subject-matter specialist in the room. The job is more demanding than ever before and calls for frequent revision of method and factual base. The capable analyst is a constant learner, continually adjusting her or his working tools, methods, and measures to a reality that never is the same tomorrow as it was yesterday.

This challenges the interface between the intelligence organisation and process, because intelligence assessments are made between the different functions of the process. The functions (direction, collection, processing, and dissemination) do not evolve in isolation. When the analyst's assignments are in constant movement, the collector's tasks move too. Their focus becomes bespoke to the requirements put to the analysis by the end user and by reality. Only when the collector understands what the analyst needs, and when the analyst understands what the collector can and cannot deliver, can this interaction work under increasing pressure and tempo.

This new reality challenges the intelligence organisation as an employer. The employees must constantly be trained and provided opportunity to develop into intelligence specialists, while still having the leeway to update their topical or discipline-specific competence. Thus, this responsibility cannot solely be that of employees.

Increasing unpredictability has, as described earlier, led to an analyst-centric intelligence process, where comprehensive relations between the components of the process are increasingly important. When this demands more from the employees' competency, an *interdisciplinary approach* has developed within intelligence which was not prominent earlier.[13]

No longer does it suffice to hire a political scientist with an interest for and knowledge about Russian politics and believe she or he will remain a relevant and experienced employee solely by further studying information on Russian politics. She or he will have to learn about other functions of the intelligence process, about the user, and about topics interfacing their own. It has to be the obligation of the organisation to develop a culture where such interdisciplinarity becomes natural and desired. Collectors, analysts, and managers must seek such creativity and insight which put the intelligence organisation in a position to create bespoke decision support that increases the user's ability to deal with uncertainty and clouded outcomes. This way, the professionals – the human beings – in the process will get closer to one another. The distinction between topic experts and discipline specialists becomes less distinct. In order to work together, these groups must learn about each other's craft. The discipline specialist must increase his subject-matter expertise, and the country or topic specialist must learn the particulars of the different collection disciplines. The analyst will need basic training in disciplines like OSINT or IMINT, while the OSINT specialist must gain sufficient topical insight to understand and identify the value of the information which is to be scrutinised. This way, the colleagues can converse better, understand the opportunities of the intelligence profession better, and, eventually, produce better, clearer, and even more comprehensive assessments for the user.

Conclusion

Over the past 15–20 years, intelligence has gone through major changes. The idea of intelligence merely unveiling secrets, finding consistent truths which the enemy attempts to hide, is rooted in Cold War experience and thinking. That perspective, however, still resides in the literature, manuals, and doctrines. Although intelligence organisations must continue to explore that which others try to hide, this is far from sufficient to provide relevant, reliable, and timely decision-making support in the digital age. Today, intelligence must relate to decision-makers who experience their security policy surroundings as increasingly complex and fluctuant. Maintaining unique collection capabilities is still a vital capacity for any intelligence organisation, but in the digital age, analysts are the core resource of intelligence. Intelligence has become analyst-centric. For intelligence, the digital age is thus also the age of the analyst. Thus, as this book has sought to demonstrate, this transformation commands far more from the analyst.

Notes

1 For more on "secrets" and "mysteries, see, for example, Michael Herman: *Intelligence Power in Peace and War*. Cambridge: Cambridge University Press, 1996, p. 103; Robert M. Clark: *Intelligence Analysis: A Target-Centric Approach*, 4th edition. Los

Angeles: Sage, 2013, pp. 348–350; Mark Phythian: "Intelligence Analysis Today and Tomorrow", *Security Challenges*, Vol. 5, No. 1, Autumn 2009, p. 68; and Joseph S. Nye Jr.: "Peering into the Future", *Foreign Affairs*, July/August, 1994, www.foreignaffairs.com/articles/1994-07-01/peering-future.

2 Jan Blom: "The Norwegian Intelligence Service in a Time of Change", in Lars Christian Jenssen, & Olav Riste (eds.): *Intelligence in the Cold War*. Oslo: Norwegian Institute for Defence Studies, 2001, pp. 167–171; and Gregory F. Treverton: *Intelligence for an Age of Terror*. New York: Cambridge University Press 2009, chapters 1 and 3.

3 Sherman Kent: *Strategic Intelligence for American World Policy*. Princeton, NJ: Princeton University Press, 1949; and Richard Betts: "Politization of Intelligence: Costs and Benefits", in Richard Betts & Thomas Mahnken (eds.): *Paradoxes of Strategic Intelligence*. London: Routledge 2003, pp. 60–61.

4 Quote taken from former Norwegian head of intelligence, Torgeir Hagen: "E-tjenesten i en omskiftelig verden [The Intel Service in a Changing World]", Lecture given to Oslo Militære Samfund, November 20, 2006, www.oslomilsamfund.no/foredrag-e-tjenesten-i-en-omskiftelig-verden/.

5 *Aftenposten*: "Trente russerne på invasjon av Svalbard? Nei, sier E-tjenesten i disse syv punktene [Did the Russians Train on the Invasion of Svalbard? No, Says the Intelligence Service in these Seven Points]", October 18, 2017, www.aftenposten.no/norge/i/6prp3/Trente-russerne-pa-invasjon-av-Svalbard-Nei–sier-E-tjenesten-i-disse-syv-punktene.

6 The Norwegian Ministry of Foreign Affairs: "Setting the Course for Norwegian Foreign and Security Policy", Meld. St. 36 (2016–2017), Report to the Parliament (White Paper), www.regjeringen.no/contentassets/0688496c2b764f029955cc6e2f27799c/en-gb/pdfs/stm201620170036000engpdfs.pdf.

7 James B. Bruce & Roger Z. George: "Intelligence Analysis: What Is it – and What Does it Take?", in Roger Z. George & James B. Bruce (eds.): *Analyzing Intelligence: National Security Practitioners' Perspectives*, 2nd edition. Washington, DC: Georgetown University Press, 2014, p. 2.

8 Thomas Fingar: "Building a Community of Analysts", in Roger Z. George & James B. Bruce (eds.): *Analyzing Intelligence: National Security Practitioners' Perspectives*, 2nd edition. Washington, DC: Georgetown University Press, 2014, pp. 295–296.

9 See, for example, Randolph H. Pherson & Richards J. Heuer Jr.: "Structured Analytic Techniques: A New Approach to Analysis", in Roger Z. George & James B. Bruce (eds.): *Analyzing Intelligence: National Security Practitioners' Perspectives*, 2nd edition. Washington, DC: Georgetown University Press, 2014, pp. 232–233.

10 Robert M. Clark: *Intelligence Analysis: A Target-Centric Approach*, 4th edition. Los Angeles: Sage, 2013, pp. 356–357; and Michael Herman: *Intelligence Power in War and Peace*. Cambridge: Cambridge University Press, 1996, Chapter 13.

11 Betts, *op. cit.*, pp. 61–62.

12 See Bruce & George: *op. cit.*, p. 5.

13 See Rebecca Fisher, Rob Johnston, & Peter Clement: "Is Intelligence Analysis a Discipline?", in Roger Z. George & James B. Bruce (eds.), *op. cit.*, pp. 72–75.

Index

Note: Page numbers in *italics* indicate a figure and page numbers in **bold** indicate a table on the corresponding page.